Physical Activities for Improving Children's Learning and Behavior

A Guide to Sensory Motor Development

Billye Ann Cheatum, PhD
Western Michigan University, Emeritus

Allison A. Hammond, EdD
Sensory Motor Development Specialist
The ResponsAble Child Clinic

HUMAN KINETICS

Library of Congress Cataloging-in-Publication Data

Cheatum, Billye Ann.
    Physical activities for improving children's learning and behavior : a guide to sensory motor development / by Billye Ann Cheatum, Allison A. Hammond.
        p. cm.
    Includes bibliographical references (p.) and index.
    ISBN 0-88011-874-1
        1. Learning disabled children--Education. 2. Problem children--Education. 3. Perceptual-motor learning. 4. Creative activities and seat work. 5. Games. I. Hammond, Allison A., 1960- II. Title.

LC4704.5 .C45 2000
371.92'6--dc21   99-041127

ISBN 0-88011-874-1

Acquisitions Editor: Scott Wikgren; **Developmental Editor:** Katy M. Patterson; **Assistant Editors:** John Wentworth and Amanda Ewing; **Copyeditor:** Anne Mischakoff Heiles; **Proofreader:** Myla Smith; **Indexer:** L. Pilar Wyman; **Graphic Designer:** Fred Starbird; **Graphic Artists:** Yvonne Griffith and Dawn Sills; **Photo Editor:** Clark Brooks; **Cover Designer:** Jack W. Davis; **Photographer (interior):** Billye Ann Cheatum (unless otherwise noted); **Photographer (cover):** Tom Roberts; **Illustrators:** Kristin Mount (medical art); Tom Roberts (mac art); Roberto Sabas (line drawings); **Printer:** United Graphics

Human Kinetics books are available at special discounts for bulk purchase. Special editions or book excerpts can also be created to specification. For details, contact the Special Sales Manager at Human Kinetics.

Printed in the United States of America   10   9   8   7   6   5   4   3   2   1

Human Kinetics
Web site: http://www.humankinetics.com/

United States: Human Kinetics
P.O. Box 5076
Champaign, IL 61825-5076
1-800-747-4457
e-mail: humank@hkusa.com

Canada: Human Kinetics
475 Devonshire Road Unit 100
Windsor, ON N8Y 2L5
1-800-465-7301 (in Canada only)
e-mail: humank@hkcanada.com

Europe: Human Kinetics, P.O. Box IW14
Leeds LS16 6TR, United Kingdom
+44 (0)113-278 1708
e-mail: humank@hkeurope.com

Australia: Human Kinetics
57A Price Avenue
Lower Mitcham, South Australia 5062
(08) 82771555
e-mail: humank@hkaustralia.com

New Zealand: Human Kinetics
P.O. Box 105-231, Auckland Central
09-523-3462
e-mail: humank@hknewz.com

To all of the children and their families who inspired us in our pursuit of helping children with learning and behavior problems; to the students in our program at Western Michigan University whose creativity and curiosity gave us opportunities for personal and professional growth; and to our families and friends who gave us endless support.

Contents

Part II – The Sensory Systems   125

Preface

Having worked for years with children who have learning or behavior problems, we felt compelled to write this book for several reasons. We have marveled at the remarkable ways in which children appear to be so similar and yet are actually so different, especially in their educational and activity needs. Children, each of them unique, deserve the best that our educational system and parenting skills can provide to help them achieve success.

Children need to be viewed as individuals. Activities and lessons directed toward classes as a whole may leave them frustrated and discouraged as individuals. Planning individually for each child in a class of 20 or more youngsters or in a family with several members takes precious time out of your busy schedule. But it may be the one step that parents and teachers can take that will make a lifetime of difference.

This is exemplified in a short story written by Canfield and Hansen in the book *Chicken Soup for the Soul*. A man stands among thousands of starfish on a beach in Mexico, and sees a native picking them up, one at a time, and throwing them back into the ocean. The man tells the native that it couldn't possibly make any difference. As the native throws yet another one in, he smiles and answers, "Made a difference to that one!" Well, that is what we hope this book will do—make a difference to not one but to the many children who have learning or behavior problems.

For either a parent or a teacher few things are more aggravating than to be told that a child has "a learning problem" or "a behavior disorder" without also being given a specific cause of, explanation of, or reason for the problem. This happens year after year during the first parent-teacher conferences of each school year. Usually a second or third-grade teacher notices that a child is not performing at grade level and tells the parents, "There is a learning problem." No helpful explanation is offered, so the first question the parents have is *why:* "Why is my child having trouble learning in class?" As a parent or teacher you may need to ask that question repeatedly until you, or someone else, can find the true cause of the child's problem.

That *why* question only leads to other questions, such as *when?* It is the cause of the problem, not its symptoms, that is important, and to know the cause it is almost equally critical to ask *when* the symptoms appear. Does the behavior and learning ability change as the day progresses? Does the child work differently between the beginning and the end of the reading period? It is only by finding the cause related specifically to when he has problems that you and his teachers can develop an educational, sensory motor program to help him.

Maybe you can remember participating in a conversation like this one, typical of parent and teacher during a conference:

Parent	*Teacher*
"You wanted to see me about my child?"	"Yes, your child has a learning problem."
"What makes you think he has a learning problem?"	"Well, Jack is performing below average."
"What makes you think he's performing below average?"	"He has trouble reading."
"Why does he have trouble reading?"	"He loses his place in reading aloud."
"Why does he lose his place?"	"Well, he reverses letters."
"Oh! Why would he reverse his letters?"	"He seems hyperactive to me."
"Why do you say he's hyperactive?"	"He's often impulsive."
"Why is he so impulsive?"	"Jack doesn't seem to concentrate well."

Unfortunately, in this example of a parent-teacher exchange no real answer is given as to why Jack is having problems in learning, and the parents do not learn when the problems appeared. The answers simply give symptoms, suggesting some underlying sensory motor problem. Neither parents nor teachers should be pressured into guessing or to listing symptoms as the cause of a child's learning or behavior problem. This kind of vague discussion isn't the "fault" of teachers. Most teachers have not had any training in sensory motor development.

Our main reason for writing *Physical Activities for Improving Children's Learning and Behavior* is to furnish parents and educators with solid, easy-to-read information on the stages of growth and development, neurological development, and various sensory systems that are often at the root of academic and movement (or motor) problems. We have tried to reduce complex neurological and developmental topics into terms that are more readily understood by people who are not trained in one of these areas. We often clarify important points through the help of illustrations, pictures, or tables. Many of the tables give the results of studies with elementary school students in Michigan (including students in the Special Physical Education Learning Laboratory at Western Michigan University) and Texas (Cheatum 1989, 1993, 1996; Cheatum and Hammond 1991, 1992).

We wrote this book as a guide for parents and teachers of children with learning, behavioral, and motor problems. It is organized to lead readers through the early growth and developmental stages that influence academic success and on to specific information about various sensory systems that also influence learning. Some symptoms of sensory motor problems appear early in a child's life and are often more easily corrected when the affected child is young.

In this book it is important to *read sequentially* through entire chapters. Without reading all the related material, it is possible to misunderstand the techniques needed to evaluate the children or the specific activities that might improve their academic and movement learning. It is our hope that parents and teachers will pick up this book, want to read through it, and then will come to better understand what is happening to their children.

In part I we discuss several medical and educational labels and motor development issues that contribute to the difficulties some children experience with behavior or learning problems. This first part concerns neurological growth and development, skill development, primitive reflexes, and tips for sensory-motor development programs. There is an overview of neurological growth and development, the reflex systems, and various motor and perceptual concepts. These early childhood experiences can all profoundly influence children in their motor development and academic learning.

To succeed in school, for example, children must understand the parts of their bodies (arms, hand, legs, feet) and how they work with each other. We focus in part I on providing readers with an understanding of the importance of a child gaining a firm awareness and knowledge of right and left sides, lateral preference, and directionality. In most cases, we provide suggestions for evaluating these developmental skills and recommend a few activities that may alleviate potential motor and learning problems.

Part II contains a general overview of sensory integration, sensory information for development and learning, and sensory dysfunction. The last five chapters of part II discuss the vestibular, proprioceptive, tactile, visual, and auditory sensory systems. Each chapter presents information on the sensory receptors, the relationship of that system to motor development, evaluation, specific problems of that system, and methods that can correct major problems.

Throughout both parts we interweave more than 100 physical activities and games related to the material in each chapter and directed toward both reducing the effects of sensory motor problems and enriching the development of children. As parents you can use all these activities at home with your children; the games require minimal equipment.

We hope that in this book you will discover why it is critical to understand growth and development, the interweaving of the sensory systems, and what is appropriate physical activity for normal childhood development and school readiness.

Acknowledgments

Many people have contributed directly or indirectly to the concepts presented in this book. Special acknowledgement and appreciation goes to Dr.Jean Pyfer and Dr. Hollis Fait (posthumously) who provided enormous advisement during the creation of the Special Physical Education Learning Laboratory at Western Michigan University.

We are very appreciative of the advice and moral support provided by Dr.Joseph Eisenbach, Dr. James Bosco, Dr. Roger Zabik, Dr. Dona Icabone, Dr. Elizabeth Patterson, and members of the Research Office during the preparation of state and federal grants that supported so many graduate students and enabled us to provide three laboratories for children with learning or behavior problems.

We are also especially thankful to Dr. Carol Heuttig and Dr. Jean Pyfer for reviewing the manuscript during the developmental stages and giving us some sound guidance.

We express our sincere appreciation for all the professional colleagues who shared their knowledge with us and our students: Dr. Robert Klein for his contributions of vision, Dr. Candace Warner for sharing her knowledge on interdisciplinary collaboration, Dr. Barbara Bennett for her unlimited proficiency in understanding infants and toddlers who have learning or behavior problems, Dr. Jo Cowden for her knowledge of the motor development of young children and Dr. Karen DePauw for her contributions in sensory motor development.

Special thanks are reserved for the following colleagues in the Michigan Department of Special Education who have been our mentors, advisors, supporters and friends throughout our experiences in Michigan: Dr. Ted Beck, Dr. Jerry Nester and Dr. James Nuttall.

Dr. Cheatum thanks all of her former teachers but is especially appreciative to Dr. Claudine Sherrill for her mentoring while at Texas Woman's University, Dr. Dorothy Ainsworth (posthumously) and Dr. Jane Mott for their guidance while at Smith College, and Ms. Evelyn Hasenmayer (posthumously) at the University of Science and Arts of Oklahoma for encouraging her to pursue graduate studies.

Dr. Hammond thanks Dr. Janet Hamburg and Dr. Janet Fisher who recognized her love of dance for children with disabilities and created a special master's program for her at the University of Kansas. Also a special thanks to Dr. Billye Cheatum who is a wonderfully generous friend and mentor.

The authors also wish to thank Eunice Kennedy Shriver for all her educational support and contributions to Dr. Cheatum and others during the sixties. Her driving force in movement and activities for children with disabilities began to open the doors for children who had problems and was instrumental in creating the special physical education program at Western Michigan University.

Last, but certainly not least, the authors would also like to express appreciation for all the cooperation and time spent by the following people who served as models for the pictures: Amber and Kyle Snodderly; Jillian and Jacob Blain; Mason and Calvin Ruzicka; Brandon Kelley; Timothy Jones; Alex, Genevieve and Browyn Halton; Max and Mollie Williams; Peter, Bryce and Christian Maurer; Emily Ouding; Isabelle Wilson; Lance and Kayleigh Harris; Tre Evans; and Brianna Wisti.

Special thanks go to relatives of Dr. Cheatum, Lee Simmons, Laura Simmons and Cameron Cheatum and relatives of Dr. Hammond, Mike and George Hammond.

Game Finder

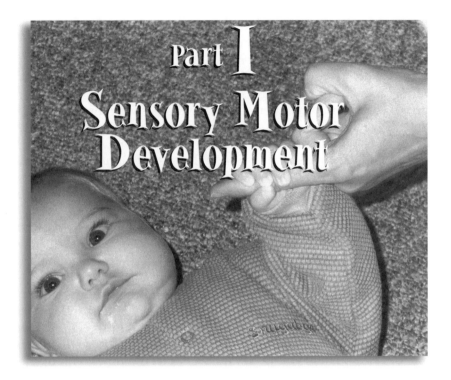

"Marty, please, sit still and listen to the story," the teacher asks for the umpteenth time. Marty is always in motion. When he should be sitting quietly, he wiggles, slides out of his seat, stands up, or lies on top of the table. Although he knows his letters and numbers, he still cannot read. The teacher continually has to remind him to keep his eyes on his book.

Jake cannot seem to walk anywhere. Once he starts out, he runs into a wall or the sofa, and he often knocks down his younger brother. Although his mother asks him to take his time going up and down the stairs, he always rushes and often falls. In school Jake can sit and listen, but he rushes in his work and his writing is sloppy.

Clara seems to have ants in her pants whenever she has to stand in line or work closely with classmates. Although she cannot seem to keep her hands to herself, she complains if another child bumps into her. Naming shapes is hard for her, and she draws her numbers and letters backward and upside down.

Emilio spends more time looking out the window or looking around the room than he does reading his assignments. He asks to go to the bathroom every time a reading lesson starts, or he spends time sharpening his pencil to a nub. When the teacher asks him to read out loud, he is very slow and cannot remember what he is reading. Although he loves to swing on the playground, he rarely climbs the play equipment; when he does he cannot figure out how to get down.

If you're a parent or teacher of a child who has learning or behavior problems, these scenes may seem familiar. You could probably share many stories about times when you have tried to help a child manage behavior and improve learning. Special learning programs and behavior management strategies may work at first, but then improvement stops. You and the child become frustrated—which causes new problems.

Many children with learning and behavior problems also appear to have movement problems, such as clumsiness. Their motor skills are below age-level, and they may show hyperactivity. You'll read in part I how *observing* a child's motor patterns and problems may be part of starting to reduce his or her learning and behavior problems. Chapter 1 discusses medical and educational evaluations of children and the reasons to consider motor problems in diagnosing children's wellness. Then chapter 2 discusses how the neurological system influences growth and motor development in young children. Chapter 3 follows with tips for providing a sensory motor program that involves other members of the family or that can be done in the classroom. Chapter 4 explains how certain reflexes strongly influence motor development. To conclude the first part, chapter 5 explains various problems associated with body awareness and a child's ability to develop a preference for one side of the body.

chapter 1
Common Behaviors and Learning Problems

The psychologist diagnosed Marty as autistic. Public school personnel told Clare's parents that she is learning disabled, and the psychologist added that the problem is dyslexia. Jake has attention deficit hyperactivity disorder (ADHD). And Emilio won dubious honors in the labeling game, with "oppositional defiance disorder" and dyspraxia. These children underwent a variety of tests and observational checklists to be diagnosed. Their parents and teachers contributed information toward the diagnoses. Although these conditions seem to indicate different levels and types of disability, the motor development issues among them are surprisingly similar.

In this chapter, we examine the differences between medical and educational labels given to behavioral and learning problems. We also take a general look at how motor problems affect these behavioral and learning problems. And we discuss the motor manifestations of a handful of disabilities, including autism and attention deficit disorders.

MEDICAL VERSUS EDUCATIONAL DIAGNOSIS

Perhaps your child or the children in your classroom have undergone assessments like Marty's, Clare's, Jake's, and Emilio's to determine the cause of their difficulties. You may have found this process frustrating; often the doctor says one thing, while teachers or other professionals say another. At some point, you may have heard the doctor say, for example, "He'll grow out of it." But you know that his problem is continuing, and now it is interfering with his ability to succeed in school.

Not only parents but also teachers, who might spend more hours interacting with children than even their parents do, should know which organizations and professionals are responsible for the various types of diagnoses. Either the medical or educational system or both may identify children as having a disability or learning problem.

Medical Diagnoses

Quentin has had many ear infections since he was two months old. The pediatrician and various medical professionals have treated his ear infections with antibiotics and eventually by putting tubes in his ears. During these treatments, the doctors' objective was to get rid of the disease and structural problems causing Quentin's ear infections. His parents did not notify Quentin's teachers of his ear infections. No one mentioned to his parents that 50 percent of the children with multiple ear infections have some hearing loss, problems with speech and language development, and problems with coordination. Quentin is now eight years old, and the ear infections appear less frequently, but he continues to have difficulty with balance and speech. These problems are affecting his schoolwork. However, since Quentin is failing reading, his teachers regard him as developmentally delayed, and they are finally addressing his problems.

A medical diagnosis can identify disabling conditions or diseases, such as Quentin's ear infection, and medical professionals then can prescribe helpful and necessary medical treatments. The medical diagnosis, however, might or might not lead toward a child's receiving special services through the public schools.

The conditions that medical doctors (pediatricians, psychiatrists, general practitioners, etc.) look for when children exhibit behavior or learning problems are generally pathological or structural causes (see table 1.1). Family doctors usually test children for infections, problems with physical growth, or other health problems. These doctors may recommend that parents take the child for specialized treatment, referring them to a specialist such as a psychologist, neurologist, or an occupational therapist. Medical professionals may find that these children need some medical treatment, which can include drug therapies or even surgery to treat the symptoms of health problems.

What medical personnel often overlook in their treatment programs for youngsters are delays in motor development. But those delays can contribute to behavioral and learning difficulties once children attend elementary school.

Table 1.1
Medical Professionals and Conditions They Diagnose

Professional	Medical conditions
Pediatricians	Disease, structural problems
Family medicine specialist	Disease, structural problems
Licensed psychologists	Psychological disorders, behavior problems, attention deficit disorder or attention deficit hyperactivity disorder, intelligence, autism or pervasive developmental disorder
Psychiatrist	Psychological problems, neuroses, psychoses, chemical imbalance, attention deficit disorder or attention deficit hyperactivity disorder, intelligence, autism or pervasive developmental disorder
Neurologists	Seizure activity, abnormal brain activity, brain injury
Optometrists/ opthalmologists	Vision problems including near-sightedness, far-sightedness, astigmatism, binocular and orthoptic problems
Audiologist	Hearing loss, auditory processing, receptive language
Speech language pathologist	Speech articulation problems, receptive and ex-pressive language, language use

Educational Categories

Like Quentin, many children are not identified as having learning problems until they reach the second grade. This is because kindergarten and first-grade teachers commonly do not use the grading scale of A, B, and C. "Suddenly" a child who seemed overly active in kindergarten no longer is just high spirited but now in the second grade is someone who receives poor grades (figure 1.1). Both parents and teachers become concerned and begin the process of looking for answers to the question of why the child is having trouble in school.

Educational professionals, specifically special educators, look at disabilities in relation to school success (see table 1.2, p. 7). They evaluate children to determine whether they are at a certain level of reading or math ability that is appropriate for their age group. If they find children who have academic delays related to a disability, they will designate them as qualified for a special education program designed to help them reach their potential.

Figure 1.1   Becoming aware of learning problems.

Educators use special terminology and labels, which vary somewhat from state to state, to designate or describe children with academic problems. These are some typical categories, using educational terminology, that qualify children for special education programs and services:

• Learning disabled
• Emotionally impaired
• Autistic
• Physically or otherwise health impaired
• Speech or language impaired
• Mentally impaired

As a teacher or parent, you may recognize that a child's clumsiness is affecting his ability to learn and to control his behavior. But a child who does not have an obvious physical disability might not receive evaluation from the teacher of adapted physical education, the occupational

Table 1.2
Educational Professionals Who Determine the Need
for Special Education Programs

Educational professional	Areas of educational problems
School psychologist	Almost all special testing, intelligence testing, behavior problems, learning disabilities, autism
Classroom teacher	Observational information, progress in school
Special education teacher	Area of suspected disability
Adapted physical education teacher	Physical ability, fundamental motor skills, motor development level, fine and gross motor ability affecting ability to learn
Occupational and physical therapists	Fine and gross motor ability affecting functioning in school and in learning situations

therapist, or the physical therapist. The underlying reason why he lacks the body control necessary to sit still or write may therefore not be discovered or determined.

Not having had a formal test of motor skills, the child may not be assigned motor development as part of a special education program. In this case, the youngster will miss the opportunity to participate in physical activities especially designed to improve his motor skills. Remember, parents and teachers have the right to demand that a child's motor development be addressed in educational evaluations and in any special programming planned for him.

To find out more about the categories for special education in your state, call your local school district or state education agency. Federal law requires that parents be given information about special education testing and programming if their child is referred for evaluation. You also have the right to—and may very well need to—ask for an evaluation of his motor development through the school system or an independent evaluation. Addresses and phone directories for these agencies are available in school administration offices or at the local public library. Contact personnel in your state capital and request the phone number for the State Department of Education. A staff member there can refer you to the Special Education Department. On the internet, you can find the phone number by using the following URL: http://www.555-1212.

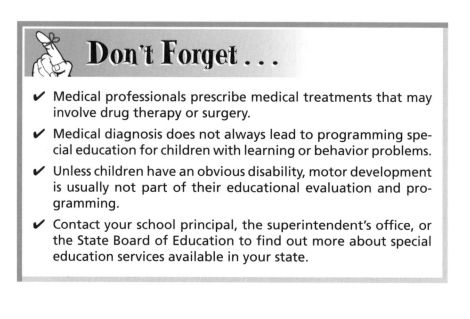

THE INFLUENCE OF MOTOR PROBLEMS ON LEARNING AND BEHAVIOR

Normally developing children have the motor skills they need to play, do homework, or interact with others. They can be attentive and enjoy learning new activities or games. These children usually experience success when attempting and practicing new activities, and often challenge themselves to do more complex tasks. When a child learns to throw a ball up in the air and catch it, he will try to throw it higher (figure 1.2). If he is successful in playing video games, he will enjoy the challenge of each more difficult level.

Once a child can sit, stand, and walk, adults take for granted that he has the motor development necessary to function in school and everyday activities. But stop and take a closer look at the child. Jill, for instance, can sit in her chair, but copying the spelling words from the chalkboard takes her twice as long as it does the other students. She just does not seem to apply himself. However, a closer look at Jill might lead to your noticing that her ability to balance (which is necessary for her to sit still) depends on her holding onto the desk with both hands. She must let go of the desk to write, however, and she then becomes a bowl of Jell-O trying not to slide out of her chair (figure 1.3, p. 10). Her inability to copy from the chalkboard has more to

Figure 1.2 Normally developing children often challenge themselves to try more complex tasks than those they have already mastered.

do with poor balance or a lack of muscle control than with a learning or behavior problem.

Children with learning and behavior problems have similar short-falls in motor development (see table 1.3, p. 11). Parents and teachers often describe these children as clumsy or awkward. They don't seem to play well with other children because their bodies just will not coop-erate. Other children may comment about how funny they look when

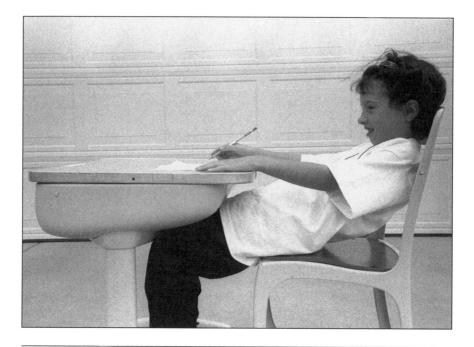

Figure 1.3 Child lacks muscle control and balance needed to sit at her desk and write.

they run. This often causes the youngsters with learning or behavior problems to become excessively silly or aggressive or to deliberately fail in activities.

We all know children who seem to be in constant motion. They crave climbing, jumping, rocking, spinning, or swinging. Some children with hyperactivity and attention problems will do cartwheels continuously—for hours (figure 1.4, p. 12). Part of the diagnostic criteria for autism is the child's exhibiting ritualistic movement patterns, such as rocking and spinning.

Other children hate to move. They never choose to play on the jungle gym or swing. Just the thought of going down a slide scares them. When these children are active, their bodies do not seem to cooperate. They may become rigid and jerky in their movements or, on the contrary, floppy and unstable. Many children with attention problems but without true hyperactivity have some of these latter motor characteristics.

Children who have a hard time with motor skills have difficulty with the everyday tasks most of us take for granted. Running Bear's parents

Table 1.3
Motor Development Problems of Children With Learning Disabilities and Behavior Problems

Diagnosed condition	Postural reactions	Balance	Body awareness	Ocular control	Locomotion	Fine motor	Endurance	Excessive movement
Learning disabilities	X	X	X	X	X	X	X	X
Autism	X	X	X	X	X	X	X	X
Pervasive developmental disorder (PDD)	X	X	X	X	X	X	X	X
High risk (*in utero* drug exposure)	X	X	X	X	*	*	*	X
Emotional problems		*	X	*		*	X	X
Attention disorder	X	X	X	X	X	X	X	X

*Not found in literature, but observed in the Special Physical Education Learning Lab at Western Michigan University.

Figure 1.4   Hyperactive children are often in constant motion.

cannot understand why their nine-year-old son takes forever to get dressed. He hangs around in his bedroom and refuses to put his clothes on. Finally, in frustration, his mother dresses him. His parents may not realize that he cannot figure out *how* to put his pants on. Somehow the pants always end up backwards. He knows his pants are on wrong; he just does not know that he needs to turn the zipper side away from his body when he steps into them.

When a particular skill needed to do a task is difficult or seems to be impossible, both adults and children become stressed. In extremely stressful situations, it gets even worse. Changes take place in the body; the heart rate, breathing, and blood pressure increase. A person's muscles tighten, and the palms begin to sweat. The stomach feels like a knot. A child's ability to eat or digest his food is reduced or even stopped.

You can step in as a parent or teacher, however, and be the initial stress meter for children! If you recognize that a child is experiencing stress, you can tell her how to change the activity or teach him how to

Figure 1.5 Child trying to avoid stress caused by academics.

ask for help. A child may not recognize stress or be able to tell you that she or he is stressed (figure 1.5). He may not think to ask for help because he does not know what kind of help he needs. For example, if a child cannot follow a ball with his eyes, he does not know why. He does not know what his eyes are doing wrong or how to use them differently. He may not even realize that his eyes are causing a problem.

During stress both adults and children commonly use two types of protective behavior—fight or flight. *Fight behaviors* may be either throwing a temper tantrum, for example, or hitting another person. *Flight behaviors* include physically leaving the activity or refusing to participate. Knowing that your child may not have the motor ability to read, write, kick a ball, or sit still can explain why he may be under stress and easily distracted, frustrated, or hyperactive.

Common fight-or-flight behaviors are listed in the chart "Expressions and Actions of Children Under Stress."

Expressions and Actions of Children Under Stress

Flight responses	Fight responses
"I need to go to the bathroom."	"I won't read."
"I'm sick. I need to go home."	Hits the nearest child.
"My mother told me I don't have to."	Throws books off the desk on the way to the chalkboard.
"I'm tired."	Trips other child during physical education.
"I don't like to do this, it's boring."	"You can't make me do it."
Deliberately falls down.	Throws books or homework.
Daydreams.	Yells or screams at the parent or teacher.
"I forgot my gym clothes."	Destroys property.

MOTOR CHARACTERISTICS OF SPECIFIC DISABILITIES

Some children with specific disabilities (including autism, learning disabilities, attention deficit disorders, and emotional problems) have been found to benefit from a program of sensory motor development. Here is a short description of how motor characteristics affect children with each of these conditions.

Autism

Children with autism often have movement you might describe as excessive or repetitive. Sometimes the movement seems socially inappropriate (figure 1.6) These youngsters seem to need movement to calm themselves or keep themselves occupied. They may avoid interaction with others. Jasmine, for instance, loves to climb on furniture and dive onto pillows. She does this continually and never seems to notice whether anyone else is around. Although she has an age-appropriate ability to climb, her walking pattern is choppy, and she seems to lock her legs with each step.

Figure 1.6 Children with autism often need movement to calm or occupy themselves. Sometimes these movements are socially inappropriate.

Learning Disabilities

Learning disabilities often stem from motor development problems that go undetected. A child with *dysgraphia* (difficulty with writing), who cannot complete writing lessons, may have difficulty not only with the fine motor (small muscle) skill of writing but also with the gross motor (large muscle) development that precedes writing. He may not have the muscle control in his torso or shoulders that he needs for holding his body still while he writes with his hand. Another child may not have control of the neck muscles that are used to hold her head still while her eyes follow a line of words in a book.

Attention Deficit Disorders

The *Diagnostic and Statistical Manual of Mental Disorders, 4th edition* (DSM-IV) of the American Psychiatric Association lists a variety of behaviors or symptoms for attention deficit disorder (ADD) and attention deficit hyperactivity disorder (ADHD). In general, to be considered to have ADD or ADHD the child must have been inattentive, hyperactive, and impulsive for at least six months. The list of behaviors for ADD or ADHD can seem to describe any child who is experiencing delays in sensory motor development. For example, a child who has difficulty paying attention to details and makes careless mistakes may have a problem with hand-eye coordination. Moreover, any child who doesn't experience success in play activities will not want to continue an activity for any length of time. Children who always seem on the go, on the other hand, may be intuitively seeking physical activities that would actually help the body and mind develop basic body-control skills. These skills must come before they can gain the body control needed to sit still.

Other Emotional Problems

People often describe a child with emotional or behavior disorders as clumsy or fidgety. Abnormal brain activity may be one factor that limits the neurological connections necessary for coordinated movements. Clumsiness, unfortunately, interferes with the youngster's ability to play and participate in sports. And this in turn reduces his opportunity to make friends and learn socially acceptable behaviors. Being uncoordinated also intensifies the difficulties he may have doing academic tasks. Altogether, it's a two-edged sword—which means he can benefit from a two-edged solution or program, medical and educational.

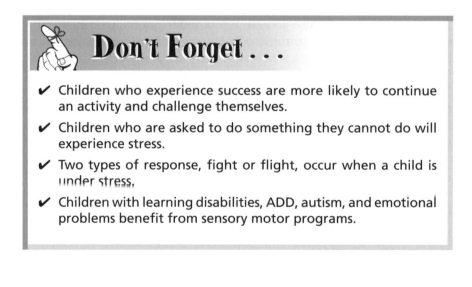

Don't Forget . . .

✔ Children who experience success are more likely to continue an activity and challenge themselves.

✔ Children who are asked to do something they cannot do will experience stress.

✔ Two types of response, fight or flight, occur when a child is under stress.

✔ Children with learning disabilities, ADD, autism, and emotional problems benefit from sensory motor programs.

chapter 2
Neurological Growth and Development

Many children who have learning problems must wait until they reach the second grade before a teacher notifies their parents of their difficulties. This is because failing grades are not usually given to children in kindergarten or the first grade. In the second grade, however, these children who move a lot no longer just "seem" (and we emphasize seem) hyperactive but may also receive a low letter grade. The teacher becomes concerned and, in turn, informs the parent, raising his or her concern.

Many parents and teachers ask, "Why is this happening to my child?" Each child's life begins the same way. How is it, then, that some children end up with one or more of the problems that teachers categorize and medical personnel diagnose (see chapter 1)? Here we help you begin to answer this question.

To fully understand a child with behavior and learning problems, it is necessary to look at what influenced the child's early development, even the prenatal stage of development! After birth, certain stages of growth and development are common to most children. They will enter and pass through these stages in approximately the same order and at about the same age as other children. By examining the stages of development, you may recognize the point at which a particular child experienced some developmental difficulties that are now limiting his academic, behavioral, or motor abilities.

DEFINING GROWTH AND DEVELOPMENT

Child development, growth and development, and maturation are three terms that people often use interchangeably to describe the stages of learning in a child's first few years. Nevertheless it can help us, in understanding the learning process, to separate these terms a bit. *Growth*, first of all, is exactly what it says. A child experiences both physical and physiological growth, or change, with the most dramatic growth rate occurring during the early years. An 8-year-old boy or girl may have the same size and maturity as a 5-year-old or as an 11-year-old, and still fall within the normal range (figure 2.1) The youngster also experiences changes in the brain as well as physiological changes, such as those that occur during the teenage years. In other words, he is said to be

Figure 2.1 Although these children are the same age, they clearly vary in height.

maturing. This period of growth continues from the time of conception to approximately 22 years of age.

Development or *child development* usually refers to a child's reaching and passing through a series of stages, which are commonly called milestones, developmental milestones, or stages of development. There are a variety of developmental charts or scales available in parenting and educational materials. Most of these charts list a series of developmental stages and give the approximate age range during which a child should accomplish each task.

DEVELOPMENTAL SEQUENCES

When you examine a childhood development chart, you should remember two basic facts. First, it is the *sequence* that is important. Children typically progress through an orderly, predictable sequence of development. One stage in the sequence leads to another. As you know, children sit before they stand, and stand before they walk. Gross motor skills (for example, walking and running) are developed before fine motor skills (such as handwriting), and babbling precedes talking. Figure 2.2 presents an example of some of the skills that lead to walking. While the order of reaching each skill seems to be recognizable and separate, a child may be involved with developing several skills at once.

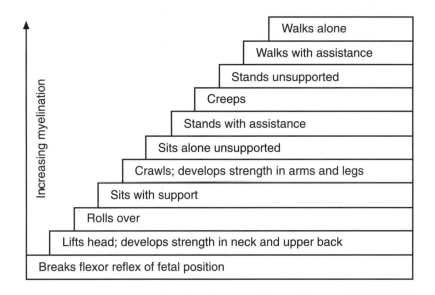

Figure 2.2 Skills that lead to walking.

For example, your child may learn to balance in sitting at the same age that she learns to stand with support.

The second fact to remember is that *each child is unique.* Each one will move through each developmental stage at an age that is right for him or her. Whereas one child may reach a milestone at an early age, another child may reach the same milestone later; yet both can be within a normal range.

Developmental charts often vary greatly. If you look at three different developmental charts, you might find that the age that a child should be able to sit with support is listed as 4 months, 6 months, or even in an age range of 6 to 8 months. For this reason it is wise to look at several developmental charts to select one that has an age range of achievement that seems more appropriate to the particular child.

View developmental milestones or stages as guidelines only! Children seem to have a set rhythm, and they move from one stage to the next only when they are ready. While some children walk as early as 8 or 9 months, most children do not walk until they are 12 to 15 months old. Twins seem to seesaw in their development. One may learn to roll over first and then seem to stop progressing for a while. The other twin may roll over later, but then move quickly through that stage and immediately on to reach the next level and sit up first (figure 2.3).

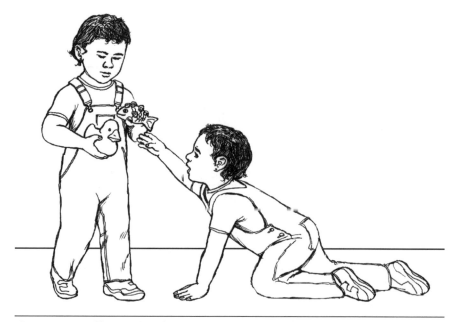

Figure 2.3 Different developmental level of twins.

Don't Forget . . .

✔ View child-development charts as guidelines only.

✔ Child-development charts should provide an age *range* for children to perform each skill.

✔ Children develop through stages in an orderly sequence.

✔ Each child develops at his own unique rate.

Progression to Cross-Lateral Movements

A newborn baby should both move and sleep a lot. The first movements are called *global movements,* and they involve moving the whole body at the same time. By interacting with the environment, babies progress through several stages of motor development until they manage to use the cross-lateral movement patterns found in creeping, crawling, and walking.

When children start to become mobile, they go through a series of movement patterns performed with all four limbs. They will typically progress from homologous to homolateral movements and then to cross-lateral patterns during creeping and crawling (see figure 2.4). *Homologous* creeping and crawling is like a rabbit hopping. Both arms move forward, and then the two legs follow.

In *homolateral* creeping and crawling, the baby moves the arm and leg on the *same side* forward (for example, both the right arm and leg), and then move the opposite limbs forward (that is, the left arm and leg). *Cross-lateral* creeping and crawling precede the movements your child will use in walking. Here the baby's right arm and left leg move forward together, as the left leg and right arm move back in opposition.

All too frequently we find that later developmental delays in the movement patterns of children who have learning problems or behavior disorders are related to problems they had during the various earlier stages of creeping and crawling. Some children never progress to the cross-lateral stages but instead remain frozen at a stage in which both arms and legs were used together or first one side of the body moved and then the other.

Stage 1:
Homologous
creeping and
crawling: both
arms move
forward, followed
by both legs.

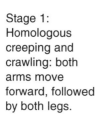

Stage 1:
Homologous
creeping and
crawling: both
arms move
forward, followed
by both legs.

Stage 2:
Homolateral
creeping and
crawling: the arm
and leg on the
same side of the
body move
forward, followed
by the opposite
arm and leg.

Stage 3:
Cross lateral
creeping and
crawling: the
right arm and left
leg move
forward, followed
by the left arm
and right leg.

Figure 2.4 Three stages of creeping and crawling.

Most children basically progress through this sequence of movement stages:

1. Moving the four limbs (both arms and both legs) in the same way at the same time
2. Moving the arms together in the same way
3. Moving the legs together in the same way
4. Moving one arm separately from the other
5. Moving one leg separately from the other
6. Moving an arm on one side of the body with a leg on the same side in the same way
7. Moving an arm on one side of the body with the opposite leg and vice versa

Quadrilateral and Bilateral Movement in Children

Surprisingly, some six- to nine-year-old children with learning problems seem frozen at the stage of development in which they still use all four limbs together, which is called *quadrilateral movement*. This is most obvious when they play catch. As a ball nears a child with quadrilateral movements, one leg and both arms move toward the ball (the other foot planted on the ground), which collapses her body in the middle. A quadrilateral movement during a kick looks like she is swinging both legs and arms toward the ball while the rear end retreats, and she nearly falls on the floor and sometimes does fall (see figure 2.5).

Other children with learning problems seem locked in the stage of development in which both arms or both legs *must be used together*. These are the same children who consistently used their two arms together and then their two legs (in homologous movements) when they were creeping and crawling. This pattern became so ingrained in their systems that catching a ball or writing without the opposite hand moving is difficult for them. This is referred to as a *bilateral movement*. Both limbs do not necessarily do the exact same movements. As children with bilateral movements try to use one hand, trace movements in their opposite hand may occur. These small movements are sometimes referred to as *associated movements*.

Children who favor bilateral movements have some major problems. For instance, they have trouble developing right- and left-side awareness, preference for one side of the body, and cross-lateral movements.

Figure 2.5 Quadrilateral movement when trying to catch a ball.

An easy way to check whether a child has bilateral movements is to watch her write on a piece of paper or the chalkboard. There should be no accompanying movement of the nonpreferred hand. Another way to check is to toss a ball to one side of the child. If he moves to one side, in order to use two hands, or if you see his opposite hand move, there could be a bilateral problem.

Cephalocaudal and *proximodistal* are terms that refer to the sequence of a child's growth and development. *Cephalocaudal* means growth occurs from the head to the tail, and *proximodistal* refers to growth from near the center of the body ("proximo-") to the outside of the limbs ("distal") (see figure 2.6). While the fetus is in the womb, the head and facial structures grow faster than the trunk, and the lower part of the body develops last. Even motor development after birth follows this trend. First, a child learns to control her head movements, followed by her trunk, and then her legs. This is why one of the first skills a child learns is to lift her head.

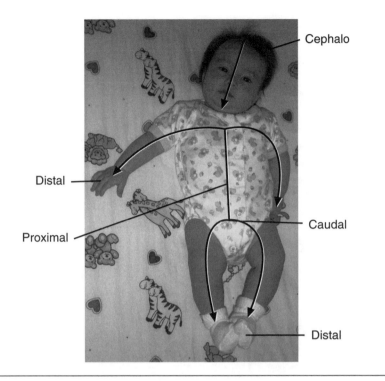

Figure 2.6 Cephalocaudal/proximodistal growth.

Proximodistal growth means learning to control movements near the center of the body before those of the extremities—the hands, feet, fingers, and toes. When you first reach for newborn babies, they cannot reach toward you. In fact, they are not even conscious that their hands and fingers are moving. At about four and a half months of age, however, babies can reach both arms toward you or toward a toy, using total arm movements starting at the shoulder. By 10 months, they can deliberately reach toward an object and grasp it with their fingers (figure 2.7).

General to specific refers to the order in which a child learns motor skills. *General movements,* such as randomly waving the arms, are learned before *specific movements,* such as rolling over, reaching for a toy, or hitting a ball. The order of skill development depends on growth in the nervous system. Children are neurologically ready for gross motor activities before fine motor or specific skills. This is why young children, and particularly those with motor difficulties, often prefer gross motor activities—such as running, jumping, and hopping—to fine motor skills—such as coloring or cutting with scissors.

Figure 2.7   Young child reaching and grasping.

Gross motor activities (using the large muscles) include throwing, hitting, striking, walking, running, leaping, jumping, and climbing, as well as coloring large circles and other designs using mainly the shoulders, arms, and legs. Fine motor (using small muscles) refers to activities that use the fingers and wrists in coloring, writing, stringing beads, and putting together toys such as Legos.

Have you noticed how 15-month-old children are often interested in scribbling? At first they use the large muscles of the shoulder to create a series of lines on a page. Eventually these random lines will resemble a circle, but a child may be three years old before she can copy a circle. Squares, rectangles, triangles, and diamonds come still later because they involve more fine motor control. When children first attempt drawing a square, usually at the age of four or five, they lift the crayon and make the line for each side separately—or the square may evolve out of a series of horizontal and vertical scribbles that turn into lines.

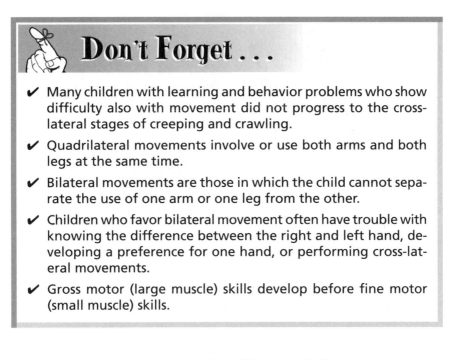

Don't Forget . . .

✔ Many children with learning and behavior problems who show difficulty also with movement did not progress to the cross-lateral stages of creeping and crawling.

✔ Quadrilateral movements involve or use both arms and both legs at the same time.

✔ Bilateral movements are those in which the child cannot separate the use of one arm or one leg from the other.

✔ Children who favor bilateral movement often have trouble with knowing the difference between the right and left hand, developing a preference for one hand, or performing cross-lateral movements.

✔ Gross motor (large muscle) skills develop before fine motor (small muscle) skills.

PRENATAL DEVELOPMENT

During the nine months of pregnancy a tremendous amount of change occurs to a developing fetus. Teachers, parents, and medical professionals have become more aware in recent years of the influence of prenatal development on the future behavior and educational ability of children. Certainly, a woman carrying a child feels the difference in the physical growth of her fetus, but she also notices changes in its movements. The first movements of a prenatal baby occur at about the 15th week. These are flutters of the legs, which are initially hard to detect. By the ninth month, however, a mother knows where each kick lands!

The sensory systems of hearing, vision, smell, taste, and touch also begin to develop during the fetal period. At approximately four and a half months old, prenatal babies will even react to sounds. Newborn babies are so adept at recognizing fetal sounds that many fathers or mothers talk to, read to, or play music to the fetus during pregnancy. Following birth, the babies continue to respond favorably to sounds that were soothing to them in the womb. Parents have even noticed that their children recognize stories that were read to them *before* birth. Youngsters in a bilingual family will often be comforted by the language that was calming for them during the prenatal months (figure 2.8).

Figure 2.8 Father talking to prenatal child in Spanish.

Sonograms indicate that some babies suck their thumbs long before birth. Through the use of sonograms, Dr. Brazelton (1988) watched a baby in the womb busily sucking his thumb. When a light was placed on the mother's stomach, the baby took his thumb out of his mouth and turned to look at the light. After a few seconds, he then turned away from the light and resumed sucking his thumb.

Throughout the nine months of development in utero, babies encounter environmental influences. These occur through the fluids within the amniotic sac, blood supplied to the baby through a mother's circulatory system, and nutrition carried through the placenta. Ideally, given the mother's proper nutrition, the growth and development of a child will proceed normally.

Doctors do know that good, consistent prenatal care increases the chance that a child will not have later academic, behavioral, or developmental problems. On the other hand, poor prenatal care often results in a higher incidence of infant mortality and an increased risk that the development of a child will be negatively affected.

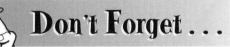

Don't Forget ...

✔ All of the sensory systems start to develop during the fetal period.

✔ Good prenatal care can have a positive effect on the development of a child.

NEUROLOGICAL DEVELOPMENT

How does the brain of a child develop before birth, and what influence does this development have on his future growth and development? Basically, as Young (1978, p. 1) states, "The brain is composed of programs that control our lives." It is made up of cells called *neurons* (see figure 2.9). Shortly after conception, the first few neurons appear in the brain of a fetus. It is estimated that the speed of neuronal creation rapidly increases in the brain, however, until some 250,000 neurons appear each minute! Neurons that have the same purpose are created at the same time, and they travel to an area where they are grouped according to their future use. Neurons that will be used for sight, for example, group together; similarly, those used for hearing group together and go to another area. Once at the new location, each neuron rapidly makes about 15,000 connections to other neurons, allowing more communication (sensations or impulses) to be sent from one neuron to another.

Exposing a prenatal baby to drugs, smoke, toxins, or even stress, during pregnancy will likely hurt the neurons that are being created and grouped at the time of that exposure. Two prenatal babies exposed to the same negative influence, such as drugs, may have two completely different sets of symptoms, permanently affecting their health, or their intellectual or physical development. An easy way to understand this concept is to visualize throwing water on several computers. The effects on each computer will be different because the water lands on different circuits of each computer. If a mother consumes alcohol during the time when the neurons that control movement are being formed, her fetus-child could eventually have coordination problems.

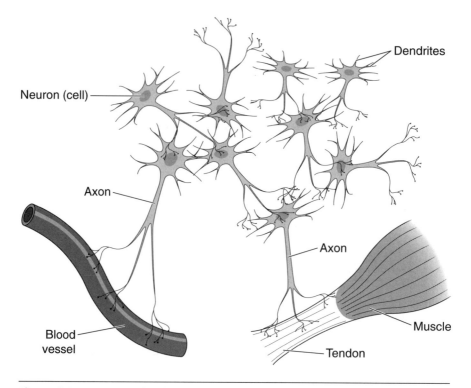

Figure 2.9   Neurons, dendrites, and the neural pathway.

Neurological Connections and Pathways

Neurons are the cells that form the basic unit of the brain and nervous system. To communicate with one another, the brain's neurons develop branches, similar to the branches on a tree. These branches are called *dendrites* (see figure 2.9) and function to receive information. Neurons connect to other neurons through the dendrites and axons. As a child grows, the number of dendrites in his or her brain also increases. That is, given an appropriate environment, experiences, and nutrition, the number of connections (dendrites) increases.

Each neuron has one axon. The purpose of an axon is to carry impulses away from the neuron to other neurons and to muscles, skin, eyes, ears, nose, and other structures of the body. The impulse delivered by an axon to a muscle tells the muscle to act. Axons can be as short as a few micrometers (particularly those that stay within the brain) or as long as several feet. One of the longest is the axon that controls the big toe. The main part of the neuron is located in the brain, but the axon extends down into the spinal cord.

When a pregnant woman moves, or when the fetus in her womb moves, sensations (actually, electrical impulses or currents) send information from one neuron to another. These sensations start the creation of a *neurological pathway*, what you might call a type of road (again, look at figure 2.9). Different movements, even in the womb, will create different neurological pathways in a baby's brain. For example, when a prenatal baby sucks his thumb, the feelings of his mouth on his thumb are sent along a set of neurons to his brain. Yet, when he responds to a light, the sensations travel along *another* pathway to his brain. These pathways or connections between the dendrites of various neurons are not located in just one place. Some connections may be between neurons that are close to each other, yet other connections may be made with neurons some distance away.

At birth, children have more neurons than they will have at any other time in their lives. Over one half of an individual's neurons are lost by the age of three! If a toddler loses so many neurons, how is he or she able to gain intelligence and develop motor skills, such as walking and running, during that time? Here is where the dendrites and their pathways come into play. There is an increase in the number of dendrites and the number and strength of the neurological pathways.

Neurological pathways are constantly being created or lost throughout life. As long as any part of a child can see, feel, hear, or move, sensations are being sent along pathways to and from the brain or spinal cord. When a child has a new experience, such as reaching for a toy held by her mother, connections are created between the dendrites and axons of various neurons in her brain (figure 2.10). She will have many partially successful and unsuccessful attempts at touching the toy before her goal is achieved. However, once she grasps the toy, it is natural for her to repeat the skill over and over. This repetition creates additional connections between the neurons and establishes a more secure pathway.

Learning to perform skills *automatically* is important to developing motor skills and eventually for classroom activities. During the process of learning a new skill, a child must think through each step as he or she attempts to do the new task (such as reaching for a mobile). Once the skill is accomplished and she creates a firm neurological pathway, the skill becomes automatic. At this stage she can perform the task without concentrating on it. This allows her to do two things at once. You will notice that she can reach for the mobile while looking at you and perhaps even while blowing bubbles. Even when a child first learns to

Figure 2.10 When a child has a new experience, such as reaching for a toy, connections are created between the dendrites and axons of various neurons in his or her brain.

hold a pencil and write, she has to think about how to hold the pencil and then how to form letters. After a lot of practice, which forms neurological pathways, she will be able to write without having to think about the techniques of holding the pencil.

If for some reason, such as severe stress or an injury, a child in the learning stages of reaching for a mobile was to stop and never again attempt to reach the mobile or another object, the dendrites would disappear and the connections would be lost. Similarly, when a child with chronic ear infections cannot hear and quits trying to make sounds, not only his neurological pathways (for hearing and speech formation) might be lost but also his future ability to hear. Say that a toddler breaks her leg just after taking her first steps; while she is confined to a cast, she could lose some of the neurological pathways for balancing and walking. As she moves about with the cast, however, she would be able

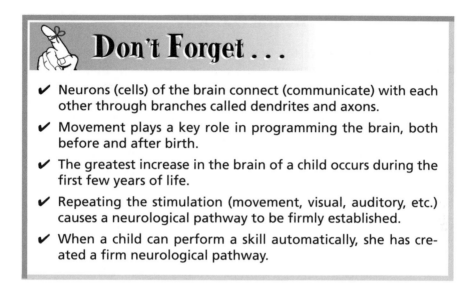

Don't Forget . . .

- ✔ Neurons (cells) of the brain connect (communicate) with each other through branches called dendrites and axons.
- ✔ Movement plays a key role in programming the brain, both before and after birth.
- ✔ The greatest increase in the brain of a child occurs during the first few years of life.
- ✔ Repeating the stimulation (movement, visual, auditory, etc.) causes a neurological pathway to be firmly established.
- ✔ When a child can perform a skill automatically, she has created a firm neurological pathway.

to develop other neuron connections, so that her balancing and walking would not be negatively influenced throughout her life.

The Nervous System and Developmental Readiness

The development of complex motor skills depends upon the nervous system's growth, a process sometimes called readiness, maturity, or developmental level. Even though babies have billions of neurons at birth, they lack the ability to perform *goal-directed skills*. As early as the first few days after birth, however, the nervous system begins to develop in a manner that allows the child to perform different actions intentionally. Growth or a change in the nervous system must precede the development of new movement or motor skills. The first obvious sign of a change in the growth of the nervous system occurs when a baby is about four and five months old and starts reaching for objects. From then until the end of the third year, many changes occur, allowing the baby or toddler to progress through skills such as rolling over, sitting up, walking, and eventually, running.

No matter what a parent or a teacher does, this particular growth of the nervous system cannot be rushed. This means that the set sequence for developing motor skills cannot be easily altered. Children cannot walk if the changes in the nervous system necessary for walking have not occurred. More advanced movement patterns and motor skills appear as the individual parts of her nervous system mature.

Neural Plasticity

Plasticity is the ability of the brain to adapt or change in response to demands of the environment. This occurs throughout life, but most easily and dramatically during a child's early developmental stages. Development occurs through plasticity, the ability of neurons in her brain to make new connections (to communicate) with a new set of neurons and to create new pathways. Through plasticity, each response of a child to a new stimulus or a more difficult demand of the environment increases the number of dendrites (connections) between the neurons. For example, say a seven-year-old girl in a physical education class faces a new task, skipping. Before she can actually perform the skill of skipping, new connections between neurons must occur in her brain.

For years we have known that rats or mice raised in an enriched environment with a variety of toys and food grow to perform better than those who receive food and water but no stimulation. Part of their superior performance is related to plasticity. As the rats played with their new toys, an increase occurred in the number of connections between their neurons.

Until recently it has been generally assumed that following birth, the number of neurons (brain cells) in the brain decrease but that no new cells develop. Discoveries from experiments involving rats and mice are causing educators to reevaluate not only their current view on brain development, however, but also their recommendations for early childhood educational programs. In recent experiments Kempermann, Kuhn, and Gage (1997) and then Kempermann, Brandon, and Gage (1998) found that certain mice exposed to a rich, active environment in just a few months had an increase in the growth of brain cells in a particular part of the brain. In one study, researchers found the increase was as much as 67 percent.

In 1993 Friend summarized the early work of many of these researchers (who are employed by the Salk Institute for Biological Studies of Genetics in California), the most interesting factor being that the growth of the cells was directly related to the type of activities performed by the mice. The mice that ran on a treadmill had more cell growth than others that swam or were inactive. This suggests that learning is affected by the environment as well as by genetics and that children may have a greater potential for learning than we have thought in the past. Note that the greatest increase in the brain cells followed the physical activity of running. If physical activity has the same effect on children, teachers and parents need to encourage vigorous physical activities as part of a child's daily life.

Aerobic physical activity also increases the blood supply to the brain. It not only forces an increase in the size of the capillaries in the brain but also creates *new* capillaries. Thus, more blood and oxygen can reach the active parts of a child's brain, which greatly increases the potential for learning.

Neurons also have the ability to change neurological pathways—another aspect of plasticity. Even though scientists think a child's brain is "wired" in a specific way, they don't consider this wiring to be set in stone. After a neurological pathway has been interrupted through injury, stroke, or disease, some connections can be reestablished or new ones can be created. The creation of a new pathway is referred to as *sprouting*, much like a branch of a tree. When one branch of a tree is lost through disease or surgical removal, the remaining tree fills in the vacant area by sprouting new branches. This action is also true in the brain. Sprouting, in the brain of a child, is a direct result of the demands of the environment and the youngster's responses to these environmental demands (such as homework, movement, interaction with others). These experiences force the individual's neurons to "sprout" (that is, to make) new connections to perform the lost skills and activities.

Sprouting is detected most obviously in the cases of children with brain tumors. You might expect that after a surgery removing part of the brain, these children would not be able to succeed in school. Some not only succeed, however, but even make outstanding grades in schoolwork. Plasticity (in the form of sprouting) has allowed them to recover many abilities. The brain that remains takes over activities that formerly had been performed by the part that was removed.

Consider something simpler. Being able to change the way one holds a pencil is also an example of creating new neurological pathways. Some children hold a pencil incorrectly when they start elementary school (figure 2.11a). The position they use feels comfortable to them. Their teacher, however, might ask them to use a different way to hold a pencil (2.11b). The youngsters must create a new skill pathway to the brain, and the old neurological pathway must be abandoned. How does this occur? Repetition and plasticity enter the scene. The children must first concentrate on holding the pencil using the new, "correct" technique. With enough repetition, this new pathway, created by connections between different neurons, is superimposed over the old pathway.

Replacing old pathways with new ones is not necessarily easy. If a child learns a skill (such as a forehand drive in tennis or a swimming stroke) incorrectly, the instructor has to teach the youngster the correct action. This involves getting the individual to repeat the new technique so often that when she starts the skill, the new pathway takes over. If

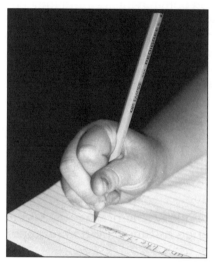

a

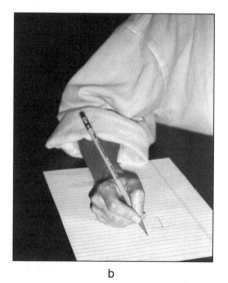

b

Figure 2.11 Creating new neurological pathways by changing pencil grip.

she does not concentrate or is stressed, she will slip back into the old pathway and will repeat the incorrect skill.

Motivation and practice are key elements in creating new pathways. A child needs to be motivated to attempt the new technique. Motivation must also be maintained during the numerous practice sessions that will be necessary for her to form the new neurological pathways. Plasticity depends on both having a stimulating environment and persistently repeating the activities.

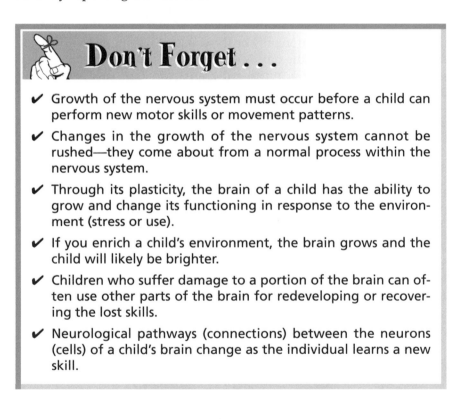

Don't Forget . . .

✔ Growth of the nervous system must occur before a child can perform new motor skills or movement patterns.

✔ Changes in the growth of the nervous system cannot be rushed—they come about from a normal process within the nervous system.

✔ Through its plasticity, the brain of a child has the ability to grow and change its functioning in response to the environment (stress or use).

✔ If you enrich a child's environment, the brain grows and the child will likely be brighter.

✔ Children who suffer damage to a portion of the brain can often use other parts of the brain for redeveloping or recovering the lost skills.

✔ Neurological pathways (connections) between the neurons (cells) of a child's brain change as the individual learns a new skill.

SENSORY MOTOR STAGE

The first 18 to 24 months of life are called the *sensory motor stage*. This is because during this stage a child learns mainly through movement and the sensory systems. A newborn baby has little control over movement. During the sensory motor stage, she changes from an infant who randomly moves her arms and legs to a young toddler who can manipulate objects and walk and run in space. You might say that in these 24 months the child gains independent movements. She passes through a series of reflexes and reactions that gradually improve her ability to control her body. By the age of two, she will have attained such skills as rolling over, sitting, standing, walking, and running, all the while maintaining balance during each of these activities.

In order for a child's brain to develop, it must be stimulated or engaged in some activity. Having a rich environment that includes age-appropriate experiences, movement activities, and interactions with others encourages the child's brain development. However, some children live in an environment in which they receive little or no stimulation. These children lack toys or other types of visual or auditory stimulation. Their only stimulation may be the constant blaring of the TV. They lie unattended most of the day. Medical and educational professionals say that under these conditions children are *sensory deprived* (figure 2.12)—they don't have the stimulation going to the brain that forces the

Figure 2.12   Examples of sensory deprivation and rich environment.

neurons to develop connections with each other or to develop pathways. And there must be some type of brain activity for neurons to make connections with each other.

Children who have been developing normally may stop progressing when they are transferred to less stimulating situations. These unstimulating conditions exist in some group foster homes and even in some hospitals (where a child might stay because of suffering a long-term injury or illness). In these cases, connections between neurons cease to be made, and the brain cells eventually die. (On the other hand, some group foster homes are a huge step up for the children living in them, in terms of access to stimulation and life-enhancing activities.)

Occasionally, parents become overly protective. They do not allow their child to explore the environment; they may tend to keep him in a playpen all day. Overly protective parents do an activity for a child instead of letting him experiment with movement through trial and error. They may insist on carrying a child beyond the age for walking or on feeding him to avoid his making a mess. These kinds of behavior tend to cause these children to be developmentally delayed.

Many children who are adopted and who are slow developmentally have suffered sensory deprivation. Even if the children were fed and sheltered in a clean environment, they sometimes had little interaction with adults. A six-month-old baby, for example, had a developmental age of only two months when she arrived from an orphanage in Columbia. After three months in a stimulating environment that included

Don't Forget . . .

✔ A child's growth during the first 24 months occurs through movement and the sensory systems.

✔ Having a rich environment and age-appropriate experiences encourages the brain's development in a young child.

✔ Children who lack a rich environment or age-appropriate stimulation may be developmentally delayed.

✔ If you do not stimulate a child's brain, it will lose connections, and part of the brain may die.

✔ Overly protective parents might be engaging in a type of sensory deprivation that interferes with their child's development.

a lot of interaction with her adoptive parents, she gained the developmental level of her nine-month-old peers. Plasticity allowed this child to catch up in development.

THE NERVOUS SYSTEM

The nervous system reaches from the brain and spinal cord to every part of the body. There are two major units of the nervous system: the central nervous system (CNS) and the peripheral nervous system (PNS). The *central nervous system* is the controlling unit of the whole nervous system and consists of the brain and the spinal cord (see figure 2.13). The spinal cord is the group of neurons within the spinal column. Involuntary activities, such as breathing, the heart beating, and blinking the eyes, are controlled here. The central nervous system also governs prenatal and early developmental reflexes and reactions that are involuntary.

The *peripheral nervous system* is the remainder of the nervous system, and it involves voluntary movements of the body (see figure 2.14). Neu-

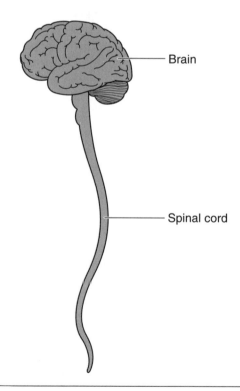

Brain

Spinal cord

Figure 2.13 The central nervous system.

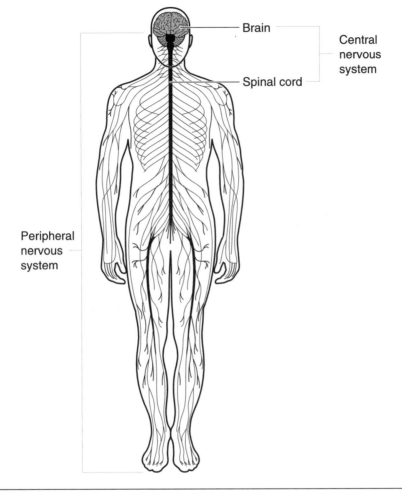

Figure 2.14 Peripheral nervous system.

rons in the peripheral system have the ability to send information back and forth to each other and to the central system. The peripheral nervous system also organizes and interprets information. In other words, it helps a child use the right motor skill for a particular movement or an activity. To write on a sheet of paper, for example, the toddler must know the shape of the pencil, where to place her fingers on the pencil, how much strength to use, where to place her hand on the paper, how much force to use to make the marks, and which muscles to use in making the designs.

SPLINTER SKILLS

We discuss splinter skills in this section to explain both the advantages your children and students in your classrooms have in progressing through movement education programs based on normal developmental sequences and to *discourage* the use of splinter skills. *Splinter skills* are the motor skills that a child learns at a higher developmental level than his age. There is a direct relationship between a child's ability to perform motor skills and the maturation of various parts of his nervous system. A child's ability to perform a splinter skill, however, has nothing to do with the rest of the child's development; it cannot be transferred to other skills with similar movement patterns.

Let's say that you receive a note from the gym teacher saying that your eight-year-old son Chang can throw a baseball but has coordination problems when he attempts to throw a basketball. The teacher includes no explanation concerning Chang's motor development level. Or say that you play catch with your child in the backyard, continuing to throw the baseball back and forth until he is fairly good at throwing. But you become puzzled because when you shift to playing basketball, he again has trouble throwing.

As another example, first-grade teacher Mrs. Whitecloud confers with the gym teacher who informs her that half her class cannot skip. Mrs. Whitecloud's training was in education, not developmental work, and she is not aware that many children are not developmentally ready to skip before they are seven or eight years old. In fact, some children cannot use their arms in a coordinated skipping pattern until they are nine. So it is perfectly normal for children in the first grade to have trouble skipping. The problem, strangely enough, is that a *few* children can learn to skip at four and a half or five years of age. These exceptional children seem to set the standard for some professionals. Sometimes professionals do not evaluate a child's developmental age before they start new activities. This tendency is not isolated to the gymnasium, and it can occur among dance teachers, sport teachers, and movement education personnel who try to push children ahead of their developmental ages.

In some cases there are a few advantages to learning splinter skills. Even though a child's nervous system may be at one level of growth, some special skills can be taught at a higher level. However, this occurs as a result of an enormous amount of repetition and hard work on the part of the child. In some cases children with motor delays are taught sport-specific skills so that they can participate in sports with nondisabled peers and thereby form friendships.

Sometimes children learn the splinter skills, but still lack the developmental movement patterns that preceded the splinter skill. A child might learn to catch a ball as a splinter skill, for example, but cannot catch a ball during an actual game that involves other factors, such as noise, teammates, and rules. Another child might have the splinter skill of holding a pencil correctly but continue to have poor handwriting because an earlier skill (stable upper-body control) is lacking.

Training children to do splinter skills is not always good. Not matching a child's activities with his or her developmental level is, in fact, a serious problem today. Many parents and teachers believe that children can be introduced to sports or other activities without regard to their developmental age—just because they are at a certain chronological age or they are in a certain grade. A clinical professor of psychiatry and pediatrics at George Washington Medical School (Greenspan 1994, p. 651) summarized the overall effects of using splinter skills this way: "Splinter skills may boost the morale of the parents, educator, or clinician, but they rarely help the child very much."

Don't Forget . . .

✔ The central nervous system controls the involuntary activities of breathing, heart beat, and blinking the eyes.

✔ The peripheral nervous system, concerned with voluntary movements, helps a child know the movements needed for an activity or a skill.

✔ Splinter skills are those learned skills that are ahead of a child's general developmental level.

✔ Splinter skills do not transfer to other similar activities.

chapter 3
Tips for Sensory Motor Development Programs

Just as building basic health and physical fitness requires daily physical activity, so too does developing the neurological connections necessary for successful learning and appropriate behavior. Although we hear many reports of the declining physical fitness of American children, we learn few, if any, facts about the negative impact a lack of daily physical activity has on children developing the motor control they need to function well in school.

Nevertheless, it is increasingly apparent that daily physical activity is critical to a child reaching important motor development milestones—and to improving health and fitness. Unfortunately, most elementary schoolchildren in the United States receive only two half-hour sessions of physical education per week. This is nowhere near what the American Alliance of Health, Physical Education, Recreation and Dance (AAHPERD, 1989) recommends: that is, at least 30 minutes of *daily* physical activity. And the trend in public schools recently, even in our nation's capital, is toward eliminating recess and concentrating solely on academic learning. At home, many children spend a lot of time watching TV or playing video games, time that is lost for motor development opportunities, whether climbing a tree, riding a bike, or playing a neighborhood game of softball.

Getting a child to be physically active may take some time and creativity. Chapter 3 discusses some recommendations we have to make the task easier both for parents and teachers. They are basic, involve your whole family, provide your child with a variety of opportunities for success, and include physical activities during the school day that relate to a classroom lesson. And when you give instructions or teach rules to a child, there are some practical basics that will make your efforts more effective.

HELP BUILD THE CHILD'S SELF-ESTEEM

All people, and especially children, need to experience success in order to build self-esteem. If children feel successful in an activity, they are more likely to continue participating in it. Eventually these children feel good about themselves and have the courage to try new activities, motor skills, or academic learning tasks.

Good physical activity does a lot for children, especially when they have success through their physical accomplishments. Even though they may exert strenuous effort and experience breathlessness during the activity, usually the youngsters have a more positive feeling about themselves at the activity's conclusion (figure 3.1). Classroom teachers no-

Figure 3.1 Physical activity can have good results for children, especially when they have success through their physical accomplishments.

tice the positive influence of physical activity on their students: after recess or physical education, most children are more alert, verbal, and ready to concentrate on their academics. Adults also benefit from participation in more vigorous activities. We all feel good after a walk, jog, or sport activity.

All too often, however, children with learning or behavior problems hear more criticism than compliments. Parents and teachers tell them what they did wrong or that they just did not try hard enough. Sensing that they are failing, many of these children tell themselves they are no good. This leads to problems with self-esteem among children who condemn themselves. They become stressed, and ultimately avoid the activity, give up, or misbehave.

Mistakes are a natural part of learning. In order to help children be successful, parents and teachers need to be realistic, recognize that mistakes happen, and assume children may fail when they try a new activity. Allow children the opportunity to experiment with a new task before saying anything about their performances. Be honest with them. Let them know that you do not expect them to do it right the first time. If you consistently interrupt their attempts at a new activity with corrections and comments, you will immediately confirm what they may think—"I can't do anything right."

Remember, practice is what strengthens the neurological pathways so that motor skills become automatic. Even though children have been successful with an activity one day, do not assume that they will automatically perform the activity correctly the next day. Avoid starting the next activity session with skills that are more difficult. Instead, begin the activity session at the level they attained in the previous session. Then, once you have seen that they can consistently do the previous skill, introduce a new skill at the next level.

Give children specific feedback about behavior and movements. Tell them what to *do* instead of what *not to do*. When you say, "You did that well," be sure to tell them what "that" was. If a child keeps missing a catch, give him both verbal and visual clues (figure 3.2). Demonstrate the skill for him. Tell him how to move his arms differently or to remember to watch the ball. However, try not to talk while the child is performing the activity. If your voice distracts him, he may end up listening to you instead of concentrating on the skill.

Sometimes children will not do an activity in the way that you planned. If the activity still accomplishes your intended goal, then avoid interrupting them. First, recall the reason you chose the activity. Does the activity meet your goal? Is it safe? Are the children being challenged and encouraged to try new things? Consider a situation: You want a child to increase body awareness by jumping on a minitrampoline.

Figure 3.2 Always try to give children *specific* feedback about their behavior and movements.

Instead, he stands in the middle of a hoola hoop and jumps in circles. The goal of increasing body awareness is still being met, but in a different way. You may either let him continue jumping in the hoop or ask him to figure out how to jump in circles on the minitrampoline. Either way, the child is successfully achieving the goal, developing body awareness or motor development.

Success also depends on using the right equipment. Choosing equipment that matches the size and ability of children is essential for success. Adult-sized bats and rackets are simply too long and heavy, making it difficult for children to hit a ball. Regular use of the wrong equipment may force children into developing skills incorrectly because of the adjustments their bodies must make for the extra length or weight.

Do something to help children feel like winners when they achieve a new skill. Compliment them for making good decisions or inventing new games. Children with learning and behavior problems may not recognize their successes without being told of them. Direct their attention to success by telling them they have improved and you are proud of them. Point out how good they must feel because of their accomplishments by asking, "How did it feel, hitting that ball for the first time?" or "How do you feel about finishing your homework on time?" Learning to reward oneself is essential for developing the self-esteem that, in turn, helps children have the courage to try new activities and challenges.

Don't Forget . . .

✔ Children need to experience success in order to build self-esteem.

✔ Mistakes are a part of learning.

✔ Practice is necessary to turn a new skill into an automatic response.

✔ When you say to a child, "You did that well," be sure to tell him what "that" refers to.

INCLUDE THE FAMILY

Children with behavioral or learning problems often have difficulty playing with siblings. Parents' dreams of watching their children play catch or teaching them to ski may disappear. It is important to realize that what you could do as a child or what your child's siblings can accomplish may be very different from what a child with learning or behavior problems can do. Family members help best by playing at the developmental level of the child with learning or behavioral problems. The thrill and joy of playing with this family member can be heightened when you take the time to find his or her strengths through play.

Having successful interactions among family members as they play together is critical. Playing with your children helps you get in touch with your inner creative playful self. And play strengthens the relationships among family members because everyone's hopes, dreams, strengths, and weaknesses are shared. Play gives you a chance to take a break from nagging and worrying about your child's academic success or undesirable behaviors.

Through physical activities and games, family members really get to know each other. You may remember how you felt when you learned a new skill or game—and perhaps better understand how your children feel about their bodies and activity. Family members see each other's limitations and strengths. Maybe dad is better at throwing and catching, while mom is good at strategy, and the children find new and inventive ways to play the game.

Family members discover what the child with behavior and learning problems *can* do. Parents and siblings become able to spontaneously choose activities that leave them all experiencing success. For example, if a family plays touch football in the yard, the child who has trouble catching might instead be the center. Another family may choose to play volleyball with a punchball balloon because by using that larger, lighter ball, the child with coordination problems can participate.

During physical activities and games family members can play different roles. Take turns being an initiator or coach of the games. Encourage your child to initiate physical activity. When he asks you to go for a walk—if the time is appropriate—do it! In games, parents should not always be the coach or referee. Each member of the family should participate as a player or official at some time. If your family is large enough, use all the officials found in a regular game. One child can be the referee, a sibling can be timer, and still another can be scorekeeper. In this exchange of duties and participation, be sure that your child with learning or behavior problems has an opportunity for team leadership.

All family members should participate at some time, as possible, in physical activities and games. Physical activity contributes to everyone maintaining physical health. Further, getting to know a child with behavioral or learning problems through a set schedule of physical activity or games makes for positive family interactions. Moreover, it is within

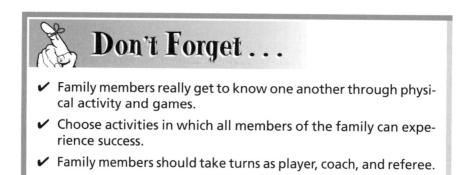

Don't Forget . . .

✔ Family members really get to know one another through physical activity and games.

✔ Choose activities in which all members of the family can experience success.

✔ Family members should take turns as player, coach, and referee.

the family unit that a child first learns how to play, take turns, follow rules, and gain a sense of fairness and team camaraderie.

ESTABLISH A DAILY ROUTINE

Parents and teachers need to include physical activities in the daily routine. Remember that often children who are uncoordinated do not choose to do structured physical activity. On the other hand, children who move constantly need to learn when physical activities are acceptable.

There are two concepts to consider as you schedule physical activity sessions: *frequency,* or how often the sessions are planned, and *duration,* or how long each session or activity lasts. Let's look first at frequency. Daily physical activity brings about the quickest results. Children benefit in many ways from improved health-related physical fitness, and daily exposure to physical activities increases their strength, endurance, and flexibility. At the same time health-risk factors (such as obesity and lack of muscle tone) decrease.

Getting a child, or yourself, used to a fixed activity schedule takes time. Planning an activity each day makes it easier for everyone to remember the schedule. A daily routine eliminates the need for anyone to ask, "Do we play today or tomorrow?" Children cannot say that they "forgot," because every day is a physical-activity day. You, your family, and even your child's teachers perhaps, will need to adjust to the new schedule. Occasionally, an activity session might need to be canceled, but avoid changing the schedule frequently because of some new event or the desire of one family member.

Doing physical activity on a daily basis reduces the time that you need to spend during a session reviewing the previous lesson. Remember that neurological pathways are strengthened through practice, so that new abilities become automatic. For example, when a child can finally focus (fixate) his eyes on a target while throwing, you still will need to repeat the throwing activity the next day. Repetition of the skill reinforces the ability of his eyes to focus. Maybe another child, for instance, walks across a balance beam for the first time at the end of a session. If you wait two or three days to have her walk across the beam again, it may take her the whole session to reach the previous level of success.

Some children benefit from intervals or movement "snacks" or breaks during the day. Parents and teachers should note when a child seems to need physical activity. Maybe the child needs a movement session *before school* to prepare him for classroom activities and a session *after school* before homework. One parent could oversee the morning activity routine, and the other parent could facilitate activities after school. School staff members may be able to arrange to have some children do specific movement exercises for part of recess. Setting a schedule helps children learn when physical activity is appropriate; it can help them learn not to start moving impulsively during dinner or homework times.

In addition to the set schedule, both parents and teachers should observe when children need a movement break from academics. Suggest that they go outside and run around the yard for 10 minutes or use a relay that can be done in the classroom. Then they can return to homework. This can be easier than arguing with them for 30 minutes about incomplete assignments!

We can turn now to the duration factor, or how long each session lasts. At first, plan for activity sessions being only 15 to 20 minutes long. By starting with short sessions, you often eliminate the reluctance some children have to participate. Initially, do not expect any child to have the strength or endurance to participate fully in an hour-long, structured exercise routine.

Extend the amount of time as their interests and abilities grow. Starting with only a few minutes a day also keeps *you* from being overwhelmed. Adding extra time for an activity session to an already busy daily routine can be stressful.

Plan a variety of activities for each session. In fact, line up more activities than necessary to fill the time. Jumping on a minitrampoline for 3 minutes, doing somersaults for 2 minutes, playing catch for 5 minutes, and stretching for 5 minutes can easily fill a session. Let children pick the activities they want, so long as their choices help meet the motor-development goals you've set. At first, even 5 minutes is an eternity to children, especially if they do not particularly like physical activity, so do not expect them to do the same activity for 15 minutes.

Sample Activity Session

Activity	Minutes
Minitrampoline (see chapter 7)	3
Blanket Rolling (see chapter 7)	2
Punchball Wall Volleys (see chapter 10)	5
Roll Out the Pizza Dough (see chapter 9)	5
Total minutes	**15**

Don't Forget . . .

✔ Make physical activities part of the daily routine.

✔ Build in movement "snacks" at home and at school.

✔ Plan several different activities for each session.

CREATE A SPECIAL PLACE

Physical activities can occur in a surprisingly wide variety of areas. If you can, create a place at home or in school where physical activity is acceptable. A special place for moving provides children a site to be active without breaking anything or disrupting others. A 10-foot-by-15-foot space, which is free of obstacles and where a ball can be tossed back and forth, contains plenty of room for most physical activities.

Classrooms have limited space; however, we give many individual activities later in this book that children can do in as little a space as 5 feet by 5 feet. In many classrooms it is possible to quickly move a few desks out of the way, creating an activity space that children can take turns using alone or with a partner. The extra time you spend providing an activity session for children with learning or behavior problems usually repays well in benefits to the class.

Most children find playing outside invigorating, even during the winter. Before planning an outdoor program, however, you might consider the distractions that might interfere with your plans. Friends drive by, other children ask to play, and dogs sometimes even take off with the balls. For these reasons, beginning activity sessions may be more successful—or at least more focused and simpler—indoors.

When you're having structured activity sessions at home or in school, keep only the equipment necessary for that particular activity or game in the space. All other equipment and toys are best put away, preferably out of sight but at least moved to the side. Set firm rules about what equipment can be used during each session. If a child tends to get overstimulated or hyperactive, the distractions of extra equipment lying around might create difficulty for him in concentrating and completing the program at hand.

You should also consider how many people can participate in the available space. The number of participants depends on the activity as well as on the ability of a child with learning or behavior problems to interact successfully. During one-on-one activities with an adult, other people in the same room divert such a child's attention. To determine the number of participants, consider the purpose of the activity and what needs to be accomplished to reach your goals.

Beware of new places. Children are very sensitive to new environments and new people. Even if you just redecorate your own home or rearrange your classroom, allow the kids some time to adjust to the difference. Expecting a structured activity session to go smoothly the first time your child is introduced to a new place is unfair and unwise.

BE CREATIVE WITH EQUIPMENT

Many items around your house or classroom are useful for physical activities. Some items that make good equipment include blankets, balls, balloons, milk jugs, scarves, stuffed animals, or buckets. Be creative and urge the children as well to discover new ways to use everyday items for games. For example, soup cans can be used as weights, or an old mattress can become a minitrampoline. Purchasing new equipment just to provide an enriching physical activity program is not necessary.

Suggested Equipment

Minitrampoline

An old mattress to jump, roll, or lie on

36-inch ball (available through physical education equipment catalogs)

10-inch balls

6-inch balls

Old ball filled with sand (1 to 3 pounds)

Medicine ball (1 to 5 pounds)

Balloons

Punchballs (without rubber band attached)

Scarves

Wrist and ankle weights

Large cardboard boxes (from appliances, moving, etc.)

Masking tape

Ping-Pong paddles
Foam paddles
Blankets
Plastic hoops
Carpet squares
Jump rope
Balance beam (a board 4 × 4 × 12 feet)

Music enlivens the atmosphere, so consider using some during physical activity. Making up songs or singing with prerecorded music can help make the time pass faster. You can do such activities as rolling, jumping, or swinging to music. There are many resources for children's movement activities available at toy stores, video stores, music stores, and your local library. One caution, however, is to use music and singing only if the child does not become distracted or overwhelmed by having so much sound.

DEVELOP SIMPLE RULES

Rules separate one game from another and help give each player a fair chance to participate. The length of "playtime" can also be governed by rules. Children with learning or behavior problems sometimes become confused and irrational when they're first confronted with rules. It helps if you introduce the rules to children slowly and simply. For example, youngsters playing softball may first need to learn the concept of taking turns before they understand that each team gets a turn at bat—and that there are rules that determine not only which team is at bat but also whose turn it is.

Start with simple rules. It's helpful to focus on one aspect of the skill or game strategy at a time. Simply rolling a ball back and forth can teach children to take turns. A child may need visual cues or sounds to remind him when it is his turn or where his position is on the field. You can set out carpet squares on the field to help him remember his position, and you can ring bells to signal that time is up.

Occasionally, it's good to alter the rules to help a child feel successful. He may need extra time, different equipment, or a different size playing area. Evaluate ways in which the rules can be changed initially to provide him with more opportunities for success. By encouraging other family members to invent different rules, you'll wind up with more creative and innovative games.

Don't Forget . . .

✔ Decrease distractions by having only the equipment you need for the activity available.

✔ Allow time for your child to adjust to new or different environments for the activity.

✔ Use music to help your child enjoy the activity session.

✔ Start with simple rules and focus on only one rule to help children remember what to do.

✔ Change rules as necessary to help a child experience success.

GIVE CLEAR INSTRUCTIONS

Giving instructions to children with learning and behavioral problems can be a challenge for parents and teachers. Since children are individual and have different problems, there may be several reasons that they have trouble following and understanding instructions. A child in an environment cluttered with equipment or excessive noise may not be able to focus on you or hear you. Here are some other things to consider:

Can the child remember?

Does he need visual demonstrations?

Does he understand what he hears?

Does he understand what he sees?

Does he understand the instructions?

Does he need written instructions?

When you're giving instructions during a structured activity session, *tell* children what you want them to do; avoid *asking*. If you ask a child who has difficulty with balance to walk across a balance beam, he will probably say, "No!" Instead simply say, "Now you are going to try to walk across the balance beam."

Some children may need you to repeat instructions using the same words. Changing the words may further confuse them, because then they have to understand two sets of instructions. Consider, for instance, what children need to interpret if they hear you say, "Throw the ball through the hoop" and then hear you say, "Aim at the center."

Sometimes you must repeat instructions for another reason: a child may be trying to avoid following instructions by engaging you in friendly conversation. After you give an instruction, he may ask, "What are we doing next?" "Why are we doing this?" "Why is the sky blue?" or "What is dirt?" Do not answer the question—repeat the directions. Once you engage in conversation, this child is probably not doing what you originally asked—and you may even have forgotten what you wanted him to do.

Children need to finish one activity before you tell them what is next. If a child can do an activity (such as jumping on a minitramp) *and* can talk, then conversation may be great. Just be sure that an interesting dialogue is not interfering with the activity or the safety in doing the activity.

Children with poor body awareness have difficulty concentrating on several body parts at a time. When you give them instructions, try to limit your comments to only one part of the body. Avoid telling them what their arms should be doing and then following that by talking about their legs and their head. An example is the overhand throw. If you tell them how to move their arms and then you say, "Step forward with your foot," they must switch their focus to their feet—then they forget what they should do with their arms.

Any child will occasionally refuse to try a new activity or follow instructions. First and foremost, try to remain calm, speak softly, and be firm. If you become agitated, you lose control of the situation. When you lose control, the child is truly getting his way. After all, this child is not doing the activity, has your full attention, and is even in control of *your* behavior. If you really cannot stay calm—stop the session, but tell him that the session will be completed at another time. He is not off the hook.

Beware of bribes. Sometimes you may be tempted to offer children rewards to get them to do something. Bribes are an external reward for an accomplishment. One problem with them is that children may cooperate *only* if they know a reward is forthcoming. Remind them that they will feel good about themselves when they overcome a challenge.

Transitions between activities can also be difficult. Some children may really enjoy one activity and not want to do anything else. So first give them a warning that the activity will be ending. This may be, "We are going to swing for one more minute," or "You can shoot the basketball five more times." The children may also need a concrete reminder that an activity has ended. Using a timer and stopping the activity when the buzzer sounds may be helpful. A visual cue might be that the lights go off.

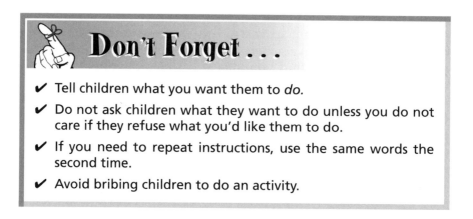

Don't Forget . . .

✔ Tell children what you want them to *do*.

✔ Do not ask children what they want to do unless you do not care if they refuse what you'd like them to do.

✔ If you need to repeat instructions, use the same words the second time.

✔ Avoid bribing children to do an activity.

chapter 4
Reflexes

Although children are born with approximately a hundred reflexes, they must lose some of the reflexes developed in the womb and instead gain new patterns. These new patterns are necessary before they can progress to skills such as sitting, creeping, crawling, walking, and running.

It is not uncommon, among elementary school children with learning and behavior problems, for some of them to retain some of their primitive movement patterns. This chapter gives you a review of several reflexes that are frequently seen in these children. You'll find evaluation techniques and a series of activities you can use to help children who still retain remnants of these primitive reflexes.

Motor development during the first two years of life depends on the child interacting with the environment and progressing through a series of primitive reflexes, postural reactions, and voluntary movements. *Reflexes* are involuntary movements that someone makes in response to a stimulus. The stimulus may be as varied as an infant's position, a movement of her head, or a touch on her cheek. *Primitive reflexes* are responsible for most of the movement patterns during a child's first few months. They emerge in a set order, and are fixed by having the same stimulus creating the same automatic response.

Many of the primitive reflexes are necessary for survival, while others prepare a child for advanced movement patterns. In order for her to progress to skilled movements, the primitive reflexes must disappear or become integrated. This occurs during the first few months after birth. At the appropriate stage of development, the various reflexes gradually weaken and become integrated within the baby's system. Eventually, voluntary movements and motor skills replace many of these reflexes. At two months, for instance, an infant should automatically grasp

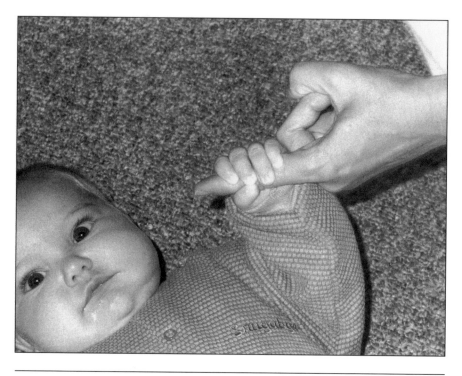

Figure 4.1 Palmar grasp reflex.

and hold a finger placed in the palm of her hand. This is called the *palmar grasp reflex* (see figure 4.1). By six months, she should have the motor skills to voluntarily grasp a toy and to release that toy to pick up another.

Retaining primitive reflexes, however, can interfere with a child's learning to roll over, sit up, crawl, creep, and walk. People in the field of child development must have knowledge of all the reflexes. In this chapter, however, we discuss only four primitive reflexes, chosen because they commonly affect learning and behavior problems:

- Tonic labyrinthine reflex prone (TLR prone)
- Tonic labyrinthine reflex supine (TLR supine)
- Asymmetrical tonic neck reflex
- Symmetrical tonic neck reflex

TONIC LABYRINTHINE REFLEX

There are two labyrinthine reflexes that are triggered by the position of the head in relation to gravity. They are the prone tonic labyrinthine reflex (TLR prone) and supine tonic labyrinthine reflex (TLR supine). The *prone tonic labyrinthine reflex* occurs when a child is placed on her stomach and gravity acts on the inner ear (labyrinthine). This causes the head, trunk, and limbs to be pulled (flexed) toward the earth. Her body seems to be curling toward the ground with her chin tucked toward the chest and her knees trying to pull under the stomach (see figure 4.2).

The TLR prone appears during the first and second month after birth and should disappear by the fourth month. The purpose of this reflex is to develop the muscles used in flexion which balance the extensor muscles that are developed when a child is placed on her back. Integration of the TLR prone must occur in order for her to gain the skills and strength necessary to lift any part of her body off the ground when she is lying on her stomach. If she retains the reflex past the first several months, she will eventually have trouble in any movement against the pull of gravity, including sitting, rolling over from her stomach to her back, and standing.

The *supine tonic labyrinthine reflex* (TLR supine) is also a combination of the position of a child and gravity. Placing her on her back allows gravity to act on the inner ear (labyrinthine). This pulls her trunk, head,

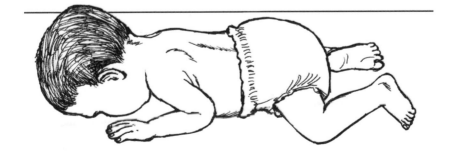

Figure 4.2   TLR prone.

Figure 4.3 TLR supine.

arms, and legs toward the ground (figure 4.3). TLR supine usually begins to diminish at about the end of the fourth month. This is appropriate, since integration of this reflex must occur before a child can roll over from her back to her stomach or perform the first goal-directed movement, reaching, which occurs at approximately four and a half months. When the TLR is active, she will have trouble lifting her head or one of her limbs against the pull of gravity. If you lift one of her arms, it feels heavy and may extend (straighten).

Older children, particularly those with behavioral and learning problems, may have some carryover from the TLR (either supine or prone). It may be so pronounced or noticeable that these youngsters have trouble doing any movement or academic activity that requires them to move the body or a limb against the pull of gravity. Some children can remain in an upright sitting position for only a short time before collapsing (see figure 4.4). Other children seem to sprawl across the desk with their head on their arms when they are writing or reading. Nine-year-old Evan, for example, tried to sit upright during an eye examination. As the evaluation progressed, he slowly sank lower and lower in the chair. By the end of the test he was so exhausted, he sighed as he slipped out of the chair and onto the floor. Any movement was heavy for him, even getting out of a chair.

A simple way to evaluate whether an older child has retained the TLR is to have him roll over. Rolling from the back to the stomach gives you an indication of his ability to overcome TLR supine, and rolling from the stomach to the back evaluates TLR prone. Observe the amount of strength needed to overcome the pull of gravity. Does he have to press down with the feet, elbows, knees, or head in order to roll over? Are there indentations in the mat that suggest he had to press down in order to overcome the force of gravity?

Figure 4.4   TLR-prone child. Gravity pulling on child.

Logrolling (rolling from the back to the stomach and from the stomach to the back) was used to evaluate the possible retention of TLR in three groups of elementary school students (Cheatum 1986, 1987, 1988, 1989, 1993, 1996; Cheatum and Hammond 1992). The results indicated that only 70 percent of group C (see table 4.1) and 75 percent of groups A and B could roll over successfully (without extra effort) from their

Table 4.1
Number and Percent of Students Enrolled in Elementary School
Who Successfully Completed Logrolls

Group	Grade	Number	Back to stomach STLP		Stomach to back PTLP	
			Number	Percent	Number	Percent
A	K–6	395	297	75.4	282	71.3
B	K–3	45	33	75.3	34	75.5
C	Third	89	63	70.8	71	79.8

A: Kindergarten–sixth-grade students enrolled in 2 elementary schools in Kalamazoo, Michigan. Students scored 0–3 on the Iowa Achievement Test in reading (scores range from 0–9) or were experiencing learning problems.

B: Kindergarten–third-grade students in Parchment, Michigan. Students scored 0–3 on the Iowa Achievement Test (scores range from 0–9 with 4.5 considered average), were recommended by the reading teacher, or had low visual and vestibular scores.

C: Third-grade students enrolled in 6 different geographic locations in Kalamazoo, Michigan. Students represented diverse academic achievement.

backs to their stomachs. Groups A and B consisted of students who were having learning problems, while Group C contained students of diverse academic achievements. This study's results demonstrated that at least a fourth of these evaluated children had a problem with supine TLR. Since retention of the supine TLR interferes with a child's ability to sit up, sit in a seat, stand, or move against gravity, it may create additional problems for school-aged children who have some type of learning or behavior problem.

The results with TLR prone are a little different. More students in group C, almost 80 percent, could roll over from their stomachs to their backs. At least 20 percent of the students in each school, however, did *not* pass the test, which indicates a possible problem with TLR prone.

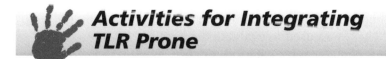

Activities for Integrating TLR Prone

The following activities create situations in which the TLR prone must be integrated in order for a child to do the activity. The pull of gravity acting on the inner ear triggers the TLR prone during

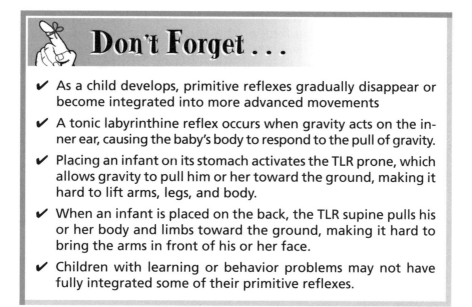

Don't Forget . . .

✔ As a child develops, primitive reflexes gradually disappear or become integrated into more advanced movements

✔ A tonic labyrinthine reflex occurs when gravity acts on the inner ear, causing the baby's body to respond to the pull of gravity.

✔ Placing an infant on its stomach activates the TLR prone, which allows gravity to pull him or her toward the ground, making it hard to lift arms, legs, and body.

✔ When an infant is placed on the back, the TLR supine pulls his or her body and limbs toward the ground, making it hard to bring the arms in front of his or her face.

✔ Children with learning or behavior problems may not have fully integrated some of their primitive reflexes.

these activities. They also develop muscular strength and endurance for holding the head and limbs away from the pull of gravity.

Saucer Spin

Individual

Appropriate Ages

Three years and up or younger than three with the assistance of an adult.

Preparation

Place a cushion in a snow saucer and set it on a smooth playing surface. Mark a large circle around the child and saucer with chalk or masking tape.

Activity

The child lies on his stomach with his hips centered on the cushion. Using his hands and feet, he spins himself on the saucer, staying within the circle marked on the floor. After 10 to 15 spins in one direction, he spins in the opposite direction. As a variation, have the child spin 5 to 10 times, then jump up, run 3 times around the saucer on the circle, get back on the saucer, and spin again. Challenge him to see how many seconds it takes him to spin 10 times in one direction and then 10 in the other. Keep track of his progress by tracking any decreases in the amount of time he takes to do this.

Some children, particularly preschoolers or those who are not strong enough, will not be able to spin themselves enough times or fast enough because of the TLR prone. If this is the case, hold the child by his feet and spin him as he holds his head and arms up like an airplane. Other family members or children can help by taking turns spinning the child on the saucer (figure 4.5).

Figure 4.5 Parent spinning child.

🖐 *Spinning on a Large Ball*

Individual

Appropriate Ages

Three years and up or younger than three with the assistance of an adult.

Preparation

You will need a large ball (at least 36 inches in diameter) or a snow-sledding saucer. Large therapy balls are available at toy stores or through catalogs of physical education or physical therapy equipment. Be sure the activity space has enough room for the child to be on the ball and for you to move rapidly around the child on the ball.

Activity

The child lies face down over the ball with his stomach over the center of the top. He looks up and holds his arms "like an airplane" as you spin the ball around. For variety, after three to five revolutions, hand the child a small foam ball and tell him to toss it into a box or at a target. See how many revolutions the child can do before lowering his head. Increase the number each time.

If you are using a sledding saucer, put a cushion in it. Have the child lie like an airplane over the saucer. His stomach must be over the center of the saucer. You can then spin him. If you put the saucer on a floor without a carpet (be warned; this will scratch hardwood floors), he will go faster. Older children can use their arms and hands to spin themselves.

🖐 *Scooter Board Surfing*

Group or individual

Appropriate Ages

Four years and older.

Preparation

Place a scooter board or a snow saucer on a smooth surface. Mark a start and finish line on the floor. The distance depends on how far your child can go. Preschoolers or children with poor strength may only go a couple of feet. A good length to try first is 10 to 15 feet.

Activity

The child lies on her stomach on the scooter board with her hips centered on the board. Using her arms, she pulls herself the length of the area. The head and feet must be held up off the floor.

For variety, set up cones at three-foot intervals for the child to "slalom" (curve in and out of the cones), or ask her to push off a wall and see how far she travels. Start by seeing how far the child can travel on the scooter board and set goals of traveling farther each time.

Activities for Integrating TLR Supine

These activities require the TLR supine reflex to be integrated for the child to complete them.

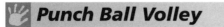

Punch Ball Volley

Individual or with partner

Appropriate Ages

Five years and older; younger than five with the assistance of an adult.

Preparation

Blow up a punchball, but do not attach the rubber band. Punchballs work best for this activity because they are heavier than balloons and tend to be more consistently round for better control of where they bounce.

Activity

Lying on their backs with the knees bent, feet flat on the floor, and toes touching the wall, children use their hands to volley a punchball against a wall. Count the number of volleys made before the punchball hits the floor or goes out of control. Two people can lie with their toes touching and volley the punchball back and forth.

A child who cannot hold his arms up against gravity will not have the shoulder and upper-arm stability to do the light tapping motions of the hands that are required to maintain control of the punchball. He may swipe at the ball with large arm movements that cause the punchball to fly out of his reach. If this happens, have the child start practicing by tapping a punchball that you hold by a string (attached where the rubber band would normally be) over his chest.

Horizontal Mountain Climbing

Group or individual

Appropriate Ages

Eight years and older.

Preparation

Assemble one scooter board and a 15-foot rope for each person. If you can't get a scooter board, substitute a snow-sledding saucer on an uncarpeted surface (but be warned: the saucer can scratch hardwood floors). As the child becomes stronger and has more endurance, increase the length of rope you use. Securely tie the rope at one end to a stable object, such as a heavy chair or desk, two to three feet off the ground. Then make sure the length of the rope is lying out straight.

Activity

Each child lies on his back on the scooter board, with his head toward the tied end of the rope. Place the untied end of the rope down the middle of the forehead and down to the belly button. Grasping the rope, each person pulls himself toward the tied end of the rope, holding his head off the ground (figure 4.6). If the head touches the ground, he must start over. Initially, the goal could be that each youngster pulls himself the length of the rope without letting his head touch the ground. Keep track of the child's progress by noting any decr2ease in the time that it takes him to go the length of the rope (or the increase in distance with his head off the ground).

For some children, it is difficult just to hold the head off the ground while lying faceup on a scooter board. You may want to

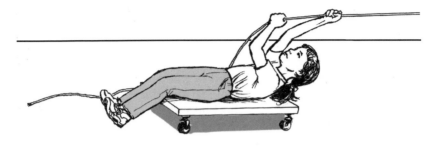

Figure 4.6 Horizontal mountain climbing.

start by seeing how long such a youngster can hold his head up and look at his toes.

ASYMMETRICAL TONIC NECK REFLEX

The stimulus for the asymmetrical tonic neck reflex (ATNR) is turning one's head, which acts on receptors in the neck. This causes the arm and leg on the same side as the turned face to straighten (extend), while the arm and leg on her skull side bends or flexes (see figure 4.7).

The ATNR can be viewed as an infant exercise program that strengthens the muscles used in both flexion and extension of the arms and legs. If you have an opportunity to observe an infant during the ATNR, you can easily see how the child learns to move one side of the body in opposition to the other. This is one of the first steps toward the alternating movement pattern of the two sides of the body used in creeping, crawling, walking, and running.

Most newborn babies do not have the ATNR. You can turn an infant's head without any other movement happening. By the second month, however, this reflex should appear and remain present until about the fourth month. Some children normally retain traces of extension on the face side and traces of flexion of the skull side until they are eight years old. However, excessive retention of the ATNR interferes with creeping, crawling, and walking. This becomes obvious when a child starts to creep. When she looks toward one side, the ATNR will cause that side to extend, but the other side will flex, causing her to collapse.

The ATNR also prevents a child from using two hands to do any activity, such as catching a ball, or from using one hand to throw a ball. As she looks at the ball, the arm on that side extends. This prevents her from being able to bend the elbow in preparation for the throw. The only way this child could throw a ball is not to look at the

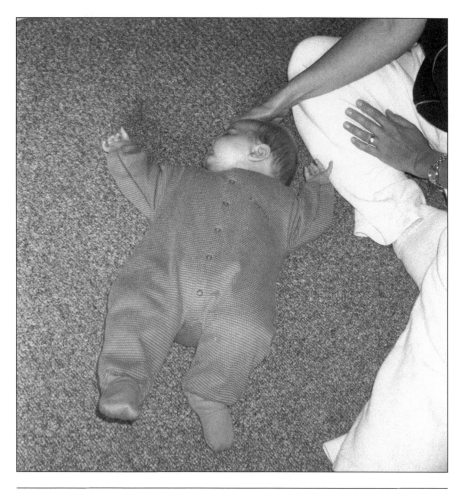

Figure 4.7 The asymmetrical tonic neck reflex.

ball. Yet, we all tell children to look at the ball! And, no doubt, most of us would think that a particular child experiencing the ATNR was uncoordinated.

In an older child, retention of the ATNR may interrupt classroom activities, especially writing. Every time she looks at the pencil, there is a slight extension of her arm. When she looks away, the arm flexes (figure 4.8). This creates a back-and-forth action on the pencil, which results in poor penmanship. To counteract this reflex, children with retention of the ATNR usually try to look away from the writing area and view the pencil only out of the corner of their eyes. Walking around the

Figure 4.8 Child writing (top): looking at her pencil triggers the ATNR; (bottom) head position enables the child to write.

classroom, you may notice a child trying to stabilize his head in a neutral position by holding his head with the opposite hand. He appears to be just resting his head in his hand, but, in fact, he is using a technique that helps him write.

To examine an infant for the ATNR, you need to turn her head and hold it in that position for a few seconds. This allows sufficient time for her body to respond to the stimulus. Observing a retention of the ATNR in older children is less obvious. A simple way to see if the reflex is still active is to turn her head and, while holding it there, try to flex (bend) her elbow on the face side or extend (straighten) her elbow on the skull side.

Don't Forget . . .

✔ ATNR causes the limbs on one side of a child's body to extend (straighten) and the limbs on her other side to flex (bend).

✔ Retention of the ATNR prevents a child from being able to use both hands together or even to use one hand effectively for such activities as throwing a ball or writing.

Activities for Inhibiting ATNR

Activities that inhibit the asymmetrical tonic neck reflex are situations in which the child must turn his head in one direction. Without the head returning to face front, he has to bring the arm on the face side toward the head, and extend the opposite arm. Remember the child can bend and straighten arms easily if the head position is facing front; therefore, the head position (turned right or left) is important during activities for inhibiting the ATNR.

Lazy Bubble Blowing

Individual

Appropriate Ages

Three years and up; three-year-olds will need assistance.

Preparation

Place a bubble-blowing solution in a shallow dish or plate. The child lies on his back with the bubble solution to the child's right or left near his waist. Be sure he can reach the solution. Hold an 8- to 10-inch-diameter hoop by the child's face on the side where the bubble is placed.

Activity

The child looks toward the bubble solution, dips the wand in the solution, and blows bubbles through the hoop.

 *Passing Pennies Down the Line*

Group activity for three or more

Appropriate Ages

4 years and up. 4-year-olds will need assistance.

Preparation

Place 10 to 20 pennies (or buttons) on a paper plate. Group members lie on their backs, side by side but at an arm's width apart. Place the plate with pennies by the first child's right side, an empty paper plate between each of the next children, and one by the last person on each team. Each participant may look only at the paper plate to his right. (When the activity is repeated, everyone will look left.)

Activity

On "Go!" the first person picks up one penny, passes it into his other hand and then onto the paper plate between him and the next team member—without turning his head to the left. That team member picks up the penny and repeats the process. This continues until all of the pennies are on the last plate. Time members of the group to see how fast they can pass the pennies from the first to the last plate. Challenge them to go faster each time. If you have more than one group, the groups can do this activity as a race to see which group (or team) can pass all the pennies first.

Side-Lying Ball Toss

Individual

Appropriate Ages

Four years and up; four-year-olds will need assistance.

Preparation

Gather several beanbags or tennis balls and a bucket. The child lies on his back with a bucket placed a few feet away from his right or left side.

Activity

The child tosses the beanbags or balls into the bucket. See how many go into the bucket. The activity could be done in groups to see which group gets the most beanbags or balls in their buckets.

A child with remnants of the ATNR has difficulty bending the elbow to initiate the toss. He either looks away, swings his whole arm, or holds the arm straight and tries to use only wrist action. You may need to remind him to bend his elbow.

Apple-Tucked-Under-the-Chin Crawl

Group or individual

Appropriate Ages

Five years and up.

Preparation

Mark start and finish lines. You need at least enough apples or tennis balls for each child to have one.

Activity

Children get in a crawling position on the hands and knees. Each child holds an apple or ball between his chin and one shoulder. Have them practice crawling in this position. You may want to see how quickly they can crawl 5 to 10 feet and then challenge them to go faster.

The activity can be a relay race, by dividing children into even groups. On "Go!" the children race by crawling to the finish line without dropping the apple. A child must start over if he drops the apple. In a relay race, have team members pass the apple to the next racer (without using the hands) or see which team can get the most apples in a bucket at the finish line. If several apples or balls are used, each person can see how many he can carry across the floor and put into a bowl within a set amount of time.

If a child with the ATNR turns his head, his arm and leg on the skull side may collapse. Have these children practice crawling with an apple tucked between their chins and shoulders before racing against others.

One-Sided Wall Push-Ups

Individual or with partner

Appropriate Ages

Younger than six years (with adult assistance) and up.

Preparation

Standing sideways to a wall, each participant extends the arm next to the wall and leans on that hand. The other hand is on the hip.

Activity

Looking away from the wall, each participant proceeds to do push-ups by bending and straightening the arm that is touching the wall. Count how many push-ups are done. For variety, have them stand farther away from the wall, lean on the arm, and look away. See how long they can hold that position. Partners could lean on the other's arm and look away from each other. See how long the partners can hold the position.

SYMMETRICAL TONIC NECK REFLEX

Stimulus for the *symmetrical tonic neck reflex* (STNR) is the positioning of a child's head acting on receptors in the neck (see figure 4.9). As you bend your child's head forward (toward the chest), her arms will bend (flex) and legs straighten (extend). When the head bends toward her back, her arms straighten (extend) and legs bend (flex). It helps to remember that the arms will do the same type of movement as the head, while the legs do the opposite of the head and arms.

Comparing the STNR to a cat going under a low fence makes it easier to visualize and understand. To get under the fence, the cat lowers its head, bends its front legs, and extends its back legs. When the upper part is completely under the fence, the cat lifts its head, extends its front legs, and bends its hind legs to complete its journey to the other side of the fence.

The STNR is active during the fourth to the seventh months. Another type of exercise program for infants, this particular reflex develops strength and coordination. Strength is needed in a child's arms and legs in preparation for creeping and crawling. Coordination enables her to develop the ability to use both arms or both legs together for

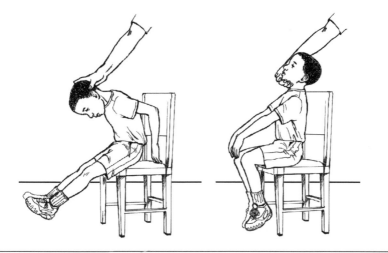

Figure 4.9 Symmetrical tonic neck reflex.

purposeful activity, replacing the random arm and leg movements of an infant.

Retention of the reflex after eight months, however, causes some problems. Children are unable to progress to activities in which they use the arms separately or in opposition. When attempting to creep and crawl, they may have to use both arms to pull the body forward, and then push with both legs ("homologous" creeping and crawling). This action resembles an inchworm's scooting or a rabbit's hopping.

One of the biggest concerns among developmentalists, parents, and teachers is that retention of the STNR will restrict a child to mostly *bilateral movements*, that is, he will be unable to use one arm without some movement of the other arm. This is also sometimes referred to as an *associated* movement. If a ball is thrown toward the middle of his body, the child can catch it since he can use both arms. If a ball is thrown to one side, he will usually not be able to catch it unless he moves over and uses both hands. The bilateral movement of the STNR also affects writing ability. Every movement of the head causes forward and backward movements (flexion or extension) of the arms, which makes fine motor control of the wrist and fingers nearly impossible (figure 4.10).

Some gymnastic movements are particularly difficult to perform. Yolanda's physical education teacher, for example, was trying to teach her to do a forward roll. The teacher would help her get into a crouched position with the knees bent, elbows straight, and hands resting on the mat. Next, she would take Yolanda's head and bend her neck forward

Figure 4.10 Child writing and looking down at paper, which triggers the STNR.

toward her chest. This action caused her arms to bend, however, and she would collapse on the mat. She was then unable to extend her arms again to push her body over in the forward roll (see figure 4.11). Repetition caused the same reaction, since it was an automatic response of the symmetrical tonic neck reflex.

Another problem that arises from retention of the STNR is the inability to perform oppositional movements. This is a skill in which one side of the body must do a movement that is the opposite of the other side's. Lacking this skill is the reason why some children cannot open lids that twist off, including those on pop bottles or juice cans. Even cutting food with a knife and fork requires the hands to do different motions and is beyond the skill ability of these children. They also find it difficult to use one hand to hold the writing paper steady while trying to write with the other hand.

Figure 4.11 STNR interfering with forward roll.

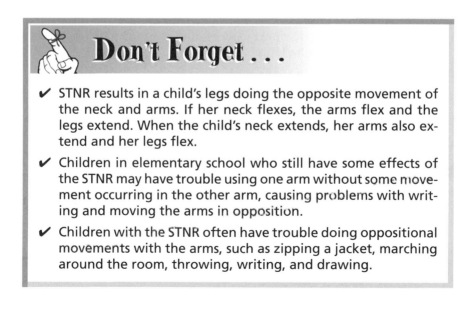

Don't Forget . . .

✔ STNR results in a child's legs doing the opposite movement of the neck and arms. If her neck flexes, the arms flex and the legs extend. When the child's neck extends, her arms also extend and her legs flex.

✔ Children in elementary school who still have some effects of the STNR may have trouble using one arm without some movement occurring in the other arm, causing problems with writing and moving the arms in opposition.

✔ Children with the STNR often have trouble doing oppositional movements with the arms, such as zipping a jacket, marching around the room, throwing, writing, and drawing.

Activities for Inhibiting the STNR

Activities that inhibit the STNR require the child to hold his head in either flexion (tucked toward the chest) or extension (bending backward) and require him to use the arms and legs independently.

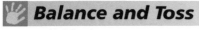

Balance and Toss

Individual

Appropriate Ages

Four years and older.

Preparation

The child lies on either the stomach or back over a 24- to 36-inch ball. Large therapy balls are available at toy stores or through catalogs of physical education or physical therapy equipment. The child lies over the ball on his stomach, with his hands and feet touching the floor.

Activity

Place several small balls or beanbags by the child's hands and a bucket a few feet away from the balls. The child picks up a ball with one hand, looks up at the bucket, and tosses the ball into the bucket. To add extra challenge have the child try this with his feet off the floor.

Next, have the child lie on his back over the ball. This time, place the bucket near his feet. Hand the child one ball at a time and have him toss it into the bucket.

Kneeling Scooter Board Surfing

Individual or group

Appropriate Ages

Five years and older.

Preparation

Mark a start and finish line about 10 to 15 feet apart. You could also place cones at 2- to 3-foot intervals to make a slalom course. Each child (or each team if you're conducting a relay race) needs a scooter board or snow saucer.

Activity

Children kneel on either the scooter board or snow saucer. On "Go!" the child holds his head up, looks at the finish line, and then uses the arms to pull himself to the finish line. The child may either use his arms together or in a crawling action. For variety, have him return to the starting line going backward.

A child with lingering effects of the STNR may collapse or have difficulty coordinating the arms to pull himself across the floor. Such a child needs opportunities to practice this activity alone before racing against others.

Beanbags in a Bucket

Individual or group

Appropriate Ages

Five years and older, though five-year-olds will need assistance.

Preparation

Children lie on their stomachs with their arms and hands ready to do a push-up (the elbows bent with the hands next to the shoulders). Place 5 to10 beanbags next to each child's head and a small bucket a few feet away from the feet.

Activity

On "Go!" each child picks up a beanbag with one hand and tucks it between his chin and chest. Replacing the hand along his side, he pushes up on his arms and, using his feet as pivot points, walks his hands around to the bucket. The beanbag is dropped in the bucket by releasing his chin. Then he walks his hands back to the starting position. Continue the activity until all the beanbags are in the bucket.

For variation, use one bucket and have the children form a circle around it. Give each participant a different color of beanbag. At the end of one or two minutes, see which child has put the most beanbags in the bucket.

Bear-Walk Soccer Drill

Individual or group

Appropriate Ages

Five years and older.

Preparation

You'll need a 10-inch ball (punchball) and cones or milk jugs for this activity. Set up the cones or milk jugs in a line at two- to three-foot intervals for the participants to go through in a zigzag pattern. Mark the start and finish lines at each end.

Activity

Each youngster gets in a bear-walk position (bent over with hands on the floor and legs extended or straightened; see figure 4.12). The children move through the cones in a zigzag pattern, each person tapping the ball with his head toward the finish line and then returning by zigzagging the ball to the starting line. Time each child to see how quickly he can complete the course, or have the children race each other.

Be sure that a child can do a bear walk without falling forward onto his head before he tries to push the punchball or race. If he cannot inhibit the symmetrical tonic neck reflex, he will collapse onto his head as his arms flex simultaneously with his head's flexing (bending) toward his chest.

Figure 4.12 Bear-walk soccer drill.

chapter 5
Body Awareness

You may have heard or come across different definitions of body awareness in talking with people about or reading books and articles on child development. Perhaps you lump together a lot of perceptions about body awareness. In this chapter, we examine body awareness by separating it into different terms to help you understand the progressive changes that young children experience in their body awareness, as well as the stages of movement patterns that lead to their academic success.

The terms you will be reading about in this chapter include *body image*, *body concept*, and *body schema* and are all a part of body awareness. A higher level of body schema is developed through movement patterns and *laterality*, *lateral preference*, and *directionality*. In this chapter you also will find useful evaluation techniques for each of these stages of development and activities that can help children overcome problems they may experience in development.

BODY IMAGE

Body image is self-image, and it involves emotions. Some professionals even refer to body image as self-concept. Body image is directly related to how children feel about themselves. Internal feelings start at birth and are greatly affected by the way children are treated. Babies who are well cared for feel warm, comfortable, and content based on their experiences with people and their environment. Their positive body image is enhanced later as they experience success in moving and controlling their bodies in the environment.

Problems with body image, on the other hand, may already have shown up in toddlers or young children through their figure drawings or verbal expressions. A child with poor body image may draw himself without body parts or draw himself smaller than he draws other people in the picture, or he may lack the motor skills needed to draw the parts. Perhaps he'll draw rain or snow always falling on him but not on the other people in the picture. A little girl might say something that sounds an alarm in her parent or teacher, such as "I feel like I am falling down a hole," "I can never do anything right," "I am ugly," or "I am no good." All children have bad days—and most children will make some of these statements. However, if a child *consistently* refers to himself in a negative manner or belittles himself, he may have a body-image problem.

Four-year-old children should be able to draw a picture of a person with several body parts (see Figure 5.1). During evaluation for kindergarten readiness, for example, four-and-one-half-year-old Ashley was found to have a problem with body image when she was asked to draw a person. She simply drew one large circle, placed a dot in the middle, and then drew two small oblong shapes that were not connected to the circle. When asked about her picture, Ashley indicated that the dot was eyes and one small circle was a mouth and the other a leg. This drawing might be a clue; it suggests a problem with body image and perhaps body concept. Although Ashley knew all of her body parts, except the elbows and ankles, she did not know where they fit on the person she was drawing. Her favorite color was black. She said she did not like to help her mother do anything around the house and did not like to play. Her evaluation indicated that she had trouble with both fine motor and gross motor skills.

A professional who observed Ashley with her family and talked with her mother could see that Ashley was overprotected. Her mother never allowed her to complete a task; the parent was afraid she would do it wrong or wouldn't be fast enough. If the mother did not immediately help her finish something, one of her two older sisters did. This caused Ashley to run to another task. Seeing these interactions strongly suggested to the observer that the child had a body-image problem along with some other concerns.

Eliminating or reducing a body-image problem can be accomplished through positive emotional and movement experiences. Parents can create an environment in which the child can feel good about herself. She may benefit from something as simple as just being held for a while. Parents can encourage good feelings in their child by praising and hugging her when she smiles, reaches for a toy, walks, runs, throws a ball,

Figure 5.1   Picture of a person drawn by a 4-1/2–year-old child.

or jumps. When a child is happy, you'll see smiles and giggles accompanying her first steps or you'll notice an older child jumping for joy when she makes a basket. It is important for parents to praise the actions of a child who behaves well when playing with other children, does errands, or participates in school or church activities. These simple but positive reinforcement techniques give the youngster a sense of accomplishment, not only mentally but also physically.

Teachers can add a lot toward building good body image. In addition to helping children do well in school, part of a teacher's role is to encourage them. Positive verbal support can enhance body image. Each child has something that is the best about him or her each day. Besides academic achievement, teachers can comment on how a child walks quietly down the hall or helps to put materials away. Looking at each child (really *seeing* the person) and in some way commenting positively ("You finished your math assignment on time," "You ran fast in that relay," "You painted that picture using my favorite color," or "That is a lovely shirt") is a simple way for a teacher to add to a student's positive body image (figure 5.2).

Figure 5.2 A teacher's positive verbal support can add to a student's positive body image.

Don't Forget . . .

✔ Body image involves the internal feelings a child has about himself.

✔ Both teachers and parents can assist a child in building good body image by giving positive verbal support.

✔ Good experiences in physical activities enhance body image.

 Body-Image Activities

These activities are great for helping children who have body-image problems. The youngsters feel not only that their own bodies are moving but also that their limbs and trunks have strength. Some of the activities also help them learn to use their bodies as part of a team or partnership.

Trampoline Jumping

Individual or group

Appropriate Ages

Younger than 3 years old *if* the child can sit up or stand *with an adult* holding the child's hands or with the child seated and the parent bouncing the child by pressing on the trampoline.

3- to 5-year-olds if holding adult's hands or adult spotter is next to the trampoline.

6 years and older *only if* adult spotters are nearby.

Preparation

Have a large trampoline, minitrampoline, or mattress, with plenty of room around the trampoline or mattress. Make sure that no hard objects, such as toys or furniture, are within five feet of the trampoline or mattress in case someone falls off.

Activity

When you first introduce trampoline activities, do not plan specific movements (such as jumping jacks or hopping on one foot). Allow children to be creative and just experience the sensations of jumping. If they need encouragement, you might use music or have them count the number of times they jump. To make the activity a game, the group can sit around the edge of the trampoline or mattress and call out different ways to jump. Each group member gets a chance to jump. Here are some ideas:

- Jump in a circle.
- Flap your arms like a bird.
- Hop on one foot.

Some children will seem to be out of control as they jump. Their arms will fly awkwardly. They may have trouble staying in the center of the jumping surface. Children have better leg control if they place their hands on their hips. Giving them a specific way to use the arms helps to decrease any wild arm waving that may throw them off balance. Sometimes having an X marked in the center of the jumping surface helps a child stay in the middle and away from the edges. However, the jumper should not stare at the X all the time while jumping. He should just glance down occasionally to see where the mark is.

Parents and teachers should also try jumping on the trampoline or mattress. Actual experience best shows you how the sensation of jumping feels and how the muscles feel as they press off the trampoline and then release. Also, after a few minutes, you will realize that jumping on a minitramp is a strenuous workout!

My Partner's a Drag

Partners or group

Appropriate Ages

8 years and older.

Preparation

Mark starting and finish lines 10 to15 feet apart.

Activity

Each person gets a partner—preferably near the same size. The partners stand facing the same direction but one behind the other, with both their backs toward the direction they will travel. The partner in back reaches under the arms and around the chest of the partner standing in front and clasps his hands together. The front partner then leans back and is held up by the partner in back (see figure 5.3). The back partner walks backward, dragging the front partner. The front partner can help either by using his legs to walk backward or can drag his heels. At the other finish line, the partners trade places and return to the starting position. Challenge the children by keeping track of how quickly the partners can drag each other to the finish line and back.

If this activity is done as a race, be sure that each set of partners first has an opportunity to practice. The partners must experience how it feels to drag each other. They need to know how much

Figure 5.3 My Partner's a Drag.

strength is necessary to hold up the partner and then drag him. Also, they need to practice coordinating their movements so they can move as a unit.

BODY CONCEPT

Body concept is the knowledge of the body parts; it involves a child really knowing what the body parts are. The age at which a child starts to identify the parts of the body stems directly from how much time family members spend teaching the youngster this information. Usually, when a baby is about nine months old, she starts to identify her nose and eyes. She usually adds other major parts of the body (ears, hands, and feet) by the time she is 18 months old. A baby first learns the body parts on herself and progresses to identifying the parts on others, on a doll, and then on a picture. Only when children are about seven years old can most of them identify more minor parts of the body such as ankles, wrists, and shins. By the age of nine years, children should be able to identify all the parts of the body.

It may not be unusual for a child to have difficulty with body concept. Results of four studies of kindergartners through sixth graders enrolled in public schools suggests that body concept is not as extensive as we might hope among young children (Cheatum 1986–1989, 1989, 1993, 1996; Cheatum and Hammond 1992). Identification of body parts usually follows the developmental trend of cephalocaudal to proximodistal (head to foot and then center to outside of the body).

As you can see in table 5.1, more students in these studies correctly identified parts on the upper body than parts on the lower body. In fact, Group C, third graders who represented all levels of academic achievement, correctly identified all of the parts of the face. Students from each group were more successful in identifying the shoulders than the elbows and more successful at identifying the knees than the ankles. The two exceptions to this trend were identification of the feet and the hips. It appears that we do not use the words hip, ankle, and elbow as much as we do other parts of the body. The large number of correct responses for the feet suggests that these extremities are a part of the body involved in a lot of interaction between the child and adults in the home during dressing, bathing, and other everyday activities or talk, such as playing this little piggy went to market.

Children with learning problems and those with learning disabilities may have similar motor characteristics. An evaluation of body concept among 68 fourth-grade students in Kalamazoo, Michigan (Cheatum 1989), supported this theory (see figure 5.4). Children with average and above-average learning ability were more successful in identifying body parts than were those considered to be learning disabled or marginal (children who were marginal were below average in learning ability and had learning problems).

Table 5.1
Percent of Students Who Correctly Identified Body Parts

Group	A	B	C	D
Head	97	95	100	97.7
Eyes	96.2	98.5	100	97.7
Ears	97	99	100	97.7
Nose	97.7	99	100	97.7
Mouth	97	98.7	100	95.3
Shoulders	92.5	90.4	96.6	95.3
Elbows	88.8	77	92.1	88.4
Hips	51.1	56.7	74.2	74.4
Knees	94	93.4	97.8	97.7
Ankles	71.8	48.1	67.4	69.8
Feet	94.8	88.3	97	93
Number	135	395	89	45

A: Third-grade students enrolled in 5 elementary schools in different geographic locations in Arlington, Texas. Students represented different academic-achievement levels based on scores received on state-administered achievement tests.

B: Kindergarten to sixth-grade students who were enrolled in 2 elementary schools in Kalamazoo, Michigan. Students scored 0–3 on the Iowa Achievement Test in reading or were experiencing learning problems.

C: Third-grade students enrolled in 6 different geographic locations in Kalamazoo, Michigan. Students represented diverse academic achievement.

D: Kindergarten to third-grade students in Parchment, Michigan. Students scored 0–3 on the Iowa Achievement Test (scores range from 0–9 with 4.5 considered average), were recommended by the reading teacher, or had low visual and vestibular scores.

A popular way to evaluate body concept is to give a child the name of the part. Someone might say, for example, "Show me your eyes." The child now has a clue, the name of the part. Instead, evaluate a child's body concept by telling him that you are going to place your hands on a part of your own body. Then ask him to touch the same part on his body and tell you the name of the body part. If he hesitates, or moves to a different part of the body, there may be a problem. Results of a body-concept test performed in this way are dramatically different from scores obtained with the naming (or clue) method. We

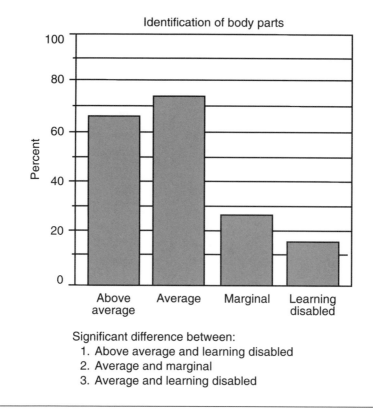

Significant difference between:
1. Above average and learning disabled
2. Average and marginal
3. Average and learning disabled

Figure 5.4 Results of identification of body parts.

found that without being told the clue of each body part, that is, naming the part to be identified, some sixth-grade students could not name some of their body parts.

You can teach children body concept in many ways. The easiest way is for parents and teachers to always refer to the particular part of the body when talking to or dressing children. For instance, you might say, "Use your right hand to hold the pencil," "Punch the ball with your left hand," "Let's put your hand in your mitten," "Let's put your coat on your arm," or "Where is your foot for this shoe?" These comments help your child gain an understanding of his body (see figure 5.5). Another way to help children learn body concept is through games and activities involving finding and naming body parts, such as the "Hokey Pokey" or "What a Miracle" (a recording by Hap Palmer).

Figure 5.5 "Where is your foot for this shoe?"

Don't Forget . . .

✔ Body concept is knowing the body parts.
✔ Children start learning to identify body parts before their first birthday.
✔ Some children cannot identify all of the body parts until the age of nine years.

Body-Concept Activities

As children use and name the various body parts in these activities, not only do they have to know where each body part is located on their bodies, but they must be able to use the body part in a controlled manner. Children feel how each part of the body moves, and they also have an opportunity to be successful and participate with others in a game.

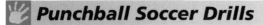 ## Punchball Soccer Drills

Individual or group

Appropriate Ages

4 years and older.

Preparation

Be sure to have an area about 5 feet by 5 feet for each child. You will also need one punchball *without* the rubber band attached. A child can do this activity alone, but it is more fun with a partner or in a small group (four or five people).

Activity

The object is to keep the punchball airborne without using the hands. If the child knows her body parts, you can call out body parts to use to tap the punchball, such as "Use your feet." "Use your elbows" "Use your head." You can also ask children (who are about five years or older) to use the same body part for a number of taps of the punchball: "Tap it five times with your knee." Or ask him to hit the punchball with a *series* of body parts: "Tap it with your head, elbow, and foot."

With a group of children eight years or older you can play "Follow the Leader." The leader taps the punchball with his shoulder, then head. He passes the punchball to the next person who then must tap it with the same body parts in the same order. Another variation is to have everyone count the number of times the punchball is tapped before it hits the floor and have a group try to increase its number.

BODY SCHEMA

Body schema is an internal (kinesthetic) awareness of where the body parts are in relation to each other. It is like a map, and it starts developing in the brain of a child around the 9th or 12th week of pregnancy. Body schema depends upon sensations received through activities involving the muscles, joints, skin, and soft tissue. Each time a child moves, plays with a toy, tenses her muscles, experiments with gravity, or is touched, the information goes to the brain and is stored in a particular place for each movement.

Body-schema problems may show up in a child's movement and activity. Children with schema problems have trouble with coordination, which spills over into an inability to play activities and sports with peers. The youngsters with the problem may not be able to figure out how to get into a chair or climb monkey bars.

An easy evaluation of body schema is to see whether a child can close her eyes and lift one of her arms to the same place at shoulder level three times in a row. Demonstrate the movement before you have her do it (see figure 8.7 on page 202). This evaluation is done first with the preferred arm, then the other arm, and finally with both arms. If she varies the height of her arm(s), then there may be a problem with body schema.

In a collection of studies, almost 40 percent of the kindergarten through sixth-grade students experienced difficulty with a body-schema test item (Cheatum 1986–1989, 1993, 1996; Cheatum and Hammond 1992). With the exception of Group A, more than half of the students lacked the ability to raise the nonpreferred arm or both arms to the same place at shoulder level four times in a row (see table 5.2). Although there were some lower-grade students in the groups, two of the groups consisted entirely of third-grade students, and one group included the upper grades. Many of the evaluated students were experiencing learning problems, which clearly suggests that

Table 5.2
Percent of Students Who Successfully Performed Shoulder-Level Arm-Raise Test

Group	A	B	C	D
Preferred arm	60.7	51.2	56.2	51.1
Nonpreferred arm	52.5	45.8	41.6	42.2
Both arms	60.7	47.8	48.3	42.2
Number	135	395	89	45

A: Third-grade students enrolled in 5 elementary schools in different geographic locations in Arlington, Texas. Students represented different academic-achievement levels based on scores received on state-administered achievement tests.

B: Kindergarten to sixth-grade students who were enrolled in 2 elementary schools in Kalamazoo, Michigan. Students scored 0–3 on the Iowa Achievement Test in reading (scores range from 0–9) or were experiencing learning problems.

C: Third-grade students enrolled in 6 different geographic locations in Kalamazoo, Michigan. Students represented diverse academic achievement.

D: Kindergarten to third-grade students in Parchment, Michigan. Students scored 0–3 on the Iowa Achievement Test (scores range from 0–9 with 4.5 considered average), were recommended by the reading teacher, or had low visual and vestibular scores.

body-schema problems may be one of the potential causes of learning problems.

Correcting body-schema problems involves using movement, but it is always important to find the cause of the problems. Sometimes the basic or underlying problem might relate to a poor knowledge of the body parts (body concept). If children cannot identify the parts of the body, they may have trouble using them effectively and knowing where the body parts are in relation to each other.

Don't Forget . . .

- ✔ Body schema is an internal awareness of where the body parts are and how they move in relation to each other.
- ✔ Body schema is developed through movement acting on the muscles, joints, skin, and soft tissue.
- ✔ Although body-schema problems interfere with coordination, sometimes the underlying cause might be body concept.

Body-Schema Activities

Children must figure out how to make their bodies move in new ways in activities intended to improve body schema. They must be able to determine which body parts are needed and how they can use the parts effectively as they move their bodies through, around, over, and under various pieces of equipment.

Follow the Leader

Group

Appropriate Ages

3 years and older.

Preparation

Choose a leader and have the others line up behind her. The group could also stand in a circle.

Activity

Everyone probably knows the game Follow the Leader. One person does a movement, and the others copy the movement. In this activity have the leader not only do a variety of locomotor skills—skipping, hopping, jumping, and others—but also do the movements with a variety of levels, directions, and speeds. Some movements can be near the ground, others can go backward, still others might be in slow motion. You can add props (such as scarves, balls, or hoops) to inspire the leader to do more creative movements. After three or four movements, change leaders. Moving to music or using musical instruments can also introduce rhythm into a game.

Under the Parachute

Group

Appropriate Ages

5 years and older.

Preparation

Get a parachute or large bedsheet (the bedsheet can be left with square corners or cut into a circle and stitched around the edge to prevent fraying).

Activity

Have the children find partners, and assign each set of partners a number (starting with #1 and going to however many sets of partners there are). You can tape number tags on the children or ask them to remember their numbers. Everyone stands around the edge of the parachute and directly across from his partner. When everyone is ready, together they lift the parachute. As the parachute goes up, partners #1 run under the parachute and switch places with each other before the parachute is lowered (see figure 5.6). Continue lifting and lowering the parachute as each set of partners is given a chance to switch places. Then, start from partners #1

Figure 5.6 Under the Parachute.

again, and this time continue until everyone is back in the same place as at the very beginning of the game.

The participants have quite a number of movements to learn, plan, and perform during the parachute activities:

1. How hard to pull upward on the parachute to help lift it
2. When to relax their arm muscles so that the parachute floats back down
3. What the timing is—when to move quickly or slowly to go under the parachute
4. How much to bend (or move) to get under the parachute
5. How fast to go to get to the other side before being trapped underneath
6. How to turn around their bodies so they can grab the edge of the parachute on the other side

LATERALITY

Laterality is an internal awareness (knowledge) that there are two sides of the body and that these sides are different. At first children do not know the names of the sides of the body even though they are aware that they are there. Children know that some body parts are the same but are on different sides of the body, such as the two arms, two legs, two ears, and two eyes. Laterality starts to appear about the fourth year. Along with an internal awareness, children develop the ability to use one side or both sides of the body to make desired movements. With laterality, children can catch a ball on the right side with the right hand, the left side with the left hand, or in the center of the body using both hands. They can also use two limbs of the body to do opposite tasks, such as using one hand to hold the paper on the desk and the other hand to write.

The development of laterality is very important for school. It is a major step in the development of children's awareness that they have both a right and a left side. This awareness plays a critical role in their academic success. Developing laterality depends on the information gained through the body-concept and body-schema stages of development.

While some basic knowledge of left and right may begin at four years of age, children still are tending to guess at age five. As you can see in table 5.3, children are seven years old before 70 percent of them can accurately identify minor body parts, such as the elbows, wrists, and heels. By the age of eight or nine, however, most children should be able to correctly identify the left and right parts of their bodies.

It's important to be aware that a few children cannot identify the right and left sides of their bodies until they are 10 years old. These children are at a learning disadvantage. For the first few years in elementary school, and perhaps throughout their education, these children will likely have academic problems. Until laterality develops, they will have trouble with the concepts of reading and writing from left to right. Even understanding many of the academic and physical education instructions will be difficult for them. This fact contradicts the checkpoints that the Council for Educational Development and Research (CEDAR) designed to help parents understand the requirements for reading in elementary school. For example, according to CEDAR, children in kindergarten should be able to identify and name the letters of the alphabet and point out letters in a text. They should know that words are combinations of letters, you read from left to right, and you hold a book right-side up.

Table 5.3
General Achievements in the Functional Development of Body Knowledge

Age in years	Identification of body parts	Laterality	Directionality	Lateral preference: handedness
0–2	Begin to "show" major body parts (eyes, nose, ears, hands, feet).			Preference changes during first year, depending on task.
2–5	80 percent identify eyes. 50 percent identify eyebrows.	Left-right discrimination is no better than chance. At ages 4–5, realize that left and right are on opposite sides of the body; unsure of which is which.	Very little knowledge of directionality.	At ages 3–5, increase in right-handedness.
5–7	At ages 5–6, 70 percent identify all major body parts. At age 7, 70 percent identify minor body parts (elbows, wrists, heels).	Consistent in response, whether right or wrong. At age 7, mistakes are infrequent.	At age 6, mirror and imitate movements. At age 7, begin to use body as directional reference of object, but are still subjective.	Handedness may shift or be inconsistent.
7–12	At ages 8–9, mistakes are rare.	Beyond ages 7–8, identify all left and right body parts.	At age 9, make objective directional references. At age 10, identify right and left of person facing them. At age 12, begin to use natural reference systems.	At ages 9–10, right-handedness stabilizes for about 80 percent. Right-eyedness increases. At ages 10–11, right-hand–eye preference increases.

Reprinted, by permission, from Jack Keogh and David Sugden, 1985, *Movement Skill Development* (New York: Macmillan), 276.

Laterality Activities

Activities that increase laterality help children use their right and left sides independently and are designed to develop an internal awareness of left and right. For example, the right hand must work independently of the left.

Toss and Catch the Magic Scarves

Individual or group

Appropriate Ages

4 years and older.

Preparation

Give two lightweight scarves or handkerchiefs to each child, and have each stand on a carpet square or in a hoop. This is the home space in which they must stay. Having a home space initially helps children to toss the scarves up—and not away—from their bodies.

Activity

Children toss the scarves up with both hands simultaneously in front of themselves; they try to catch one or both scarves in one hand. The scarves will float down at different rates and in different directions, causing the children to have to move the arms and hands independently to catch each scarf. For example, the right hand may need to catch its scarf before the left hand does its catching. You should try this to better understand how differently the scarves move. Count the number of times the children catch one or both scarves. If more than one child is playing, have them toss the scarves back and forth. When tossing the scarves back and forth, the element of aiming correctly adds to the activity's difficulty.

Balance and Scribble

Individual or group

Appropriate Ages

4 years and older.

Preparation

Hang a large piece of drawing paper on the wall at a height that the child or children can easily reach to draw on. Give each child a crayon or pencil.

Activity

The child stands on one foot, using his nondominant hand to brace himself against the wall for balance. Then he draws a large squiggly doodle on the paper. He can color in the squiggles with crayons or markers. If you place a bright light source behind the child, he can trace his shadow on the paper and fill in his facial features and clothes.

For a group activity each child starts a doodle on one piece, and then, on a signal, everyone moves to another doodle to add more lines or colors in the spaces of another child's doodle. This gives children an opportunity to rest and to cooperate on some wonderful visual art.

Push-Up Pivot

Individual or group

Appropriate Ages

6 years and older.

Preparation

Using masking tape, mark a dot on the floor and a circle around the dot that has a radius about the height of your child or the children. Place beanbags around the taped circle. Have each child put his feet on the dot and lean forward into a push-up position with his hands on the circle.

Activity

When you say, "Go!" the child walks his hands around to each beanbag and sets it off the tape line outside the circle. Keep time to see how fast he can get all the beanbags off the taped circle. Start with four or five beanbags and add more as the child improves.

Especially with younger children, if a child cannot hold a push-up position, make the circle around the dot smaller so he can do the activity from a knee push-up position or bending at the hips and waist. Or place a snow saucer in the center of the circle and have the child lie on his stomach and turn on the saucer.

Lateral Preference

Lateral preference is a term used when a child favors the use of one eye, hand, or foot over the other. It is an expected result of a child progressing through a normal developmental sequence, and it should occur naturally. Lateral preference is being able to use one side of the body more proficiently than the other, and it plays an important role in future academic learning and success in motor skills. *Pure lateral preference* is a situation in which a child *prefers* to use the eye, hand, and foot on the same side of the body.

During the first few months of life, an infant has a tendency to use the left hand. This stage is followed by an ambidextrous stage in which no preference is apparent. By the beginning of the seventh or eighth month, however, he begins to favor one hand, which is usually the right-sided one. At this stage, his preference may shift back and forth, depending on whether the desired object or person is near the left or the right hand. If you always feed an infant from his left side and he wants to grab the spoon, he will naturally reach up with his left hand. Lateral preference is usually established by the age of three or four, with most children preferring the right hand.

A child who has developed lateral preference will have a different feeling in the side of the body that he favors. This innate feeling enables him to *automatically* know which hand, arm, foot, or leg to use for a particular academic or motor task. Activities performed with the nonpreferred limb will not feel the same. For instance, if you try to write your name or throw a ball with your nonpreferred hand and arm, it will not feel natural to you. The feeling in that limb is different.

This awareness or feeling developed in the preferred side of the body is the foundation that children need in order to determine which objects are up, down, right, or left of their bodies or other objects.

Children who have not established lateral preference have difficulty using the nonpreferred hand to assist the other. This assistance is necessary in activities such as moving the limbs in opposition when throwing the ball, cutting food, or holding a bottle steady while unscrewing the lid.

To evaluate lateral preference, look at the way a child moves when performing several tasks. Ask him to throw a ball, write his name, draw, cut with scissors, kick a ball, balance on one leg, catch a ball, and dribble the ball. You can determine eye preference by having the child look through a tube (see chapter 10 for a more detailed discussion).

Helping elementary schoolchildren develop lateral preference involves creating a different feeling in the limb that is to be preferred. This includes doing numerous activities with the hand that you think each child favors. For example, during a physical education class if you want to encourage a child's lateral preference for the right side of his body, ask him to use just the right side. Have her dribble balls, throw balls, and catch balls with her right hand. Then have her kick balls, push a scooter board, and hop on her right foot. Do this the whole period and for several days. Avoid the temptation to have her alternate with the left side or she will continue to feel that both sides of her body are the same.

Mixed preference exists when a child does not favor the eye, hand, and foot on the same side of the body. In other words, there may be a preference for the right eye, left hand, and right foot. Lack of preference for one side of the body will affect the ability to develop a solid knowledge of left and right. There is some controversy over what type of corrective measures to take in the case of mixed preference—or even whether to take any action at all. If a child has mixed preference and consistently has trouble in school, an effort should be made to establish lateral preference. However, if he or she has mixed preference and is succeeding in school and movement activities, there should be no cause for concern.

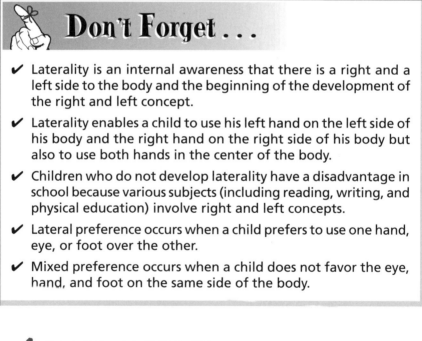

Don't Forget . . .

- ✔ Laterality is an internal awareness that there is a right and a left side to the body and the beginning of the development of the right and left concept.

- ✔ Laterality enables a child to use his left hand on the left side of his body and the right hand on the right side of his body but also to use both hands in the center of the body.

- ✔ Children who do not develop laterality have a disadvantage in school because various subjects (including reading, writing, and physical education) involve right and left concepts.

- ✔ Lateral preference occurs when a child prefers to use one hand, eye, or foot over the other.

- ✔ Mixed preference occurs when a child does not favor the eye, hand, and foot on the same side of the body.

Lateral Preference Activities

Activities that increase lateral awareness or knowledge of a difference between the right and left sides of the body cause the child to really feel one side or the other. These activities also encourage children to use the preferred hand and leg. Switching sides, such as practicing a movement with the right and then the left hand, will defeat the purpose of these activities. Therefore, if possible, determine the child's preferred hand and leg and concentrate on the use of these activities on only that side of the body.

Jack-and-Jill Relay

Individual or group

Appropriate Ages

4 years and older.

Preparation

Fill three one-gallon buckets with water. Add more or less water depending on how much the child can lift. Place the buckets at a starting line. Mark a finishing line about 5 to 10 feet from the starting line. Increase the distance for older or stronger children.

Activity

The child picks up one bucket with his preferred hand and carries it to a finish line where he leaves it. Then he returns, picks up a second bucket, also with his preferred hand, and carries it to the fin-

Figure 5.7   Children doing Jack-and-Jill Relay.

ish line. Continue with the third (or more) bucket. The object is to avoid spilling any water. This is a great summer game and can be done as a relay race among several children (see figure 5.7).

One-Arm Tug-of-War

Partners

Appropriate Ages

5 years and older.

Preparation

Mark a three-foot line on the floor.

Activity

Two children stand on opposite sides of the line and grasp each other's preferred wrists. On "Go!" they try to pull each other over the line. Time the intervals of pulling to allow about 20 seconds each. Remind children not to let go of each other unless they pull each other over the line or unless the instructor tells them to stop after 20 seconds. The children should use a slow, steady pull, and not jerk one another's arms.

Paper-Ball Soccer Drills

Individual or group

Appropriate Ages

5 years and older.

Preparation

Each child gets a paper ball (simply use an 8 × 10 piece of paper and wad it up). Mark a starting line. Set up 4 or 5 cones in a straight line at two to three-foot intervals, using 2 cones set about four feet apart as the goal at the finish line.

Activity

The children assume a crab-walk position (on the ground with their hands placed behind them, knees bent, feet flat, and their bottoms lifted off the floor). Then, using only the dominant leg, they kick the paper ball in zigzag patterns around the cones. At the finish line they use their preferred leg to kick the paper ball through the goal. For added challenge, see how quickly they can go through the cones and then shoot for the goal. This activity can also be done as a race.

Some children will not be able to hold their bottoms off the floor to crab-walk very far or to kick the paper ball. Try keeping track of increases in distance they can travel without needing to rest.

Scramble Around

Individual

Appropriate Ages

6 years and older.

Preparation

Using masking tape, mark a dot on the floor and then a circle around the dot that has a radius about the height of your child.

Activity

The child places his preferred hand on the center dot and extends his other arm toward the ceiling. Leaning on his preferred hand, the child walks his feet around the tape circle. See how far the child can go around the circle without resting. Try to increase the distance each time. If the child can go all the way around, see how many circles she can make.

Thumb Wrestling

Partners

Appropriate Ages

6 years and older.

Preparation

Seat the children in pairs near one another at a table. The participants place their preferred hands on a table, with the little fingers just touching the table and their palms open and facing the opponent's palm.

Activity

On, "Go!" both participants hook their fingers with their opponent's fingers. Each person tries to get his thumb on top of the opponent's and pin it down. This can also be done in a standing position without the use of a table (see figure 5.8).

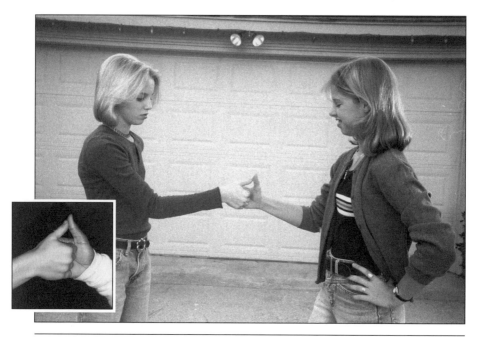

Figure 5.8 Thumb Wrestling.

Midline

Midline relates to laterality. In the early stages of development, the midline is like a wall that keeps a child from crossing one arm or leg across the center of his body into the other half. When a baby is a few months old, he will grasp a block in one hand, move it to the center of his body and then transfer it to the other hand. Between 8 and 12 months, most children gain the ability to reach *across* the midline of their bodies to pick up a toy or snack.

Parents and teachers should be somewhat concerned when a child reaches the age of five and cannot cross the midline. Crossing the midline occurs automatically after the child has developed lateral preference, which is sometimes delayed until a child is about seven years old. If a seven-year-old child still cannot cross his midline, he may be considered to have a *midline problem*. Retaining a midline problem in elementary school interferes with his everyday classroom and physical education activities. Bobby, for instance, obviously exhibits a midline problem when he erases a chalkboard. He erases one side of the chalkboard and then places the eraser in the other hand at the middle of his

Figure 5.9 Midline problem prevents child from moving arm across front of his body when erasing the chalkboard.

body to erase the other side of the chalkboard. In this way, he accomplishes the task of erasing the board without having crossed the midline (see figure 5.9).

The best way to see if a midline problem exists is to observe children doing activities in the classroom or in the gymnasium. If they do not naturally reach across the body to catch a ball, do not follow through after throwing, or do not perform dance steps that cross one leg in front of the other, for example, you should suspect a midline problem. Young children doing deskwork may also transfer the pencil at the midline, using the right hand on the right side and the left hand on the left side.

Inability to cross the midline also affects the visual system. Children with midline problems use the right eye to read or write on the right side of the midline and the left on the left side. This switching of the eyes leads to confusion. During the act of reading, the left eye reads to the middle of the sentence; then the right eye takes over. Angelo has this problem. His right eye may not know where his left eye stopped in the middle of a sentence, which causes him to keep losing his place or to skip lines.

Often, a child with a midline problem places papers on the right side of his desk in order to use only his right eye and to avoid crossing his midline with his pencil. The position of the paper on the right side even helps him avoid using the left eye. This child may also cover his left eye with his left hand to literally block out his left eye.

When examining children for a midline problem, keep two facts in mind. First, even though a child may have a midline problem, if you ask him to cross the midline, he may be able to do so. This may not be a natural skill or a comfortable movement for him; he really has to concentrate to cross the midline because the skill is not automatic for him. Second, children with a midline problem find crossing their feet or some lower part of the body easier than crossing the arms. Therefore, just because a child sits cross-legged or can walk sideways, crossing the legs, do not assume that that a midline problem does not exist.

Children with a midline problem may appear to have the ability to write and perform activities with either hand equally or be *ambidextrous*. These children seem stuck at the midline level. They will usually be delayed in developing laterality, lateral preference, cross-lateral motor patterns, or even learning left from right on their bodies and on other objects. They often use either side for catching or batting, but the two sides of the body have no relationship to each other. This prevents co-ordinated activities with the two hands. When you toss balls to such a child, she can catch it with the right hand on the right side and the left hand on the left side. However, if you toss balls toward the midline, the two sides of the body and the visual system usually cannot coordinate enough for the child to be able to catch the ball.

When evaluating a child for lateral preference or a midline problem, make sure that the particular test item accurately measures what you want. Some tasks involve more than one skill. For example, if you ask a child to take his right hand and touch his left toe, you are examining his right-and-left awareness but you are also assessing whether or not he can cross his midline. If he uses his right hand and touches his right toe, he may know which is the left toe but have a midline problem (therefore he cannot cross the midline).

Evaluations of four groups of elementary schoolchildren indicated that many of these children still had a right-left awareness or a midline problem (Cheatum 1986–1989, 1989, 1993, 1996; Cheatum and Hammond 1992). Notice in table 5.4 that more than two thirds of the children in Group C failed to do the initial task, touching the right hand to the left foot. However, about half of them were smart enough to realize their mistake, and when asked about it, they correctly touched the left hand to the right foot. This indicates that the second set of figures, touching the left hand to the right foot, more accurately tells you which students have more serious problems with laterality. The second set

Table 5.4
Percent of Elementary Students Who Correctly Passed Midline and
Right-and-Left Awareness Test

Group	Grade	Number	Touch right hand to left foot	Touch left hand to right foot
A	K–6	395	61.8%	61.5%
B	3	89	79.8%	86.5%
C	3	135	32.6%	86.5%
D	K–3	45	88.9%	86.7%

A: Children with learning problems or in kindergarten.
B: Above-average, average, and below-average students.
C: Above-average, average, and below-average students.,
D: Children with learning problems or in kindergarten.

shows that either they did not know they failed the first item or they could not cross the midline to touch the left hand to the right foot. Therefore, there was a problem in one or both the areas of right-and-left awareness and midline skill.

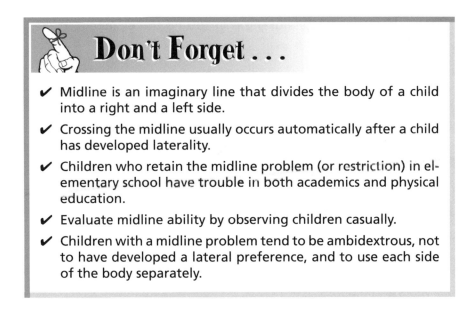

Don't Forget . . .

✔ Midline is an imaginary line that divides the body of a child into a right and a left side.

✔ Crossing the midline usually occurs automatically after a child has developed laterality.

✔ Children who retain the midline problem (or restriction) in elementary school have trouble in both academics and physical education.

✔ Evaluate midline ability by observing children casually.

✔ Children with a midline problem tend to be ambidextrous, not to have developed a lateral preference, and to use each side of the body separately.

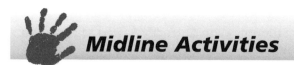

Midline Activities

For an activity to be successful in encouraging children to cross the midline it should be child initiated. The child needs to be put in a situation in which he must cross his midline to successfully complete the activity. Repeatedly practicing marching and or touching the right hand to the left knee and vice versa may result only in developing the splinter skill of performing that particular movement. Therefore, these midline activities create a situation in which the only way the child can be successful is to cross the midline.

Cross Toss

Individual

Appropriate Ages

5 years and older.

Preparation

Get about 10 beanbags. Have the child lie on her back, and place 6 to 10 beanbags right next to the elbow of her nonpreferred side (she must be able to reach the beanbags without rolling her body toward them). Place a bucket by her preferred side. The distance depends on how successful she is at tossing the beanbags in the bucket.

Activity

The child picks up and tosses the beanbags, one at a time, into the bucket using her preferred hand. She must keep both shoulders on the ground. See if she can increase the number of beanbags she can successfully toss into the bucket each time. You could also start to move the bucket farther from her body to increase the distance she must toss.

Minitrampoline Jump and Twist

Individual

Appropriate Ages

7 years and older.

Preparation

Use a minitrampoline, with plenty of space around it. Make sure no hard objects are within five feet of the trampoline.

Activity

The child begins by jumping with hands on hips and feet together. Next he "scissors" the legs back and forth, keeping the hands on the hips. Have the child continue doing this until you notice that the shoulders are shifting in opposition to the feet and a slight twisting movement is observed at the waist. (The right shoulder shifts forward while the left foot is forward and vice versa). When you observe this occurring consistently for 10 to 15 consecutive jumps, ask the child to try jumping with the arms lifted to shoulder height, elbows bent, feet together and twisting at the waist. If the child begins to do a side-to-side jump with the whole body facing the same direction alternately—return to jumping with hands on hips, feet together and progress to the legs scissoring again. In order for the child to jump and twist consistently, he must be able to cross the midline naturally with the arms and legs.

DIRECTIONALITY

Once a child has developed a well-defined sense of laterality and knowledge of the body, he or she can build directionality. During this developmental step, the youngster transfers knowledge of the right and left sides of the body into space. Directionality involves three references: right and left, up and down, and before and behind (in front of and in back of, or forward and back). A child first learns all three of the directional references in relation to his or her own body, and then projects this knowledge into space and onto other objects.

Knowledge of directionality enables a child to become the center of her universe. From this point on, she learns to refer to people and objects in relation to the center of her body. This is called *egocentric localization* (location of objects in relation to one's self), and acquiring this sense is a gradual process that usually occurs between the ages of 6 and 8. A child begins to make references such as, "The ball is on my right," "The dog is in front of me," and "Barbara is in back of me." Between the ages of 8 and 11, a child should progress to the stage of *objective localization,* which is the ability to refer to objects and people in relation to each other. She can observe, "The ball is in front of the desk," "The dog is on top of the couch," or "John Paul is standing behind Devon."

Children are commonly 10 years old before they can identify the right and left parts of people who face them. In terms of the developmental steps of directionality, our educational programs often expect too much, too soon, of children in this area. In fact, we may be guilty of prematurely foisting learning-problem labels on children in early elementary schools because of the way we give instructions and what we expect them to learn.

References to directions are used all the time in teaching, which means that having a clear understanding of directionality is critical for children to be able to do many classroom tasks. Teachers and parents routinely use directions when giving instructions for assignments. However, many children in the first and second grades do not understand what is meant by the top-right corner of the paper. In fact there are two tops: the top side and the top half of the paper. Even simple directions like folding the right side of the paper toward the left is confusing for some first-grade students. If they do not know the right and left sides of someone facing them, how will they be able to identify the right and left sides of papers on their desks? As an example of a directionality problem, some children may take an entire semester to remember how to get from one place in the school to another. For these youngsters, just going out the classroom door and turning left to get to the library can be overwhelming.

A look at developmental charts shows that some normally developing children may be in the upper elementary grades before they have matured enough to understand more complex directions. These are examples of complex directions for an elementary school-aged child: "Place your name in the upper left-hand corner of the paper" or "The math problem is the third one on the left side of the paper in the fourth row." Think about putting on a coat; it actually involves all the components of directionality. Children must know the front and back, top and bottom, and right and left side of both themselves and the coat.

Sports and games are difficult for children with directionality problems. These children are often accused of not listening or not paying attention, but in reality they do not understand what they are supposed to do. A child might hit the ball and run to third base instead of running to first base. Or he might run to the wrong goal in soccer. "Pass the ball to the right" or "Throw the ball behind you" are confusing instructions to him.

Directional discrimination problem is a phrase you might hear used to describe the difficulty a child has with directionality. Directional discrimination depends on a firm knowledge of laterality and directionality. Has she really internalized a knowledge of the body, the right and left concepts in laterality, and the three directional references in directionality? In learning situations, both academic and sports, the way in which directional discrimination problems affect a child is very subtle but profoundly influential. Learning depends on a knowledge of directions.

As young toddlers, children learn *constancy*. Objects are constant. That is, a chair is a chair—even if it is in a book, upside down, on the TV screen, or on its side. This is also true of books, forks, dolls, and all the other objects in a child's world.

Enter the academic phase of a child's life! When she starts to learn the alphabet, the concept of constancy breaks down. This is particularly true when you look at the letters *p, q, b,* and *d.* All these letters are similar except for facing different directions. Teachers talk about the straight line going in one direction, with the rounded part facing another direction. Children who can discriminate between the directions begin to understand what the teachers are talking about—but those who can't discriminate, don't understand what teachers are talking about. A child who is still in the laterality stage (does not know right and left) or lacks directionality (has not gained a sense of up and down, before and behind) will continue to get these letters confused. So he will not be successful in learning the academic material, but instead will become frustrated and perhaps resort to inappropriate behaviors.

English is meant to be read from the top to the bottom and from the left to the right sides of the paper. When you ask children to read from the left to the right or to "move your finger left to right across the page," it has no meaning for a child who lacks directional discrimination. Even reading simple words, such as *bed*, involves reading each letter from left to right. Yet, this child may read it from the right to left as *deb*. Or he may read part of the word in one direction and then go back. Words such as *mom* may become *wow*. Such directional discrimination problems are often called *dyslexia, dysgraphia,* or *dyspraxia.*

Copying work from a chalkboard confuses many early elementary schoolchildren, and it can be even more troublesome for children who are left-handed. If the teacher writes the capital letter *B* on the chalkboard, left-handed children will try to write the letter from the midline of the body toward the outside as the right-handed teacher does. This results in a backward *B.* You may think these children reversed the *B,* but in fact they are copying the teacher's movements in a way that is natural for them. If left-handed children also have directional discrimination problems, copying work from the chalkboard becomes nearly impossible.

Several concepts relating to body awareness, laterality, and directionality have been presented in this chapter. The box titled "Developmental Problems and Symptoms Related to Body Awareness" summarizes these problems, which are often seen at home and in the classroom.

Developmental Problems and Symptoms Related to Body Awareness

Developmental Stage	Problems
Body image	Child knows when he or she cannot move efficiently—is aware that other children shun him or her—and often experiences fight-or-flight reactions when tasks are beyond his or her age of neurological development.
Body concept	Child cannot identify parts of body—even when he or she is elementary school aged.
Body schema	Child is unable to form a mental map of the body and how the body parts move, preventing him or her from making coordinated movements.
Laterality	Child is unable to coordinate the use of one hand or two because of lacking internal awareness of right and left.
Bilaterality	Child experiences associated movements, two arms or two legs moving together, and hasn't progressed to cross lateral movements.
Midline problem	Child retains dividing line down the middle of the body, using the right hand for activity on right side of body and the left hand for the left side. He doesn't normally cross the midline and can't use two hands or arms together. The child has some difficulty crossing midline with his eyes.
Lateral preference	Child lacks neurological information that helps him develop lateral preference; lacks the internal feeling that one side of the body is different than the other.

Directionality	No projection of laterality into space; no mental map of up-down, right-left, and before-behind.
Directional discrimination	With no directionality cannot develop directional discrimination; makes learning letters difficult (b, p, d, q are all the same); blocks or delays ability to read and write.

Don't Forget . . .

✔ Directionality involves the concepts of up-down, right-left, and before-behind.

✔ Egocentric localization is the ability of a child to locate objects in relation to her own body.

✔ Objective localization is the ability to locate objects in relation to each other.

✔ Children are often in upper-elementary grades before they can understand complex directions.

✔ In order to read or write, a child must be able to break down the constancy concept and also have a knowledge of directions.

Directionality Activities

Activities that increase awareness of directionality cause children to move their bodies up, down, around, under, or in specific directions through space. The children need to sense which way is appropriate to move in order to complete a task. Each of these following activities creates a situation in which the children must determine which direction to move and then move that way. In addition, while children are doing these activities, they will begin to label directions.

Refrigerator Box Obstacle Course
Individual or group

Appropriate Ages

As soon as children can crawl.

Preparation

For those with a big budget, elaborate obstacle courses made of nylon are available commercially. But it also works well to use large cardboard boxes from refrigerators or other large appliances to build your own course. Any other props that inspire building an inventive obstacle course are wonderful to add. For example, you might use scarves, blankets, or chairs. You can decorate the obstacle course using scissors, tape, crayons, or paint.

Activity

The number of ways to build an obstacle course is as vast as your imagination. Children can tape the boxes together, then cut out doors, windows, or gates. Smaller boxes can create smaller spaces to crawl through or step over. If they are careful, the children can take apart the obstacle course and rebuild it in new ways. For a more lasting obstacle course reinforce the corners of the boxes with duct tape. Adults may need to build the obstacle course for younger children, but with older children, you can build in all kinds of concepts for this activity. They can help measure the size to make doors, figure out the directions, how to attach one box to another or help write the plans for building it, and so forth.

After the obstacle course is built, the children can ask each other to go through the course in certain patterns. You might at first suggest to them, *go in the door, crawl through the first box, come out and stand up, then jump over the shoe box.* This activity also helps develop body schema.

Have fun!

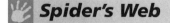
Spider's Web
Group

Appropriate Ages

4 years and older.

Preparation

You'll need at least three children for this activity and a space at least 10 feet by 10 feet. Give each child a different color ball of yarn or ribbon. Assign each child a place in the room to attach the end of their "web," such as a chair leg or a drawer handle. Each person then stands at the beginning of his web.

Activity

The leader tells the participants to move in various ways (crawling, hopping, walking backward) through the activity space to another place to attach part of the web. Encourage them to move over or under each other, objects, and so forth. Use music or sounds if you like. When the music stops, the children change the direction in which they are weaving the web. Keep this up until a nice web has been formed. About five or six changes for each web usually is enough; more than that and the web will become too tangled.

When the web is complete, have the children take a moment to see where their pieces of the web go and how they interweave with others. When the leader says, "Go!" all the participants work to rewind their web substance and undo the web.

Milk Crate Statues

Partners or group

Appropriate Ages

4 years and older.

Preparation

Give each participant a plastic crate or bucket that is strong enough to stand on. The crate can contain other props, such as scarves, balls, and small hoops. Have a way to play music (radio, tape, CD, piano, other instruments) and some recordings or examples to use.

Activity

Play some music. When you stop the music, each participant freezes in a shape using his crate and props. The leader gives suggestions, such as "Move under the crate" or "Stand on the crate." Ask the children to describe how other statues look. For example, a child might say, "Derek is standing on his crate with a hoop around his waist and a scarf on top of his head."

Children can work with partners, for instance, with one acting as the sculptor, and the other the clay. The sculptor tells the clay how to pose. "Hold the crate over your head with your knees tucked under your chin."

Directional Discrimination Activities

In these activities, children must not only determine how and where to move their bodies, but also how and where other people and objects must move. For example, they may know that they need to move under something, but another person may need to move in a *different* direction in order to complete the game.

The Human Knot

Group

Appropriate Ages

8 years and older.

Preparation

Three or more children stand in a circle and stretch their arms toward the middle of the circle. Each person takes hold of two hands (neither of which is their own).

Activity

On the signal "Go!" the children proceed to figure out how to get their arms untangled and try to end up standing in a circle holding hands. The arms may be in such a knot that they cannot be totally untangled. Have the group decide (that is, figure out) when they come to a place where no more untangling is possible.

Each child in the human knot must understand not only the direction his body needs to move to get untangled, but also where the other children need to move. Each child must be able to mentally picture what the outcome of each move will be. Will someone become more tangled as a result of his move?

Children need to solve the following problems during the activity:

1. Do I need to move under or over another person's arms?
2. Do I need to turn around, and, if so, should I turn right or left?
3. Which directions do the others need to move in relation to my body and to each other?

Blindfolded Soccer

Partners or group

Appropriate Ages

8 years and older.

Preparation

Set cones in a straight line, marking a start and finish line at each end. Participants choose partners and one partner puts on a blindfold.

Activity

The partner without a blindfold directs the blindfolded partner to dribble a ball in a zigzag pattern through the cones.

What Did You Spell?

Partners or group

Appropriate Ages

8 years and older.

Preparation

You will need 8-inch-by-10-inch cards made from posterboard, one for each letter of the alphabet. Scatter the letters around the floor. Participants will need a partner.

Activity

Without saying the name of each letter, one partner will direct the other to step on a series of letters. For example, step on the letter to your right (which might be a B), then the letter behind that one (an A), then step on the letter (which might be a T) to the left of the first one. When the directing partner says, "What did you spell?" the other partner in this example would respond, "bat."

Part II
The Sensory Systems

Noriko hates to go to school on Tuesdays and Thursdays because those are physical education days. Just the thought of going to gym class makes her sweat. She cannot catch or throw well, and she can hear the other children moan under their breaths whenever she ends up on their teams. Whenever she tries to run faster, she feels as if she's going to fall on her face, and tumbling activities make her feel nauseous.

Carl, on the other hand, can hardly wait to go to physical education class. Sitting in a chair in the classroom is a major chore to him. If he is not shaking his legs, he is tapping his pencil eraser on the desk. Reading gives him a headache and watery eyes. He does not know why but standing in line is very uncomfortable because he hates feeling other kids standing so close. Once he gets into the gymnasium, the physical education teacher seems to always be reminding him to listen to instructions and wait for his turn, but Carl just needs to move!

Rosetta is good at reading and would sit with a book all day if she could. In fact, she becomes so involved in books that she does not hear her mother call her for dinner. Her teacher must tap her on the shoulder and look directly at her when giving instructions if she wants Rosetta to pay attention. She appears overweight and fatigues easily during physical education. Every chance she gets, she seems to melt down, wanting to sit or even lie down on the floor. Although she could tell you all about history, geography, and horses, she does poorly on tests because of poor handwriting and an inability to remain focused on test items.

All the children in these examples have problems with at least one of their sensory systems, and the problems interfere with their classroom or movement activities. Children who have trouble with their sensory systems also usually have one or more developmental problems. As you observe children like these at home or in a classroom, you may notice behavior or learning problems that are caused by underlying developmental delays. These delays are often related to an inability to use the information that enters the sensory systems. The developmental problems, in turn, may cause them to have more trouble using sensory information.

To help these children, their parents and teachers must understand how an inability to process sensory information contributes to learning difficulties and undesirable behavior. Therefore, part II examines the sensory systems responsible for the way a child responds to gravity and moves, feels touch, sees, and hears. Material relating to each individual sensory sytem appears in separate chapters. Each chapter includes a description of the sensory system and its receptors, the influence of the system on a child's development, problems with the systems that affect a child's behavior and learning ability, and ways to manage the problems. You'll also find methods for screening for problems, as well as activities to assist the child in alleviating the problems.

chapter 6
Overview of the Sensory Systems

In this chapter we discuss the development of the sensory systems, explore perception (how sensory information is understood), and consider the influences of external and internal stimuli on sensory development. We also describe three sensory dysfunctions, or problems: sensory overload, hypersensitivity to stimuli, and hyposensitivity to stimuli.

The five basic senses are the vestibular, proprioceptive, tactile, visual, and auditory, and each has a sense organ through which information is gained and primary actions are initiated (see table 6.1). These systems seldom, if ever, operate in isolation. They depend on each other for interpretation of information and movement. For example, although balance is strongly influenced by the vestibular system, balance also depends on the other systems.

An infant doesn't just suddenly start using his or her sensory systems at birth. As early as nine weeks after conception, the vestibular system (described in detail in chapter 7) begins to develop. During the prenatal period the fetus also develops the ability to hear, see, smell, taste, touch, and move. By the time of birth, an infant can be said to be in a state of *sensory readiness*—ready to learn and to seek information from the environment and the movement of his or her body.

Each sensory system (sometimes referred to as a *modality*) has its own neurological networks, pathways, and location or site within the brain. Children hear sounds, obviously, but they do not *smell* sounds or *listen* to pictures.

As you may recall, neurological networks are created when neurons form connections to other neurons through the axons and dendrites.

Table 6.1
Overview of Sensory Systems

Sense	Sensory organ	Sensory system
Balance	Ears	Vestibular system
Movement	Joints and connective tissue	Proprioceptive system
Touch	Skin	Tactile system
Sight	Eyes	Visual system
Hearing	Ears	Auditory system

And the more opportunities that a child has with various sensory experiences, the more the brain develops, forming connections between neurons. These connections, in turn, increase the youngster's ability to use sensory information.

SENSING STIMULI

Children receive both external and internal information in the form of stimuli (sensations). An *external stimulus* occurs, for instance, when Jane looks out the classroom window and the picture of the janitor mowing the lawn enters her visual system. Jimmy, on the other hand, does not turn his head in that same classroom to see what is happening; he uses his ears (auditory system) to hear the mower (external stimulus) and registers what is happening.

An *internal stimulus* can occur through the positioning of body parts, movement of muscles and tendons, pain, pressure, balance, or temperature. Most children do not look at their feet to walk because sensory information to the brain about the position and movement of their feet comes through their muscles and joints. When a child walks across a balance beam, internal sensations give his neurological system information on how high to lift his foot and where to place it. He will unconsciously adjust his position to keep his body upright.

Similarly, if a child is learning to hold a pencil or throw a ball, there are certain joint positions that provide *internal stimuli* to make his skill more accurate. However, accuracy depends also on an internal, intricate knowledge of the positions of the involved muscles and joints. It is up to his neurological system to separate the feeling of the correct movements and positions from those that are uncoordinated.

Perceiving Stimuli

Perception depends on the brain recognizing sensory information and understanding what it means. Once a *stimulus* (sensation) enters the neurological system, it travels to the brain. In the brain, it is related to past memories and recognized, which is when the perception of the stimulus occurs (see figure 6.1).

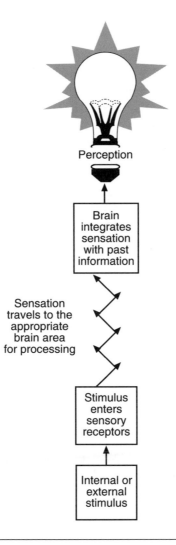

Perception

Brain integrates sensation with past information

Sensation travels to the appropriate brain area for processing

Stimulus enters sensory receptors

Internal or external stimulus

Figure 6.1 The stages of perception.

Several events must happen before a child can respond to either an external or an internal stimulus. To begin with, the stimulus must occur and be received by his particular *sense organ* (such as the eyes). Let's use the example of a visual stimulus and follow it through the sensing process to better understand how perception works. When a baby first opens his eyes, none of the toys or objects in his room are familiar. His eyes may receive the stimulus of a cuddly bear, but this image has no meaning to him. That is, he has never seen a bear before, so he has no past visual image, or picture, with which to match the present visual stimulus.

After repeated interactions with the bear, however, the baby will recognize it as a familiar sight. This is because the visual stimuli, passed along the *neurological pathways* as *sensations* (electrical impulses) that went to his brain, have created memories. In his brain, the baby interpreted or *integrated* (associated with past memories) the sensations, and *perception* occurred. The area of the baby's brain concerned with perception constantly undergoes changes and modifications as he has new experiences and builds new areas ("files") full of different memories.

Dr. Gerald Getman, a leading authority on child development, saw perception as the ability to make the most sense out of something with the least amount of information. The brain works in some ways like a computer. If someone shows you something that you have never seen before, the stimulus goes in and becomes a sensation. When the sensation reaches the brain, you try to make sense out of it by consciously or unconsciously running through the files in your memory. When you finally recognize the sensation, you have reached the perception, or the "I know what it is," stage. The more frequently you interact with a stimulus and store information about it, the less time it takes for perception to occur.

Imagine that you see someone approaching you from down the street. You recognize that it is a person, but do you know that specific person? When the visual sensation reaches your brain, you start going through past memories to locate that face and make an *association*. Was the person someone you knew at camp? A friend at school? A former teacher? When you finally make the association, you have reached perception. If you do not match the face to a past image (experience) no association is made and your mind is blank.

You have probably observed a similar reaction occurring in some children with learning problems. She or he cannot make the association and the mind becomes a blank. This interrupts his or her behavior and ability to learn.

Responding to Stimuli

Perceptual motor act refers to a motor response that follows perception. When the sensory information sent to the brain requires a *motor response,* the information is sent by the brain through neurological pathways to the muscle or muscle groups that should respond (see figure 6.2). When a baby sees and reaches for a teddy bear, he is experiencing a perceptual motor act. Copying the word *dog* off the chalkboard is another example of a perceptual motor act. The child must see and recognize the word or at least the letters in *dog* by associating the visual information with past memories. Messages are then sent along neurological pathways to the muscles needed to perform the act of copying the letters on a sheet of paper.

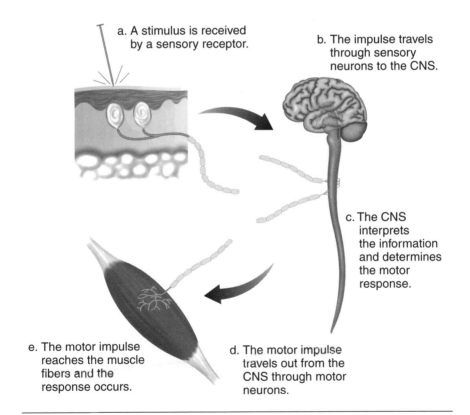

a. A stimulus is received by a sensory receptor.

b. The impulse travels through sensory neurons to the CNS.

c. The CNS interprets the information and determines the motor response.

d. The motor impulse travels out from the CNS through motor neurons.

e. The motor impulse reaches the muscle fibers and the response occurs.

Figure 6.2 Sensory integration process.
Reprinted, by permission, from Jack H. Wilmore and David L. Costill, 1999, *Physiology of Sport and Exercise*, 2nd ed. (Champaign, IL: Human Kinetics), 71.

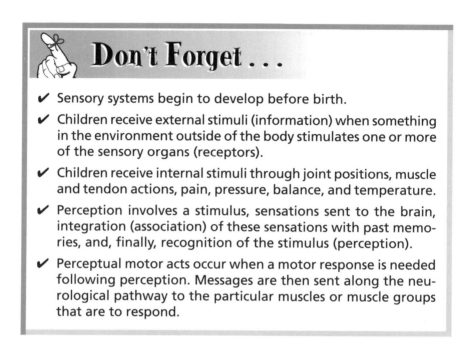

INTEGRATING STIMULI FOR DEVELOPMENT AND LEARNING

Sensory integration is a phrase used to describe the process of perception and perceptual motor activities. It involves the ability of the brain to receive, organize, interpret, and use the vast amount of sensory information that enters the body and neurological system through both external and internal stimuli. To do this, information from each of the senses, movement of the body, and gravity must be integrated (pulled together) and interpreted before children can successfully function in the world around them.

We do not use just one sensory system at a time. Consider the environment you are in as you read this book. You have information entering your body through your skin, ears, eyes, muscles, and joints. Although you may not be paying attention, your skin is still telling your brain what your clothes feel like. The sounds around you are received by your ears, your eyes see the words, and your muscles and joints are holding the book and maintaining your posture. On a conscious level, nevertheless, your neurological system responds only to the sensory information necessary for you to read. It ignores the other information.

Even before babies are born, they use more than one sensory system. During the early months of life, they love to look at and listen to anything new in their environment. In this way, they are using their visual and auditory systems (sometimes known as *far receptors*) to learn about the world around them. When they can, they want to touch and taste everything they can reach. In these ways, they add the knowledge gained through the senses of touch and taste (*near receptors*) to what they have already learned from the visual and auditory systems.

The need to combine information from one sensory system to help a child understand information from other systems often continues in elementary school. Many young children seem driven to touch every object on their desks and on the desks of students next to them (see figure 6.3). Although some teachers call this hyperactivity, experienced teachers view this behavior as a clue that this child may be immature. That is, he is still in the developmental stage of learning about objects through touching them. He cannot rely on just seeing the object. He has to feel it, to use the near receptor of touch.

Combining information from different sensory systems is a normal part of learning. We all do this at one time or another. When buying a piece of clothing or a billfold made of leather, we often feel it in order to know what it is really like. We don't want to use just our eyes. Artists, particularly sculptors, are notorious for feeling objects. If they are look-

Figure 6.3 Immature child needing information from sense of touch in order to understand objects and environment.

ing at a sculpture, they have an almost uncontrollable drive to *feel* the sculpture as well! The sense of touch gives them a more complete image of the piece of art.

During physical activity, such as jumping over a high bar, parts of sensory integration will function as a subconscious act. The child needs to perceive the height of the bar. Then, his brain associates this information with past memories about how high to jump. Specific directions are then relayed to his muscles and joints so he can clear the bar successfully. If the sensory integration were not automatic and unconscious, he would probably miss the jump: he does not have time in midair to consciously think through the jump.

Observe a child writing. Try to count the number of sensory integration activities that she must go through to use her eyes, sit still, hold the pencil and paper, and move her fingers, hands, and wrist to write. The visual system takes in the letters and words, while the vestibular and proprioceptive systems keep her head steady and maintain her balance in her seat. In the meantime, the tactile and proprioceptive systems must work so she can hold the pencil and paper. Even the auditory system must function to write silently. Some children mentally say each word, so they are internally listening to memories of how words sound as they write quietly (figure 6.4).

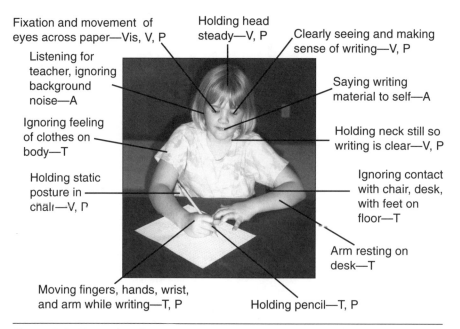

Figure 6.4 Example of some sensory motor activities involved with writing. Key: V = vestibular, P = proprioceptive, T = tactile, Vis = visual, A = auditory.

When a child has a learning problem and the cause is found to be in one of the sensory systems, it is often helpful to use other sensory systems during remedial activities. For instance, a child of six should be able to focus (fixate or hold her eyes steady) on a page or object for a period of 10 seconds. If she cannot, try having her add the help of two of the more primitive systems, the senses of touch and movement, to the visual system. Have her move her index finger out to touch the word. This uses the muscles of her shoulder, arm, hand, and fingers (the proprioceptive system) and the tip of her finger (the tactile system) to bring it all together for her; it increases her ability to focus.

If a child has trouble moving his eyes across a page during reading, visual-motor therapists often have the youngster place a finger under the line of words and move the hand across the page as he reads. This is a simple but effective way to use three sensory systems to increase the child's learning and to decrease the stress.

👆 Don't Forget . . .

✔ Sensory integration is the ability of the brain to receive, organize, interpret, and use the information that enters the body.

✔ Multiple sensory systems are operating at any given time—we do not use just one system.

✔ We often use one sensory system to give us additional information about another system (for example, when we hear a loud noise and look in that direction, we are adding the visual system to the auditory one).

✔ Children who have trouble reading can benefit by adding the use of other sensory systems.

SENSORY DYSFUNCTION

Sensory dysfunction occurs when children have an underlying problem in one or more of the sensory systems. Either sensory information does not reach the central nervous system or the information is not processed correctly.

Any difficulties with receiving, organizing, interpreting, or responding appropriately to the vast amount of information that enters the sensory systems can create problems. As children age, the academic and motor skills they need to function well in school and society become more complex. Children with sensory dysfunction have less success and become more frustrated. They often have poor self-esteem (body image) and feel defeated before even trying new things.

The most important thing to understand is that each child with sensory dysfunction is different. Sven may have problems with vision, while Mark cannot process auditory information efficiently. Therefore, a thorough evaluation by appropriate professionals of each of the sensory systems and underlying development stages of body concept, body schema, laterality, and directionality is necessary to find the underlying cause of the problems and to plan intervention activities to help the child. Evaluations should be completed by trained professionals such as visual specialists, speech and language personnel, physical therapists, adapted physical educators, physicians, or occupational therapists.

An estimated 10 to 20 percent of elementary schoolchildren in the United States have behavior or learning problems that prevent their learning successfully. Many children do not show any signs of sensory dysfunction until they reach elementary school. As infants and toddlers, they play with friends and family and basically live in an environment adjusted to their needs. During these years, children have more freedom to choose activities they can do and enjoy. The activities in which they participate during preschool are not as complex and demanding as those they encounter in grade school.

As children enter elementary school, however, expectations for performance change. Many new demands are placed on their neurological systems. Besides being able to stand in line and sit quietly at a desk, children must write on the proper side of the paper, remember a series of instructions, and learn abstract concepts (such as math story problems). And the push toward stronger requirements for early education these days can create more stress. Some programs have academic standards above the developmental level of average children.

Often, the cause of a child's behavior and learning problems lies with poor functioning of one or more of the sensory systems. As evaluators, teachers, and parents, we tend to look at the symptoms (characteristics) of a child, instead of locating the actual cause. Finding the cause requires determining first which sensory systems are involved and then where a child is developmentally. For example, Larry frequently falls out of his chair. He may not be hyperactive, a simple and popular label these days. Perhaps, observing him more closely, he has a problem controlling his muscles (involving the vestibular and proprioceptive systems).

Amber has trouble catching a ball. School staff members have noted on her physical education records that she is "uncoordinated" and "clumsy." However, she may have a midline, body identification, or muscle-strength problem. Any of these problems suggest or indicate that the cause is in the proprioceptive or the vestibular system. She might also have a visual or auditory problem. Can she see the ball clearly? Can she concentrate on the act of catching with all of the outside noises assaulting her auditory system?

Many times, vague terms are used to describe the behavior of children. Words such as "impulsive," "hyperactive," and "inattentive" are a few examples of vague labels. They focus attention on what the child is *not* doing: she does not sit still, he cannot complete homework, he holds the scissors improperly. If you want to get some clues to what sensory-system obstacles are present, you need to focus on what the child *is* doing. Is there a pattern to his impulsive behaviors? Does the behavior occur at the same time each day? Observe what he chooses to do when he is impulsive. Does he run? Rub his eyes? Talk out loud? (See figure 6.5.)

Figure 6.5 Inattention of a child who sees double.

It is helpful if you can observe what the child does even up to a few hours before the misbehavior or learning difficulties appear. Has the youngster experienced an accumulation of sensory stimuli or increasingly demanding tasks? When Bill hits Susie, for instance, it may have nothing to do with Susie and lots to do with his extreme stress over hearing too much noise on the playground.

When children are overwhelmed by stimuli, they can experience *sensory overload.* Part of sensory integration is the brain's ability to *inhibit* or *ignore* a large amount of the information entering the sensory systems. Some children, however, lack this ability in their neurological systems. A normal amount of stimulus in a classroom or at home can instead be overpowering for them.

When the neurological system cannot process or inhibit all the information entering the sensory systems, it does not organize the information into a useful schema. It is almost as if the brain of a child reaches a high level of stress and triggers a fight-or-flight reaction. The child cannot focus on tasks and wants only to get out of the frustrating situation. He becomes so intent on relieving the stress that he ignores the instructions of parents and teachers, resorts to aggressive behavior, or withdraws from the situation.

Fight-or-flight behavior is often labeled as *attention deficit disorder, hyperactivity,* or *attention deficit hyperactive disorder.* The disorganized

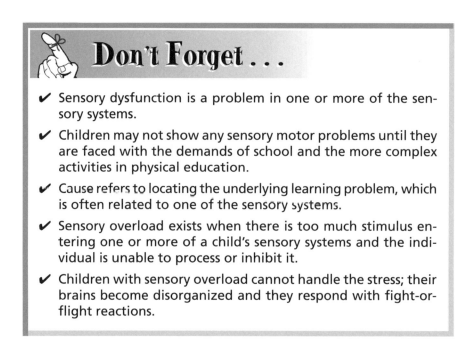

Don't Forget . . .

✔ Sensory dysfunction is a problem in one or more of the sensory systems.

✔ Children may not show any sensory motor problems until they are faced with the demands of school and the more complex activities in physical education.

✔ Cause refers to locating the underlying learning problem, which is often related to one of the sensory systems.

✔ Sensory overload exists when there is too much stimulus entering one or more of a child's sensory systems and the individual is unable to process or inhibit it.

✔ Children with sensory overload cannot handle the stress; their brains become disorganized and they respond with fight-or-flight reactions.

brain causes a child with sensory dysfunction to choose inappropriate responses to situations, such as hitting people nearby, tearing up papers, breaking pencils, running around the classroom, rubbing his eyes, or even hitting his head on the desk.

Hypersensitivity to Stimuli

Hypersensitivity is a condition which causes a child to overreact to a normal amount of sensory stimulation. For example, a child who has a hypersensitive auditory system will immediately have a negative response to a normal level of noise. This could occur in the classroom, dining room, hallway, or playground. A gymnasium or shopping mall, where the acoustics leave much to be desired, are particularly unsettling for these children.

Sometimes hypersensitivity can be cumulative, that is, it builds up over a period of time. Initially, a child may seem to adjust to a normal amount of sensory input, but as the day goes on, hypersensitivity accumulates. Finally, the child can no longer process or inhibit any additional stimuli and becomes distressed.

Simon, who is hypersensitive to tactile stimulation, offers a good example of these cumulative sensory effects. He usually wears loose-fitting cotton clothing, but one day he wore stiff blue jeans to school. At the beginning of the day, he was able to handle the tactile stimulation. However, the stiffness of the jeans eventually caused an overload of tactile information to his neurological system. By the end of the school day, the teacher said that he appeared to be highly distractible and that he refused to participate in class activities.

Fernando, who has trouble with the visual system, may be able to read during the first few minutes of the reading period. As his visual system becomes stressed through overload, however, he loses his focus and starts rubbing his eyes. He goes on to look out the window, bother the students next to him, or throw his book (figure 6.6).

Fernando and Simon are not consciously choosing to misbehave; they are experiencing automatic neurological responses to the situation. Since they have no control over their actions, attempts to modify their behavior through reasoning or offering rewards would be of little value. Saying to them, "You can pay attention if you try" or "You can hit the ball if only you would concentrate on watching it," or "You have to finish copying the words before you go out for recess" may only compound the unfortunate situation.

Hyposensitivity to Stimuli

Hyposensitivity, or an underreaction to sensory stimuli, occurs when the child's nervous system does not process—or incorrectly processes—

Figure 6.6 Progression of stress behavior.

the sensory information. The underlying reason for the hyposensitivity might be that the nervous system does not (a) receive the stimulus through the sensory organs, (b) process the sensations along the neurological pathway, (c) associate the sensation with past memories (integration), or (d) send the appropriate information to the muscles and joints. In other words, the reason might lie anywhere in the process.

Some children who are hyposensitive appear to be unaware of the surrounding environment. For example, Isabella looks at and appears to see a step in her path—but trips over it anyway. Why? Not because she lacks visual acuity, but because her visual input does not get integrated with her muscles and joints to allow her to alter the size of her stride and avoid the step. Cleatus, who is hyposensitive to tactile information, never notices when he bumps into classmates, which adversely affects his ability to interact socially with his classmates. Why? It isn't that Cleatus does not care that he touched his classmate; rather it's because he is not aware that he touched anyone. His classmates do not understand the situation, and avoid this clumsy kid who keeps running into them!

Don't Forget . . .

✔ Hypersensitivity is a condition which causes the nervous system to have little tolerance for a particular type of stimulus (such as visual, auditory, or tactile).

✔ Hyposensitivity is a condition causing the nervous system to underreact to a stimulus.

chapter 7
The Vestibular System

The vestibular system is the sensory system considered to have the most important influence on the other sensory systems and on the ability to function in everyday life. It is the unifying system in our brain that modifies and coordinates information received from the visual, proprioceptive, auditory, and tactile systems. The vestibular system functions like a traffic cop, telling each sensation where and when it should go or stop.

Without an individual's being conscious of it, the vestibular system informs his nervous system where it is in relationship to the pull of gravity so that the person can maintain equilibrium. In combination with the proprioceptive and visual systems, it helps him know when he is upright, upside down, or lying down. He knows if he is moving or still, speeding up or slowing down, through messages received from the vestibular system. Controlled movements—whether rolling over, crawling, sitting still, standing, moving through space, or performing sport skills—all rely on information received from the vestibular system.

To help the reader understand the vestibular system within the space constraints of this chapter, we have placed the material in five sections. First comes a basic overview of the organs in the ear that serve as the vestibular receptors and the way in which they are stimulated. Next is a discussion of the vestibular system and motor development. The following three sections include a few tests to evaluate the vestibular system, an overview of some vestibular problems, and activities you can use to help children who have vestibular problems.

VESTIBULAR SYSTEM RECEPTORS

The ear contains three parts: the external, internal, and middle ears. The external and middle ears are involved only with hearing and will be discussed in chapter 11. The inner ear is concerned with both hearing (auditory system) and equilibrium (vestibular system). Located within the inner ear are the receptors (sense organs) for the vestibular system: the semicircular canals and the vestibule.

Semicircular Canals

Each ear contains three semicircular canals that are filled with fluid and rest at right angles to each other (see figure 7.1). The canals are shaped like tunnels, with one end of each canal opening into the *utricle* and the other end opening into an enlarged area called the *ampulla*. At the connection between the ampulla and the semicircular canals is a gelatin-like mass that contains *hair cells*. These hair cells are the actual receptors. When the fluid in the semicircular canals moves, the hair cells are stimulated.

Rotation of the head causes the fluid in the semicircular canals to move, which stimulates the semicircular canals. Rotation can occur as spinning, circular, or turning types of movement of the head. The greatest amount of stimulation occurs when the movement is started or stopped or when there is a change in the speed of the head as it is turning.

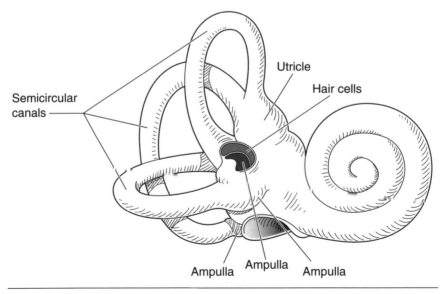

Figure 7.1 Semicircular canals.

Postrotational stimulation of the semicircular canals occurs when the rotation stops. This sensation is the cause of nystagmus, vertigo, and falling. These are the responses of the vestibular system that are the most obvious to a child whose head has been rotated during activities such as a series of forward rolls, logrolls, turning in dancing moves, or spinning around in a chair.

Nystagmus is easy to observe in a child with normal vestibular awareness who holds her head upright and spins in a circle. When she stops, her eyes will usually move rapidly back and forth (see figure 7.2). However, if she spins with her head on one shoulder or the other, nystagmus will be up and down. Her eyes will move in a diagonal fashion if she is rotated with her head only partway toward her shoulder.

Vertigo also occurs during repeated rotations of the head, and it is the spinning sensation that causes dizziness or a nauseous feeling. Children

Figure 7.2 Three types of nystagmus.

experiencing vertigo often feel as if they are going to throw up. *Falling* occurs because the spinning has thrown off a child's ability to use her eyes (visual system) and body parts (proprioceptive system) to sense where she is. If she wants to move forward, her body and eyes tell her she is moving to the right, and she corrects for it. However, since she was not moving to the right but was moving forward, the corrections cause her to go off to the left (figure 7.3). You can observe this by asking a child to stand and turn rapidly in a circle 10 times. Or you can ask two students to hold one another's hands and rapidly turn around in a circle. Then ask them to stop and walk toward you. They will not be able to walk straight and will probably show signs of nystagmus in their eyes.

Vestibule

The inner ear (figure 7.4) has an enlarged area that is shaped like a chamber and is known as the vestibule; it contains the utricle and saccule. The utricle and saccule are often called *sacs* since they resemble two little bags or balloons. One end of the utricle is connected to the semicircular canals, and the other end leads to the saccule. The remaining end of the

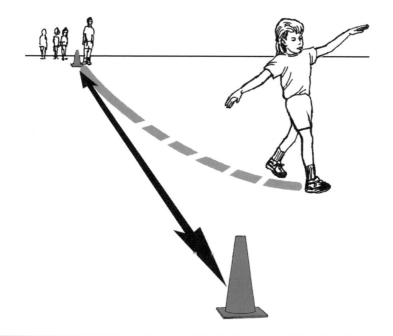

Figure 7.3 Falling after spinning.

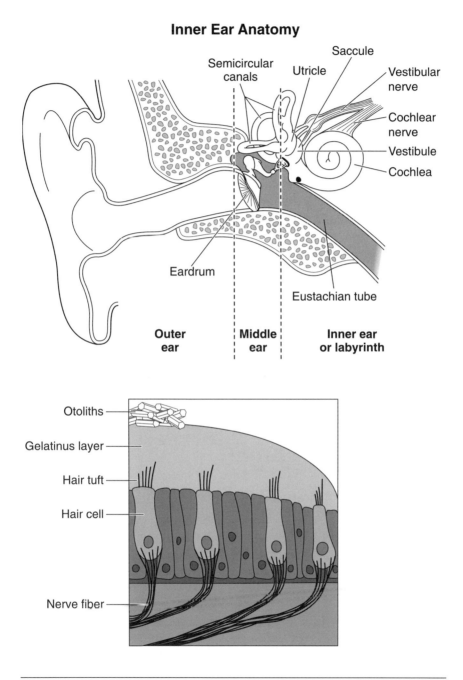

Figure 7.4 Receptors of the vestibule (utricle and saccule).

saccule is connected to the *cochlea*. Both the utricle and saccule have a group of hair cells that lie in gelatinous masses. On top of each gelatinous mass rest particles of calcium carbonate called *otoliths (statoconia).*

As your child moves his head, gravity pulls on the statoconia and gelatinous mass and stimulates the utricle and saccule. Stimulation occurs in two ways: either when the child's head is tilted or when the head is moved in a straight line. When a child's head is tilted, gravity acts on the vestibule and tells him the position of his head. This means that each movement of his head from any static (nonmoving) position or any change in the speed of the head tilt will stimulate his vestibule. Again, the greatest stimulation occurs at the beginning and the end of his tilting movement. In between, there is a constant speed and therefore little stimulation.

Straight-line movements that stimulate the vestibule can be in horizontal, vertical, or diagonal directions. These stimulations include acceleration (starting) and deceleration (stopping) of linear movements, as well as any change in speed that an individual encounters in going up and down (for example, in elevators), walking, running, or riding in cars, trains, and planes. The most stimulation occurs when a person starts the movement and when he or she suddenly stops. In between starting and stopping, there is little stimulation. For this reason some sports, such as soccer or basketball, create an abundance of vestibular stimulation because they require continual changes in positions, starting, and stopping.

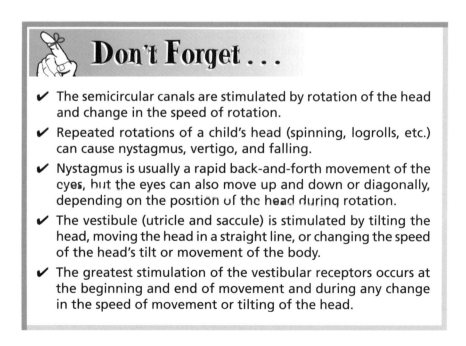

Don't Forget . . .

✔ The semicircular canals are stimulated by rotation of the head and change in the speed of rotation.

✔ Repeated rotations of a child's head (spinning, logrolls, etc.) can cause nystagmus, vertigo, and falling.

✔ Nystagmus is usually a rapid back-and-forth movement of the eyes, but the eyes can also move up and down or diagonally, depending on the position of the head during rotation.

✔ The vestibule (utricle and saccule) is stimulated by tilting the head, moving the head in a straight line, or changing the speed of the head's tilt or movement of the body.

✔ The greatest stimulation of the vestibular receptors occurs at the beginning and end of movement and during any change in the speed of movement or tilting of the head.

THE VESTIBULAR SYSTEM AND MOTOR DEVELOPMENT

The semicircular canals, utricle, and saccule are often referred to as the *balance sense organs*. Overall, their purpose or action is to communicate a sense of where the body is in space and to maintain the posture and equilibrium (balance) that is necessary for the individual to be able to perform motor acts. To do this, the vestibular receptors—along with the eyes, muscles, and joints—constantly monitor movement. The vestibular receptors let the person (child) know whether he is maintaining balance against the pull of gravity, moving fast or slow, or whether he or the room is moving. Through the vestibular receptors, the child knows, for instance, whether his head is rotating or his body is bending or remaining static in an upright position. You can find a summary of the actions of the vestibular system in table 7.1.

Table 7.1
Overview of Sensory Systems

Receptors	Action
Semicircular canals	Organize information for the tactile, proprioceptive, auditory, and visual systems.
	Monitor rotation of the head.
	Respond to the pull of gravity in both stationary and moving positions.
	Help control posture and balance in all positions.
	Inform you when you or the room is moving.
	Stabilize skeletal muscles.
	Influence muscle tone and eye-hand coordination.
	Tell you where you are in space: right-side up, upside down, sideways.
	Have an arousal (excitatory) effect during and after activities that cause the head to turn rapidly.
	Control eye movements and ability to focus.
	Stabilize neck muscles, which helps ability to focus.
Utricle/saccule	Monitors head's tilt in relation to gravity.
	Responds to linear acceleration and deceleration in horizontal, vertical, and diagonal directions.
	Monitors position of head in relation to the body: above, under, to the side.
	Has calming (inhibitory) effect on child.

Muscle Tone

The vestibular system has a strong influence on the muscles that control posture. This includes muscle tone and the strength needed to sit in a chair, hold the neck steady for academics, or compete in sport or recreational activities. We often take postural muscle control for granted, but a child must indeed have the automatic control of his or her skeletal muscles in order to sit or stand still. The youngster must be able to stabilize the body to move an arm, hand, leg, or foot independently during fine and gross motor activities.

Tonic Muscle Control

Tonic *(static)* muscle control is established when children can contract a muscle or a group of muscles and hold them in that position for several seconds. Control of their skeletal muscles and static muscle control are essential for them to be able to maintain a variety of positions in the classroom and in physical education.

You can check for tonic muscle control by asking a child to lie on her back, keep her legs straight, lift them about 20 to 30 degrees off the ground, and hold the position for 10 seconds (figure 7.5). A six-year-old child with a vestibular system that is functioning normally can do this. On the other hand, a child who lacks tonic muscle control because the vestibular system is not functioning properly cannot do this.

Tonic muscle control has a strong influence on cocontraction. *Cocontraction* occurs when all of the muscles surrounding a joint are in a state of tonic contraction; they are contracting together statically. Simple activities (for instance, standing still) require the muscles surrounding the hips, knees, ankles, and feet to be in a state of cocontraction.

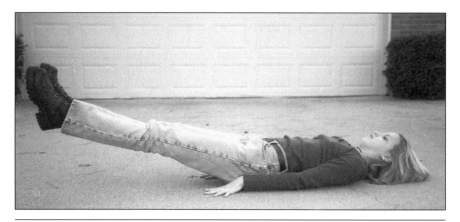

Figure 7.5 Tonic muscle control.

If you observe the students whose vestibular systems are not functioning normally, you notice that their feet and other parts of their bodies are constantly moving. They lack the cocontraction of the muscle groups necessary to sit or stand still. It is impossible for them to be still! They are moving first one foot and then the other, falling forward, backward, and sideways, with the arms going every which way. These children may also seem to tire quickly and need to sit down or rest their heads on their desks.

Reflex Response

In some actions, such as turning rapidly, children receive a forceful stimulation that causes the postural muscles to have an automatic *reflex response* against the pull of gravity. This response is so strong that they cannot stop it voluntarily. The reflex response can occur when a child lying prone on a scooter board, for example, rides down a ramp. At the end of the ramp, the vestibular stimulation will cause his legs, arms, and head to automatically lift up like an airplane. His body parts are automatically lifting up against the downward pull of gravity. This is similar to a child going down a playground slide.

You might notice a similar sensation if you accelerate a car driving down a hill and suddenly hit a place in the road that levels out. You would feel your head and shoulders respond upward against the pull of gravity, and this would tend to pull the rest of your body into an attention position. Roller coaster rides can be dramatic examples of the reflex response. As the cars accelerate down one of the hills, the stimulation causes an automatic response in the participants against the downward pull of gravity.

Arousal

The vestibular system has yet another important feature, its influence on the prearousal part of the brain. In a child you see the effect of this part of the brain because it's what controls alertness and the ability to focus. Depending on the type of vestibular stimulation, the influence can wake up (arouse) or calm a child's nervous system. Vigorous movements, such as spinning or jumping, excite the youngster's brain and enable her to focus.

You may notice that when children are struggling to stay awake, they tend to stay active by running around. Or you may have experienced the necessity to shake your head in order to stay awake while you're driving. These vigorous movements stimulate the vestibular system, which activates the arousal part of the brain and wakes it up.

Some children have not only an inner drive to arouse their system but the awareness that it benefits them. When Henri was a boy, his mother could not understand why he was constantly moving his head up and down while he was studying. His movements were so vigorous that his shoulders and upper body also moved. She said, "How can you study like that?" He replied that "It is the only way I *can* study."

Inhibitory Response

Slow vestibular activities, and particularly movements in a straight line, have a calming effect on the nervous system of children. Activities such as swinging or rocking are calming. Some children may seem sleepy when they come back into the classroom from the playground. This might be a result of fresh air or it might also be caused by their earlier slow swinging. We all know that slow rocking will work wonders in helping a young child or a baby get to sleep.

Many children and adults are almost tranquilized by the motion of their body moving in a straight line. Haven't you heard of your students getting drowsy or falling asleep in the school bus or in their parent's car on the way to or from school? The slow motion of a car, train, bus, or airplane moving in a straight line seems to have a magic effect on most fussy children.

Ocular Muscle Control

The vestibular system plays a key role in controlling eye movements and fixation of the eyes. Each eye is controlled by six pairs of muscles that receive stimulation from the vestibular system. Just as the vestibular system affects tonic muscle control in the skeletal muscles, it also acts to control the eye muscles. It provides tonic muscle control to keep the neck muscles steady and the eyes focused on the original target.

Movement of the head will always cause some corresponding movement or readjustment of the eyes. You can observe how the vestibular system influences the eyes in the "doll's eye maneuver." When children turn their heads 60 degrees to the left, their eyes will try to remain focused on an object in front of them. When their head is quickly rotated 60 degrees first to the right and then to the left, their eyes will be 90 degrees out of synchronization with their head (figure 7.6). Ask your children to try these movements and observe the action of their eyes.

During academic tasks, such as reading or writing, the vestibular system helps students keep their eyes focused on the teacher or on assigned schoolwork. Injury to or dysfunction of one of the semicir-

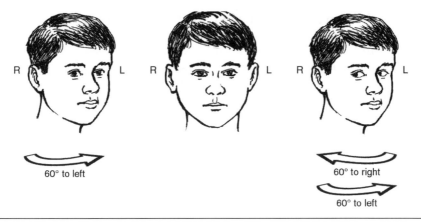

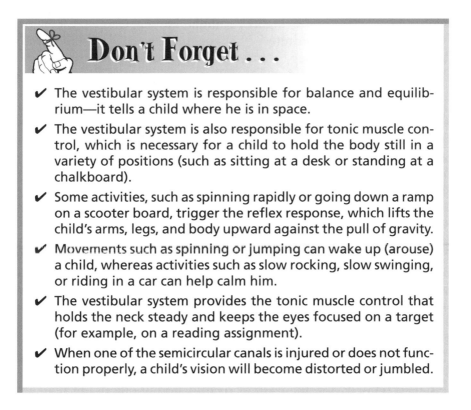

Figure 7.6 Doll's eye maneuver.

cular canals causes a child's vision to become distorted or jumbled when he moves his head. Then he has trouble focusing on his tasks, not because he does not want to concentrate on them but because *neurologically he cannot.*

Don't Forget . . .

✔ The vestibular system is responsible for balance and equilibrium—it tells a child where he is in space.

✔ The vestibular system is also responsible for tonic muscle control, which is necessary for a child to hold the body still in a variety of positions (such as sitting at a desk or standing at a chalkboard).

✔ Some activities, such as spinning rapidly or going down a ramp on a scooter board, trigger the reflex response, which lifts the child's arms, legs, and body upward against the pull of gravity.

✔ Movements such as spinning or jumping can wake up (arouse) a child, whereas activities such as slow rocking, slow swinging, or riding in a car can help calm him.

✔ The vestibular system provides the tonic muscle control that holds the neck steady and keeps the eyes focused on a target (for example, on a reading assignment).

✔ When one of the semicircular canals is injured or does not function properly, a child's vision will become distorted or jumbled.

EVALUATING VESTIBULAR FUNCTION

The vestibular system can be evaluated through several fairly simple tests: The Manns test, the one-leg test, postrotary-nystagmus, and the visual-stimulation test. The *Manns* is a heel-to-toe test. It requires a child to stand on a straight line with the heel of one foot against the toe of his other foot and close his eyes (see figure 7.7). A six-year-old child should be able to hold this position for about seven seconds.

You should always use caution when doing vestibular evaluations because children with vestibular problems may fall over while trying to balance or spin. Always be prepared to catch them! Do the Manns test with your child's eyes open first. If he cannot hold his balance with the eyes open, you may not need to have him close his eyes, which would probably cause him to fall over.

The *one-leg test* consists of having the child stand only on his preferred foot, with his opposite leg bent at the knee and his eyes closed. You then have the child repeat the action standing on his nonpreferred leg (see figure 7.8). A six-year-old child should be able to hold the position for 10 seconds. In order to remain still and in an upright position when the eyes are closed, the child is basically forced to rely on the information he receives from his vestibular system.

Table 7.2 shows the results of 45 students who had learning problems in trying the one-leg balance test (Cheatum and Hammond 1992; Hammond 1992). You can see the difference in their vestibular ability during this test. Seventy-five percent of the students could maintain a one-leg standing balance with their eyes open for 10 seconds on their preferred leg. This dropped to 64 percent when these students used the nonpreferred leg. However, with their eyes closed, only 17 percent could maintain balance on the preferred leg—and only 4 percent on the nonpreferred leg. This indicates that many of these children may be experiencing difficulty with their vestibular systems and controlling their bodies in relation to gravity. They will have a reduced ability to sit up in a chair, move about the room, hold the head up, and perform other academic and movement tasks.

The *postrotary-nystagmus* evaluation is a modification of the Ayres Southern California Post Rotary Nystagmus Test (1975), which is a modification of the still earlier Bárány Test (1906). Dr. Bárány, known for his tests to determine vestibular problems and their relationship to equilibrium and muscle control, received a Nobel prize for his work in this area in 1914. The postrotary (or after-rotation) test examines the length of time nystagmus lasts following rotation of a child. The child

Figure 7.7 Manns test.

Figure 7.8 One-leg test.

Table 7.2
Number and Percent of Students Who Maintained Balance
for 10 Seconds

	Preferred leg		Nonpreferred leg	
	Number	Percent	Number	Percent
Eyes open	34	75%	29	64%
Eyes closed	8	17%	2	4%

sits in a chair with her head slightly bent toward her chest and is rotated 10 complete turns in one direction for 20 seconds. Rotation is stopped and the child's eyes are checked for movement. After a rest of one or two minutes, the test is repeated in the opposite direction.

Following rotation, children whose vestibular systems function normally will usually have nystagmus that lasts from 7 to 14 seconds. Anything below 7 is considered *hypovestibular* (below normal), whereas scores above 14 are considered *hypervestibular* (above normal). Children who are hypovestibular often show no nystagmus on rotation to the left or on rotation to the right. This indicates that their vestibular system is not processing the information. As mentioned previously, these are the children who do not get dizzy. On the other hand, hypervestibular children have an excessive amount of nystagmus, and their eye movements might continue as long as 30 seconds.

When you evaluate postrotary nystagmus, be aware of the following issues. Many children have nystagmus for a longer time (more seconds) following the second rotation because the first rotation provided vestibular stimulation (see figure 7.9). An example of this can be seen in the

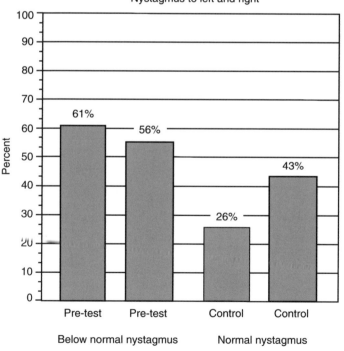

Figure 7.9 Nystagmus to the left and right.

scores of kindergartners to third graders with learning problems who were tested at Spring Valley Elementary School in Parchment, Michigan (Cheatum 1986–1989, 1989). Among these children with learning problems, 61 percent of them had below-normal nystagmus to the left, which was reduced to 56 percent following rotation to the right. Only 26 percent of the students had normal nystagmus after rotation to the left, but this increased to 43 percent following rotation to the right.

Visual-stimulation tests can also arouse the vestibular system and cause nystagmus. In this type of test, the child is in a stationary position, and a series of objects (such as vertical straight lines) move across his visual path to trigger his vestibular system (see figure 7.10). This causes the same effect as rotating him on a chair or scooter board. NASA uses a similar test to examine the ability of prospective astronauts to withstand motion sickness; examiners put them inside a capsule with dots covering the interior walls. The capsule spins around, triggering a visual vestibular stimulation.

As you work with children in the classroom or view your child at home, there are some clues that can help you determine whether a hypovestibular problem exists and whether a child should be further evaluated. These include your noticing a frequent loss of balance, an inability to sit still, low muscle tone, or general clumsiness in the child, as well as his or her seeking spinning activities. To determine the extent of the problem it is always wise not to rely on just one test or evaluation, but to gather information from several evaluations.

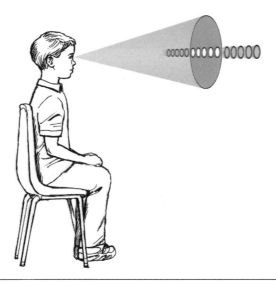

Figure 7.10 Visual stimulation of the vestibular system.

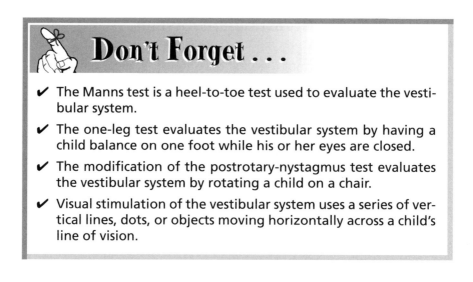

Don't Forget...

✔ The Manns test is a heel-to-toe test used to evaluate the vestibular system.

✔ The one-leg test evaluates the vestibular system by having a child balance on one foot while his or her eyes are closed.

✔ The modification of the postrotary-nystagmus test evaluates the vestibular system by rotating a child on a chair.

✔ Visual stimulation of the vestibular system uses a series of vertical lines, dots, or objects moving horizontally across a child's line of vision.

Physicians who specialize in evaluating vestibular disorders are neuro-otologists and otolaryngologists. In general, they see people who have severe dizziness or balance problems. Examinations usually involve several tests, including testing hearing and monitoring eye movements while the child is in a series of positions, balancing on a platform (posturography), and rotating in a computer-controlled chair ("rotary-chair testing").

VESTIBULAR SYSTEM PROBLEMS

Maria craves vestibular stimulation and disrupts the class when she becomes excessively preoccupied with rocking during story time. Gunther, who has attention problems and cannot sit still, lacks the postural muscle tone to maintain a static body position. Yet Gunther may not even be aware that he is continually bouncing around in his seat. Teachers classify Latissa as a daydreamer. She cannot concentrate on reading, and during recess she is either on the merry-go-round or standing there watching the rotation. These children all test positive for difficulties with the vestibular system.

The two basic types of vestibular problems are hypervestibular (an oversensitivity) and hypovestibular (an undersensitivity). Both conditions usually result in neurological and motor development problems but for different reasons. This is why it may be important to evaluate your child's vestibular system or to recommend evaluation of a child in your classroom.

Hypervestibular Problems

Hypervestibular reactions to vestibular stimulation occur when a child's neurological system cannot regulate the amount of information bombarding the central nervous system. Too much stimulation is reaching his semicircular canals or the utricle and saccule (or all three) and causing *sensory overload*. The child's brain is unable to ignore all the vestibular information entering the system. Children who are hypervestibular may return from the playground or gymnasium complaining of an upset stomach or dizziness after normal physical activity.

Children with normal vestibular function will feel the sensations of motion when a car starts to move. But eventually their systems will not notice or respond to the motion of the car. A child who has a hypervestibular system continues to feel the sensation of even the smallest amount of motion. They do not have the ability to suppress (inhibit) vestibular stimulation, and as a result they end up with motion sickness.

Children who are hypervestibular can even experience vertigo during normal daily activities, such as running, riding down an escalator, or jumping. Watching the trees, telephone poles, buildings, or people passing by their eyes as they ride on a subway, bus, or train can be overstimulating (figure 7.11). Images flashing across their vision, such as those on a movie screen, can also trigger a reaction.

Figure 7.11 Overstimulation of vestibular system by common everyday activity.

Just watching other children spin or play on a merry-go-round sometimes will make children with hypervestibular problems uncomfortable. Forget about taking them to the amusement park to enjoy the rides. Even the thought of riding on a Ferris wheel or doing a somersault in physical education can trigger nausea or cause a stomachache or headache.

Children who are hypervestibular frequently have a problem interacting socially with relatives or friends of the family. They seem to leave the room or run outdoors when Grandpa, Uncle Seto, or Aunt Jane comes over. They do everything they can to avoid the relatives who pick them up, toss them in the air, or swing them around. Some adults seem to have an uncontrollable urge to do these things. Even though the hyperactive child may like the relative, his system cannot handle the stimulation, so he leaves the room.

Interestingly, children who are hypervestibular do not seem to have difficulty with verbal skills or reading. Since they prefer to sit and observe, they spend time reading and talking. These children are very good at describing exactly how to do an activity, but avoid actual participation. Coordination problems arise from a lack of experience in physical activity. Since they avoid movement and may become dizzy, they often have poor balance, hand-eye coordination, and locomotor skills. These can cause future difficulties with weight control and sedentary lifestyles.

Hypovestibular Problems

When a child has a hypovestibular problem, his central nervous system does not receive or correctly process information about movement,

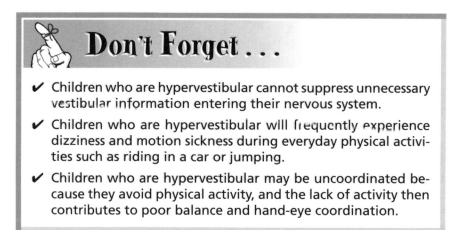

Don't Forget . . .

- ✔ Children who are hypervestibular cannot suppress unnecessary vestibular information entering their nervous system.
- ✔ Children who are hypervestibular will frequently experience dizziness and motion sickness during everyday physical activities such as riding in a car or jumping.
- ✔ Children who are hypervestibular may be uncoordinated because they avoid physical activity, and the lack of activity then contributes to poor balance and hand-eye coordination.

changes of direction, or his relationship to gravity. It receives only a limited amount of vestibular stimulation. This results in the child's diminished ability to react to the pull of gravity, to earth, or to the space around him. Neurologically, his vestibular system has trouble telling him whether he is lying down or standing up.

Most of the children in a classroom subconsciously feel the force or the pull of gravity. This is a constant force. They do not need to look at their bodies. They know where they are and when they are sitting, standing, or lying down. The pull of gravity gives them a reference to the world and space. Children with a hypovestibular problem, particularly those with learning or behavior problems, have a diminished reference source to the world and space.

Since hypovestibular children receive little information about the pull of gravity or whether or not they are moving, they are not aware of falling. They lack the ability to realize that they are in motion or to be able to catch themselves when they start to fall. These are children who might fall out of their seats in your classroom for no apparent reason. They just fall and then wonder how they ended up on the floor. They get very frustrated, naturally, when you ask them what happened—because they really do not know. They may act as if they did it on purpose to be silly or they may accuse another child of pushing them. If you notice a child who cannot seem to sit up straight, who frequently falls out of his seat or who falls a lot in physical education, you should always suspect a hypovestibular condition.

Hypovestibular children crave movements that feed the vestibular system. They are constantly asking you to spin them, to let them stay on the merry-go-round, to pull the wagon faster, to swing them in a circle, or to toss them up in the air. Amazingly, they never get dizzy. Observe these children at home, on the playground, in your classroom, or even walking around town. You may notice them watching objects spin, turning in a circle, or even moving their hands back and forth across their face in order to stimulate the vestibular system through vision (figure 7.12).

Hypovestibular problems are common among children with learning and behavior problems. In the classroom, you may find in some children that a lack of internal reference to gravity and space causes them to be unaware of the difference between up and down, top and bottom, or left and right. The consequence is their confusion with laterality, directionality, and directional discrimination. They will have trouble knowing which part of the paper to use for their assignment or remembering to read and write from the left side of the page to the right. In playing a sport, they puzzle over which hand to use to catch, throw, or hit a ball.

Figure 7.12 Child gaining vestibular stimulation by watching spinning activities.

Dr. Julio B. de Quiros (1976), an early pioneer in the field of learning disabilities, believed that vestibular disorders are the cause of learning disabilities. He further recognized that children with these problems are not identified until they enter school. As a physician, he was able to evaluate newborn infants as early as an hour and a half after birth. Dr. de Quiros examined more than two thousand children during the 1950s and 1960s and tracked a group of normal and vestibular-disabled infants for three years. He found that children with vestibular problems had delays in motor development, balance, acquisition of language, reading, and writing. Auxter, Pyfer, and Huettig (1996) emphasize that children who lack normal vestibular function have difficulty with balance, with gross motor activities that demand the use of both sides of the body, and with movements that require the coordination of the hands and eyes.

Astronauts are also subject to the lack of vestibular information reaching their nervous systems. Medical studies of the effect of weightlessness on astronauts have focused on the function of the vestibular system in space. In outer space, astronauts experience symptoms of poor body awareness similar to those of youngsters with vestibular problems. Since there is no gravity to stimulate the vestibular system, astronauts have no awareness of motion, where they are in space, or whether the body is upright or upside down. If the astronauts close their eyes for a time, when they open them, they may be in another part of the spaceship and in a different position! They will have no idea how their bodies got there.

People of all ages are subject to vestibular disorders and dysfunctions. Fortunately, these problems respond to vestibular therapy. For example, in past decades numerous hospitals have routinely rotated premature babies two or three times a day. These babies ate better, slept better, and showed better development than babies who were not rotated.

In recent years, a few geriatric institutions have used vestibular stimulation. Senior citizens sit in a motorized rocker for a selected amount of time. After experiencing the vestibular stimulation of the rocker, the residents have been less distressed and more alert, manageable, happy, and responsive to people around them.

Low Muscle Tone

The lack of muscle tone that accompanies a hypovestibular condition can create academic and social problems for children. These problems concern their parents as well as their classroom teachers. The problems can damage the children's self-esteem or body image. In addition to having other children tease or ignore them, the youngsters with hypovestibular conditions end up disliking themselves. Since they do not know where they are in relationship to space and other people, they often stand too close to other students or run into them (figure 7.13). These children are clumsy and seldom successful in sport activities. As a result, they avoid sports and resort to playing with children who are younger than they are. Numerous books have been written on

Figure 7.13   Child unaware of space standing too close to others.

the symptoms and problems of clumsy children. Most of the time, their problems revolve around the vestibular system.

Low muscle tone can cause a child to be unable to control himself against the downward pull of gravity. When you try to lift him, he is not able to help you. Therefore, he feels much heavier than his actual weight. As you lift him, it feels as if you are picking up a sack of flour or a very young baby. The parts of his body that you are not supporting will just flop toward the ground.

Poor Phasic Muscle Control

Some children do not have enough tonic muscle control or strength to hold a body part steady. When this happens, they rely on *phasic muscle control*. This means that they have to repeatedly contract and relax a group of muscles (that is, in phases). It is hard for them to maintain a steady contraction or cocontraction to stabilize the body or a part of the body. If you ask a child with phasic muscle tone to lie down on her back and lift her legs for 10 seconds, her legs will bob up and down (figure 7.14).

However, a child with phasic muscle control is unable to sit still in his seat in school or at home. He cannot stand at the chalkboard or stand still long enough to catch a fly ball. His feet and other parts of his body are constantly moving. It is physiologically impossible for them to be still! He moves first one foot and then the other, falling forward, backward, and sideways with his arms going every which way.

Many activities in classrooms and in physical education classes require children to hold one part of the body steady while using other parts. When a child sits at his desk, for instance, and reaches his hand forward to write, his trunk and shoulder girdle must remain steady. If the whole body follows the arm, the child may fall forward on the desk or the excess motion may interfere with smooth control of his pencil. In physical education, kicking requires a child to stabilize his upper body and opposite leg so

Figure 7.14 Phasic muscle tone.

that his kicking leg can swing freely. If he cannot do this, his whole body will follow through—and he may end up sitting on the ground.

If children with vestibular problems concentrate on sitting still, they can consciously contract their muscles and hold still. However, the minute you ask them to do any other task, such as reading or writing, their concentration shifts to the new task. The symptoms of hyperactivity (such as wiggling, rocking, or shifting in their seats) will reappear. Thus, their hyperactive behaviors stem from a problem with tonic muscle control caused by poor vestibular function.

Poor Equilibrium

Any type of movement, as well as sitting still, always involves maintaining equilibrium (balance) in relation to gravity. Hypovestibular children, who do not subconsciously feel the pull of gravity, will have trouble with equilibrium and overall body control. When their equilibrium is disturbed, they will not have enough postural muscle control to maintain their balance while sitting, standing, or moving. Unlike children who are not hypovestibular, they cannot rely on the subconscious functioning of the vestibular system to sit still. They must mentally concentrate and focus all their efforts and attention on sitting still. This prevents them from being able to take in any new information that the teacher may be presenting. If they shift their concentration to what the teacher is saying, they immediately lose their balance and start moving around in their seat, appearing hyperactive.

When walking, a child's body continually goes forward out of balance, and he must automatically move the next foot forward in order to break the fall. Running relies even more on information received from the vestibular system. Consider the fact that the neurological system must have accurate information about the position of the body in relationship to gravity during the airborne phase of a running stride in order for an individual to automatically respond with just how, where, and when to put the foot down.

Without adequate vestibular function, a child may lack the automatic reactions needed to contract or relax muscles in order to maintain a body position or prevent falling. Thus, if a child starts to fall sideways, his neurological system does not know which body parts need to move to prevent the fall and return his body to an upright position.

The lists in the following box summarize common symptoms you can observe in children who have hypervestibular or hypovestibular problems.

Symptoms of Vestibular Problems

Hypervestibular	Hypovestibular
Cannot inhibit vestibular information entering the system.	Low muscle tone causes poor body awareness.
Dislikes seeing or doing spinning activities.	Poor balance and frequent falls.
Experiences dizziness going down slides, riding in a car, or jumping.	Has clumsy and uncoordinated movement patterns; usually not successful in sports.
Avoids the playground and sports (such as gymnastics) that provide too much stimulation.	Poor static muscle control; unable to sit or stand still for academics or activities.
May feel that he is constantly in motion and losing balance.	Has trouble knowing his position in space (standing, sitting, falling, etc.).
May get dizzy or nauseous when riding on buses, trains, or subways.	Craves doing or watching spinning activities.
	Never gets dizzy.
Prefers to ride in front seat of cars.	Has laterality problems—knowing and using body parts in a coordinated way.
Feels dizzy on escalators, elevators, and entrances to and from escalators.	Often has delay in language, reading, and writing.
Avoids relatives and adults who toss him in the air.	Trouble moving arms and legs against an unstable trunk (the whole body moves).
Usually uncoordinated since he avoids sports and activities.	Lacks ability to control eye muscles, which interferes with academics and movement.
Retreats to books and usually does OK in academics.	Usually not successful in sports.

The vestibular system's influence on equilibrium is not restricted to children. More than five million people visit a physician each year complaining of dizziness. By the time most people are 70 years old, balance disorders are a common reason for their seeking medical assistance. And although a vestibular virus can result in nystagmus and balance problems, some other common causes include whiplash, a trauma to the head, an infection of the inner ear, the long-term use of antibiotics, caffeine, alcohol, and nicotine. The Vestibular Disorders Association (VEDA) has an online home site (http://www.vestibular.org) that provides information about balance and hearing, and some of it may be helpful to you.

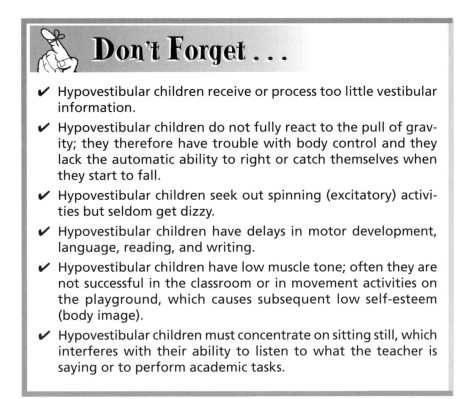

Don't Forget . . .

✔ Hypovestibular children receive or process too little vestibular information.

✔ Hypovestibular children do not fully react to the pull of gravity; they therefore have trouble with body control and they lack the automatic ability to right or catch themselves when they start to fall.

✔ Hypovestibular children seek out spinning (excitatory) activities but seldom get dizzy.

✔ Hypovestibular children have delays in motor development, language, reading, and writing.

✔ Hypovestibular children have low muscle tone; often they are not successful in the classroom or in movement activities on the playground, which causes subsequent low self-esteem (body image).

✔ Hypovestibular children must concentrate on sitting still, which interferes with their ability to listen to what the teacher is saying or to perform academic tasks.

CORRECTING VESTIBULAR PROBLEMS

The first step in developing a program to correct vestibular problems is to determine whether the child is hypervestibular or hypovestibular. Remember that children with vestibular problems are either receiving or processing too little *or* too much vestibular stimulation. A child's inability to receive the necessary amount of vestibular stimulation may be caused by the semicircular canals, utricle, saccule, or some combination of these. For this reason, it is usually impossible to tell exactly which part of a vestibular system is causing the underlying problem. Table 7.3 lists vestibular-stimulating activities.

Table 7.3
Movements That Stimulate the Vestibular System

Movement	Example of activity or sport
Hypovestibular	
Spinning	Merry-go-round, diving, gymnastics
Swinging	Swing set
Jumping	Minitrampoline, basketball, gymnastics
Accelerating/decelerating	Shuttle run, soccer, basketball, hockey
Changing directions quickly	Running zigzag through cones; soccer, hockey, tennis
Rocking	Fast rocking in chair or on rocking horse
Tumbling	Somersaults, cartwheels
Rolling	Leg-roll relay race
Hypervestibular	
Slow swinging	Swing set
Rocking	Slow rocking in chair
Slow linear movements	Riding on sled that is being pulled
Jumping	Minitrampoline
Directional change	Dancing
Linear walking	Golf
Linear movement	Swimming, baseball

Often, children with vestibular problems engage in exactly the kind of vestibular stimulation they need. Peter, for example, needed to run in circles around his room every night in order to relax and fall asleep. Initially, his parents thought this was unusual behavior and attempted to discourage this nighttime ritual. After several nights of Peter's getting out of bed and waking family members, his parents relented. The first night he was allowed to run laps around his room, he fell right to sleep—and the whole family was more rested the next day.

Sometimes parents come up with unique solutions to homework problems. Matthew was having trouble with math. He did not understand the concepts. His mother noticed the way he needed to move in order to study, and she set up a study area in the basement. She bought a minitrampoline and then taped math symbols and problems on all the walls of the basement. As Matt bounced on the minitramp, he was able to complete his math assignments!

Many parents ask, "How long does it take to make a change in my child?" This depends on how low the nystagmus scores are and the design or intensity of the sensory motor program that is set up to help. Sometimes, a slight change occurs after administration of the tests used to evaluate the vestibular system. Many parents and teachers have noticed changes in a child after a few weeks. However, progress depends on the number of times a week the youngster receives specially designed sensory motor training and the sport or recreational activities that complement the vestibular program.

Correcting Hypovestibular Problems

Vestibular problems have been found to decrease when children participate in a systematic program of sensory motor activities. Activities that stimulate the vestibular system are easily administered to a child by a classroom or physical education teacher, parent, physical therapist, or occupational therapist. The most beneficial of these activities keep the child's body and head in constant motion or alternate between acceleration and deceleration. Swinging, spinning, jumping, running, stopping, and starting stimulate the system. Whatever activity you choose, the child should frequently change direction in moving or turning. Alternating between these movements allows him to experience a wide variety of vestibular stimulation.

Changing the position of the head stimulates the vestibular system. The best way to determine the motions that will help a child is to watch the youngster. A child knows when a particular rotation or linear movement feels good or makes him or her feel ill. You may see the youngster get in a swing and rotate herself around for some time, stop that action, put her head in another position, and continue turning around. Even a few minutes of such stimulation will often have a dramatic effect. Following stimulation, the child has more static muscle control, and teachers frequently report that a child also seems to be able to concentrate for a longer period of time.

Here's an example of how strong the effects of vestibular stimulation can be on hyperactivity of children with learning problems. A study involved 45 kindergarten to third-grade students in a small urban town in Michigan (Cheatum 1986–1989, 1989). Researchers administered the postrotary-nystagmus evaluation on these children who had learning problems. They were also grouped by their teachers based on whether they (a) were usually or always hyperactive, (b) had increased hyperactivity with stress, or (c) were seldom or never hyperactive. On the pretest, 61 percent of the students had below-normal nystagmus to the left and 56 percent had below-normal nystagmus to the right (see figure 7.15). Among the children, 33 percent were (a) usually or always hyperactive, 36 percent (b) increased their hyperactivity under stress,

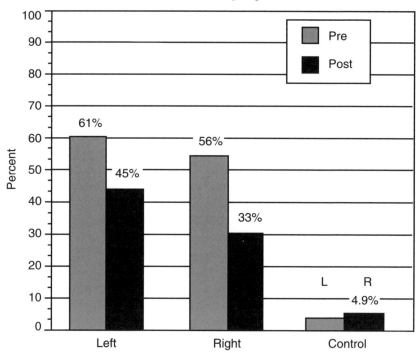

Below normal nystagmus

Figure 7.15 Nystagmus scores before and after a 10-week sensory motor program.

and 29 percent were (c) seldom or never hyperactive. After this evaluation the students participated in a 30-minute sensory motor program for 10 weeks, with the first 15 minutes of the program devoted to vestibular activities (figure 7.16).

At the end of the sensory motor program, 16 percent fewer students had below-normal nystagmus to the left and 23 percent to the right. In addition, 11 percent fewer of the students fell in the groups of "usually or always hyperactive" or having increased hyperactivity with stress. There was also a 16 percent increase in the number of students who were seldom or never hyperactive. These numbers may not seem impressive. However, if you are a teacher or parent who has experienced hyperactive children in groups, you can appreciate the enormous amount of time, energy, and stress you spend trying to get even one child to concentrate and produce work up to his potential. Remember the story in *Chicken Soup for the Soul* of the native throwing back the starfish one by one?

A sensory motor program can have dramatic effects on children's academic ability in even a short time. The teachers of the 45 students in the study in Michigan recorded the reading, math, and spelling scores of their

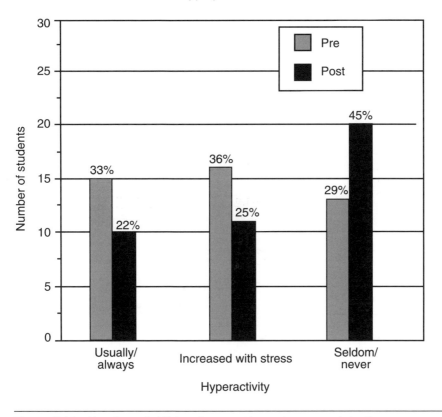

Figure 7.16 Number of children hyperactive at inappropriate times.

students before, during, and after the 10-week sensory motor program. The program not only used activities that addressed specific problems of each child, but it also emphasized 15 minutes of vestibular activities each day. At the end of the program, 11 percent of the students had raised their reading and math scores above 70 percent (see figure 7.17).

Often, however, the signs that a sensory motor program may be working are more subtle. A child may be sleeping better and eating better. He may be having fewer tantrums, experiencing less hyperactivity, getting along better with peers, and feeling better about himself. One indication that a program is beginning to work is when a child starts to get dizzy! Remember that these are the children who had no or little nystagmus and previously showed no reaction to spinning. Therefore, any sign of dizziness suggests that the vestibular system is beginning to process the information.

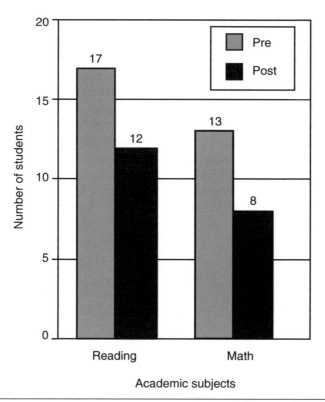

Number of students scoring below
70% in academics

Figure 7.17 Percentage of students scoring below 70 percent in academics.

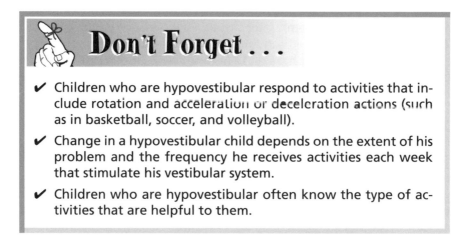

Don't Forget . . .

✔ Children who are hypovestibular respond to activities that include rotation and acceleration or deceleration actions (such as in basketball, soccer, and volleyball).

✔ Change in a hypovestibular child depends on the extent of his problem and the frequency he receives activities each week that stimulate his vestibular system.

✔ Children who are hypovestibular often know the type of activities that are helpful to them.

Hypovestibular Activities

If a child has a hypovestibular problem, it is important that an activity session *start with vestibular activities*. The following activities involve spinning, swinging, jumping, or stopping and starting to "wake up" the vestibular system. Through these movements children begin to sense direction, speed of motion, and the relationship of their bodies to gravity. These activities also promote the development of muscle control. Although most involve vigorous movements, a couple of balance activities are also included, which give children a short break from high-energy exercises as well as a chance to practice adjusting muscle tone and body position to maintain balance. Observe the children carefully during spinning activities. If they receive too much stimulation, they may become flushed, pale, dizzy, or hot with moist skin.

Vestibular Circuit

Circuit activities or a group of activities similar to these benefit youngsters by providing a variety of sensations to the vestibular system. During a *circuit,* children spend one minute at each "station," going three times around the circuit. Or they may spend 30 seconds at each station and go around it four times. For best results, try to set up six stations (see figure 7.18).

Station 1: Hammock Swing

Individual

Appropriate Ages

Infancy and older.

Preparation

Hang a hammock by a heavy-duty rope from the ceiling. The hammock should be 12 to 18 inches off the ground. Place a mattress or mat underneath it. Fold the hammock lengthwise like a taco so that the child rides inside it.

Activity

The child lies with his body through the hammock and swings like Superman or sits inside. Swing and spin the child in a variety of

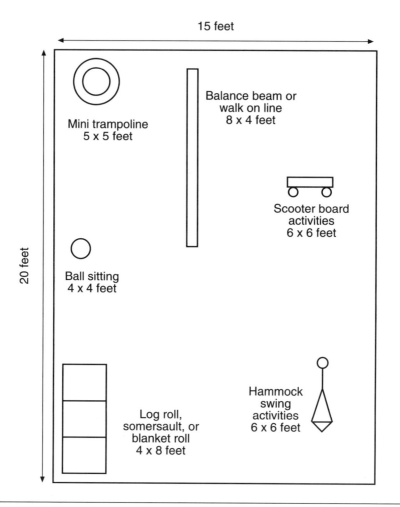

15 feet

20 feet

Mini trampoline
5 x 5 feet

Balance beam or
walk on line
8 x 4 feet

Scooter board
activities
6 x 6 feet

Ball sitting
4 x 4 feet

Log roll,
somersault, or
blanket roll
4 x 8 feet

Hammock
swing
activities
6 x 6 feet

Figure 7.18 Example set-up for vestibular circuit.

directions. Some older children may prefer to use their hands or feet to propel themselves. Do not include the amount of time for the child to get situated in the hammock as part of the activity. At first, a youngster may take the entire 30 to 60 seconds just getting into the hammock!

If you do this activity with an infant, be sure he is lying supported with pillows inside the hammock. Watch all infants or children closely for any sign of stress, which may include frequent yawning, crying, or flushing.

Station 2: Scooter Board

Individual

Appropriate Ages

10 months and older

Preparation

Be sure the area is free of obstacles. Use a snow saucer if you do not have a scooter board or for children younger than two years old.

Activity

The child can sit or lie on the scooter board and use his hands to spin himself, or you can hold his hands or feet and spin him. Be sure to alternate the direction after 5 to 10 spins. After a few times pull the child in a straight line. If you get dizzy, you may need to have other family members take turns spinning the child.

Some children do not have the postural control to stay on the scooter board because they cannot maintain a stable body position. In this case, spin the child slowly and stop when he begins to lose his balance. Adjustable belts can be used to secure the child onto the scooter board.

Station 3: Minitrampoline or Mattress Jumping

Individual

Appropriate Ages

10 months and older.

Preparation

Set up a minitrampoline or mattress in an area free of obstructions. If you use a minitrampoline, place it on a mat.

Activity

Infants who are able should sit in the center of the mattress or minitrampoline. An adult gently bounces them. Children under about three years of age should hold hands with an adult while they jump.

Older children can start by jumping with hands on hips and the feet fairly close together. Gradually work into other movements, such as the legs opening and closing or scissoring. More advanced movements to try are jumping jacks, running in place, or cross-country skiing motions. Whenever the child loses control, have him return to jumping with hands on hips and the feet together.

 Station 4: Rolling

Individual

Appropriate Ages

10 months and older.

Preparation

Place floor mats or a mattress on the floor if it is not covered with carpet. This activity can also be done outside on a grassy area.

Activity

Infants and children who cannot roll themselves can be rolled by an adult. Children who are able to roll do so, moving across the floor with the arms extended straight overhead and the legs held straight. If a child cannot roll in a straight line, put two parallel lines on the floor and have him roll between them. For this particular activity, the purpose is to roll quickly to stimulate the inner ear. Therefore, perfect form is not necessary. You should also encourage forward and backward somersaults if children can do them.

Station 5: Ball Sitting

Individual

Appropriate Ages

10 months and older.

Preparation

Place a large ball (24 to 30 inches in diameter) in an area free of obstacles.

Activity

With infants and children who cannot sit on the ball alone, an adult should hold the child by the torso or hands. A child who can sit on the ball alone should extend his arms out to the side. Increase the challenge of the activity by having him pick up one foot, close his eyes, place his hands on the floor behind the ball, and lift both feet off the ground. He can also lie on his stomach over the ball and balance with only his feet or hands on the floor. Many children begin to create their own new ways to balance on the ball.

Station 6: Balance Walking

Individual

Appropriate Ages

3 years and older.

Preparation

Set up a low balance beam (this works with a piece of wood 4 inches by 4 inches by 8 feet). If the child has trouble with balance, start by marking a line right on the floor. Have some beanbags handy to use with the children who have already had experience with this activity.

Activity

The child walks forward, backward, or sideways on the beam. To add complexity, have the child step over beanbags or pick up beanbags that you have placed along the beam.

An adult might need to hold hands with some children. Have them put their hands on their hips if their upper body is wobbly. For some children, putting the arms out to the side for balance only complicates the movement for them because they have to concentrate on keeping the arms in position rather than on balancing.

Station 7: T-Board Balance

Individual

Appropriate Ages

3 years and older.

Preparation

A T-board is a wooden board about 11 × 14 × 1 to 2 inches with an 11 × 1 × 1-inch piece attached in the center of the board.

Activity

The child tries to stand on the T-board and not allow either side edge of the board to touch the floor. See how many seconds the child can hold this position. For added upper-body control, have the child either hold your hands or put his hands on his hips.

Other Vestibular Activities

These activities can be done alone or as part of the vestibular circuit. Children can also do these activities as movement "snacks" during the day. They can easily be done in the classroom or family room.

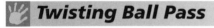 Twisting Ball Pass

Partners

Appropriate Ages

4 and older.

Preparation

Have enough balls for each set of partners to have one between them. The size of the ball depends on the ability of the participants. A larger ball (8 to 10 inches) is easier to handle.

Activity

Partners stand back to back, with one partner holding a ball. The partner with the ball twists to her right as the other partner twists to the left. The ball is passed, and then the partners twist the other way and the ball returns to the first partner. Try to twist and pass the ball as quickly as possible. See how many times the partners can pass the ball in a minute (figure 7.19).

Another way to do the activity is for the first partner to pass the ball to the other *overhead* and then receive the ball back between the legs. Partners will stand up and bend over to pass the ball alternately overhead or between the legs. Stop the game if either partner gets dizzy.

Blanket Roll

Partners

Appropriate Ages

18 months and older.

Preparation

You need a large blanket or sheet. Lay the blanket out flat on the floor in a space at least 6 feet × 6 feet.

Activity

The child lies along one edge of the blanket and grasps the edge. A partner squats down by the opposite edge and grasps it. The child then rolls up in the blanket toward his partner. When the child, rolled in the blanket, reaches his partner, the partner stands up

a

b

c

d

Figure 7.19 Twisting Ball Pass.

and pulls the edge of the blanket (see figure 7.20). The rolled child will quickly unroll from the blanket and return to his starting position. The partners can change places after 5 to 10 rolls. Younger children may need help to roll up into the blanket. An adult who is an "unroller" must be sure not to pull too hard, which could flip the child across the room.

Shuttle Run

Individual or group

Appropriate Ages

4 years and older.

Preparation

Mark start and finish lines on the floor about 10 to 15 feet apart. Place 5 to 10 beanbags on the finish line. The child stands on the starting line.

Activity

On "Go!" the child runs to the finish line and picks up a beanbag. He runs back to the starting line and *places* the beanbag on the line (he does not throw it). Have the child repeat the shuttle run until all of the beanbags are on the starting line. Keep track of how quickly each child completes the shuttle run.

Figure 7.20 Blanket roll activity.

👋 *Partner Spin*

Partners

Appropriate Ages

4 years and older.

Preparation

Pair up the children with partners. The partners face each other.

Activity

Partners cross their right arms over the left and grasp each other's wrists. The partners begin sidestepping quickly in a circle and spinning. On a cue (such as a music change or a whistle), the partners change the direction of their spin. See what happens if one partner rises to his tiptoes and the other bends his knees, and they then alternate. The partners will feel a kind of roller-coaster sensation. Children who get dizzy easily should focus on their partner's forehead. They need to tell each other if they are getting too dizzy. Warn the partners not to let go of each other until they stop.

Correcting Hypervestibular Problems

Children who are hypervestibular should avoid activities that overload their systems. Generally, hypervestibular children benefit most from slow, linear movements such as they might experience riding on a train or in a car. This kind of movement includes slow rocking, horseback riding, and activities that are linear. Some sport activities can be beneficial, such as swimming and some of the specific activities in golf, dance, or track and field events. These activities help participants organize the vestibular system. Introduce these activities slowly and for very short periods of time. If the child becomes pale or flushed or complains of dizziness, discontinue the activity for that session.

If your child or the children in your classroom frequently complain of being dizzy or nauseous, keep track of the activities that happened just before the complaint. Then eliminate or reduce the negative influence. Did the physical education class include a lot of logrolls, somersaults, or zigzag-type relays? Even though a slow car ride can be calming to some youngsters, many of these children get an upset stomach or headache riding in a car.

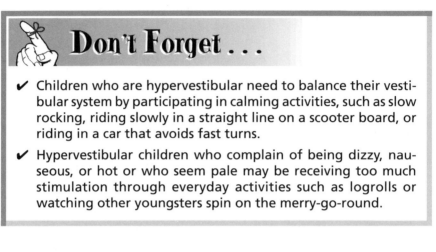

Don't Forget . . .

✔ Children who are hypervestibular need to balance their vestibular system by participating in calming activities, such as slow rocking, riding slowly in a straight line on a scooter board, or riding in a car that avoids fast turns.

✔ Hypervestibular children who complain of being dizzy, nauseous, or hot or who seem pale may be receiving too much stimulation through everyday activities such as logrolls or watching other youngsters spin on the merry-go-round.

Hypervestibular Activities

Children who are hypervestibular are easily overwhelmed by motion and may even experience headaches or nausea. The activities in this section provide vestibular stimulation that begins to help the neurological system inhibit sensations of motion that cause the hypervestibular children dizziness or increase falling.

Blanket Slide

Individual or group

Appropriate Ages

10 months and older.

Preparation

Find a large space at least 15 × 15 feet that is clear of obstacles. Lay a blanket out on the floor and have one person sit or lie in the center of it. Have two people grab the corners of the blanket.

Activity

The blanket holders run across the room dragging the blanket. For variety, on a signal the blanket holders drop the blanket, and the person in the center hops up and changes places with one of the holders. Keep exchanging places until everyone has had several turns in the blanket.

🖐 Swinging

Individual

Appropriate Ages

10 months and older.

Preparation

Take the children to a park that has swing sets. For infants, be sure to use only swings that have a safety seat with a safety bar across the front of the seat.

Activity

Slowly swing the children. Watch the child's face and actions for signs of stress, which include crying, looking fearful, or becoming flushed.

🖐 *Minitrampoline or Mattress Jumping*

Individual

Appropriate Ages

10 months and older.

Preparation

Set up a minitrampoline or mattress in an area free of obstructions. The minitrampoline should be set on a mat.

Activity

Children who are hypervestibular may start out simply by bouncing, without really jumping up and down on the minitrampoline. Infants who are able to sit up on their own should sit in the center of the mattress or minitrampoline while an adult gently bounces them. Until children are about three years old, they should hold hands with an adult while jumping.

Older children can start by jumping with hands on hips and the feet together. Gradually they can work into other movements, such as the legs opening and closing or scissoring. Advanced movements they can try include jumping jacks, running in place, or cross-country skiing motions. Whenever the child loses control, have him return to jumping with the hands on hips and the feet together.

Partner Rocking

Partners

Appropriate Ages

4 years and older.

Preparation

Partners sit facing each other, with their legs crossed or spread out to the side with the feet touching. They hold each other's wrists.

Activity

Slowly, one partner leans forward as the other leans backward; they then reverse the action. The partners rock back and forth at least 20 times.

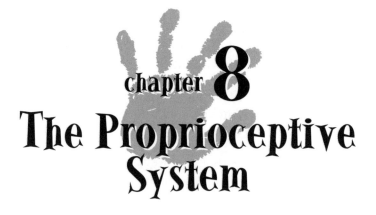

chapter 8
The Proprioceptive System

P_roprioceptive_ applies to the actual awareness of sensations that come from receptors in the muscles, joints, skin, tendons, and underlying tissue. The body may be still or in motion; the prefix _proprio_ indicates information about any type of static position or dynamic movement felt or received from _within the body_. A near synonym to proprioceptive is the term _kinesthetic,_ and although the two terms have somewhat different meanings, they are frequently considered the same. You may hear either one of these terms, because they both are frequently used.

This chapter briefly discusses the proprioceptive receptors and the way in which stimulation occurs. Then it reviews the proprioceptive system and its development. You'll find techniques to evaluate children and their proprioceptive systems. Next we provide an overview of proprioceptive problems and symptoms you may see at home or in the classroom. The last section gives instructions for some activities that may help reduce these problems.

PROPRIOCEPTIVE SYSTEM RECEPTORS

The receptors or sense organs that professionals mention most often for the proprioceptive system are the muscles, tendons, and joints of the body. Part of the proprioceptive system's function is to maintain an individual's posture in an upright position, however, so the vestibular system must also be involved. In fact, Sherrington (1906) discusses the vestibular receptors as part of the proprioceptive system's receptors. So we can distinguish five different types of receptors within the proprioceptive system: (1) joint capsules and ligaments, (2) tendon receptors, (3) muscle spindles, (4) connective tissues, and (5) vestibular receptors.

Joint receptors are nerve branches located in the joint capsules and joint ligaments. They are also found in the fibrous cartilage, hyaline cartilage, and fat pads of a joint (see figure 8.1). Various kinds of stress placed on the nerves stimulate the receptors, and they are affected by the joint's position (angle), movements, and any change in its position. Pain also stimulates the receptors.

The *tendon receptors* are found where the muscles and tendons unite— and sometimes only within the tendons. Tendon receptors are stimulated any time a muscle is shortened (contracted) or stretched beyond its resting length. *Muscle spindle receptors* get their name from their spindle-shaped forms. They are located in cells within the belly of the muscles and respond to tension, compression, and movement of a muscle. *Connective tissue receptors* are found in the connective tissue surrounding the muscles and bones and in other soft tissue under the

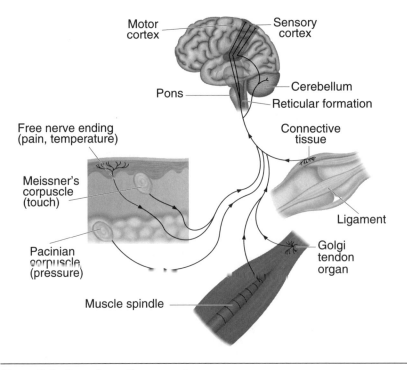

Figure 8.1 Proprioception receptors.

Reprinted, by permission, from Jack H. Wilmore and David L. Costill, 1999, *Physiology of Sport and Exercise*, 2nd ed. (Champaign, IL: Human Kinetics), 72.

skin. Any type of pressure (compression) of the area may activate the connective tissue receptors. This includes pressure caused by contraction of a muscle across a joint located in the same area. The last group of receptors, the *vestibular receptors,* include the semicircular canals, utricle, and saccule. Rotation and tilting of the head and movements of the head in a straight line will stimulate these vestibular receptors.

You might think of the proprioceptive and vestibular systems as operating in a cooperative but somewhat separate fashion. Once a child's sensory receptors receive a stimulus, the sensation travels to his central nervous system (CNS) where it is interpreted (refer back to figure 6.2 on p. 131). When a muscle response is needed, his CNS (including the vestibular system) sends the information in the form of a motor impulse to motor neurons that tell his specific muscle or group of muscles to perform the desired skill or motor act. His proprioceptive system then performs the movement, monitoring the movement of his muscles, joints, and other proprioceptive receptors. Then the information about the result of the movement is sent back to the brain and vestibular system. In this way, the proprioceptive system constantly tells the CNS exactly what is happening within the body and to the body.

THE PROPRIOCEPTIVE SYSTEM AND ITS DEVELOPMENT

Each of the proprioceptive receptors provides specific information about the body. This information includes the relationship of the body parts and joints to each other in both stationary (static) and moving (dynamic) positions. Table 8.1 offers a summary of the location and actions of each proprioceptive receptor. Trying to separate each receptor into specific actions during various movements of the body is far beyond the scope of this book. It is more appropriate for parents or teachers who have children or students with learning problems to focus on the function of the proprioceptive system *as a whole.*

At any one time, the proprioceptive system sends information to the brain concerning the (a) location of the joints and body parts; (b) movement of the joints and muscles; (c) pressure on the skin and underlying tissue; (d) pain felt in the joints, tissue, or muscles; and (e) temperature (figure 8.2). This information helps children to subconsciously know the exact amount of force to use when throwing a baseball, serving a volleyball, balancing on skates, reaching for a pencil, writing, drawing, or just sitting still in a chair.

Basically, the proprioceptive system plays a key role in helping a child maintain equilibrium, progress through the motor development stages,

Table 8.1
Functions of the Proprioceptive System

Receptors	Location	Action (functions to tell brain)
Joint	Joint capsule, ligament, fibrous cartilage, hyaline cartilage, and fat pads.	Position of joint (both static and dynamic), joint speed, pressure and pain.
Tendon	Junction of muscle tendon and tendon.	Muscle tension, strength of muscle contraction.
Muscle spindle	Muscles.	Muscle tension; monitors stretching of a muscle.
Connective tissue	Connective tissue around the joint; skin and tissue under the skin.	Pressure on tissue caused by joint movement, compression of skin or tissue under skin.
Semicircular canals Saccule and utricle	Inner ear.	Position of head in relation to gravity; rotation and changes in the speed of head rotation.

and later perform complex motor skills. It acts, in cooperation with the vestibular and visual systems, to keep his body upright and balanced. These three systems are so intricately related that when one system is not working, the other two systems can provide sufficient information to the brain to keep the body in an upright position. This is why a child who is blind (and receives no visual information) uses his vestibular and proprioceptive systems to function in an upright position. A child whose vestibular system is not functioning will usually have a proprioceptive system that is also not functioning. He must rely instead on his visual system to tell him where he is in space.

Neurological Feedback

Feedback is the ability of the nervous system to monitor intended movements of the body and body parts, to keep a neurological record of the movements, and to change the intended movements when necessary. Feedback may be internal or external. *Internal feedback* consists of tracking and recording all the information received from the proprioceptive system and all of the other sensory systems involved in a movement and its outcome. *External feedback,* on the other hand, involves information received from outside the body, especially information received through the visual or auditory systems. You might consider verbal feedback that a parent or teacher gives a child another important type of external feedback.

Photo courtesy of Gary Loyd.

Figure 8.2 There is a lot of proprioceptive information sent to the brain in order to hit a volleyball: locations of joints and body parts, parts of body and muscles needed, exact movements needed, amount of force required, balance (with vestibular) while in act of hitting ball, combining visual information with movements so contact is made, contacting ball (also tactile), and the pressure on hand and arm as contact is made.

Feedback is as critical for improved academic performance in the classroom as it is for motor skill development. As a child learns new academic skills that involve any movement of the body, the proprioceptive system comes into play to perform the movements and record the action. A student learning to progress from printing her words to writing in script must rely on her proprioceptive system. In this case, her voluntary motor system has been programmed to print. When she tries to shift to script writing, the proprioceptive system (body parts) must learn to make the necessary adjustments. This includes the way that she holds the pencil and then moves her hand, wrist, and forearm across the page. If you observe a child really struggling to make this transfer or having trouble with both printing or script writing, it is realistic to suspect that the youngster is having a problem with the proprioceptive system.

There is also internal feedback occurring after an action has been started but before the intended action takes place. This may occur in several ways. Subconsciously, a child can use internal feedback to help maintain his equilibrium. Let's say that she is walking across a field, places her foot forward, and accidentally steps on a rock. As she starts to fall, she receives internal feedback from her sensory systems, which relay this information to her neurological system in time (usually) for her proprioceptive system to readjust her foot and correct her balance (figure 8.3).

Skilled athletes also use internal feedback to change an intended motor skill. Laura, as an example, is serving the volleyball toward a weak opponent when she sees (external feedback through her visual system) that the players have recognized where she planned to serve the ball and have changed places. Even though she is in the middle of her backswing for the serve, up to a certain point in her serve she has the ability—through internal feedback—to redirect her serve to the new position that the weak opponent took in swapping places.

Verbal feedback from a teacher or parent is often beneficial when children are learning new motor and academic skills. Some typical suggestions are "Swing at the ball earlier," "Make the letters smaller," or "Concentrate on following through with your arm to make the ball travel farther." These examples of feedback can help direct a child's attention toward the parts of his proprioceptive-vestibular systems that are needed to correct the movement (figure 8.4a). However, beware of giv-

Figure 8.3 Internal feedback.

a   b

Figure 8.4 Verbal feedback.

ing too much verbal feedback while someone is attempting the particular skill. He can become confused and overwhelmed (figure 8.4b).

Body schema forms the basis, along with the vestibular system, for posture and equilibrium. A child's body schema (see chapter 5) develops through actions of the proprioceptive system and its feedback processes. It is an internal awareness, or map, of the relationship of the body and body parts to each other. It is somewhat like a mental picture in our minds of the body and the way it moves.

Body schema evolves through neuromuscular information sent to the central nervous system (CNS) during static and dynamic movements. Although body schema information is generated and transferred primarily by the proprioceptive system, other sensory systems assist in contributing information. Body schema contains information based on past actions. Changes and modifications or corrections are made throughout one's life. As the child starts a new movement, motor impulses are sent to his proprioceptive receptors based on his past movements. Each time he moves, the new proprioceptive information created by that movement is sent to the CNS to continually fine-tune his body schema.

It is important to understand how both active and passive movements influence the development of a child's body schema and the proprioceptive system in general. *Active movements* are those the child controls. Her own neurological system receives the stimulus and sends information to various parts of her sensory systems to perform the appropriate action or skill. Throughout the motor skill, her CNS is not only actively monitoring the action but also receiving sensory information about every phase of the activity. In this way, the information from her current motor skill is compared to past actions to evaluate whether the movement was successful and to make changes in her neurological pathways. This information is then used to perform similar skills or movements in the future.

Passive movements, in contrast, are ones that are controlled by something or someone other than the child. Mike, for example, stands behind his daughter, Allison. He takes the bat in his hands and moves it through the path of a swing. Even though her hands are resting on the bat, Allison has not initiated any action, and therefore her sensory motor system (including her proprioceptive system) does not receive much stimulus (figure 8.5). Assisted movements (such as this one with the bat) result in little change in a child's proprioceptive system or in the ability to learn the motor skill.

Figure 8.5 Passive movement.

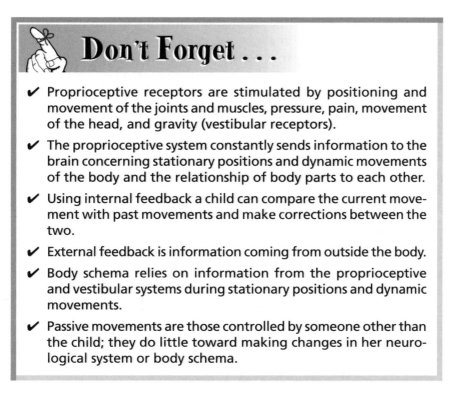

Don't Forget . . .

✔ Proprioceptive receptors are stimulated by positioning and movement of the joints and muscles, pressure, pain, movement of the head, and gravity (vestibular receptors).

✔ The proprioceptive system constantly sends information to the brain concerning stationary positions and dynamic movements of the body and the relationship of body parts to each other.

✔ Using internal feedback a child can compare the current movement with past movements and make corrections between the two.

✔ External feedback is information coming from outside the body.

✔ Body schema relies on information from the proprioceptive and vestibular systems during stationary positions and dynamic movements.

✔ Passive movements are those controlled by someone other than the child; they do little toward making changes in her neurological system or body schema.

Motor Planning

Motor planning or *praxis* is the ability to plan, organize, and complete a series of movements that are directed toward some purpose. It must occur before the development of motor skills or purposeful action. Motor planning allows children not only to learn new skills but also to combine skills into new and more complicated motor acts. This does not occur at birth. Rather, it is a process that develops over a period of time as the sensory system matures. During the first few months of life, an infant uses the arms and legs in involuntary movements and experiences a series of reflexes. Motor planning by the child appears as he starts to experiment with voluntary movements, such as reaching for an object. This motor planning involves a thought process as well as a resulting movement or action.

Children who have good coordination rely on the close relationship between the sensory systems and muscle action. Each movement involves the correct amount of muscle force, timing of the force, and length of time that the force is applied. As children repeat a correct movement pattern over and over, their coordination continues to improve and the movement becomes automatic. Once children have developed more movement patterns, they find it easier to add additional skills that have similar characteristics. They also have a wider movement vocabulary from which to choose if they need to react to external changes when they are performing motor skills.

You can see the motor-planning process in simple movements, such as buttoning a shirt or tying shoelaces. With these actions the child must think through each step at first, but after he repeats the action and the skill becomes coordinated, he can perform the task automatically. Even though the movement becomes automatic, the proprioceptive system continues to monitor the movements and notify the central nervous system when an error occurs. This can be seen when a student is typing and makes a mistake. He does not have to look at the screen to know that he hit the wrong key. His proprioceptive feedback system sent the message to his CNS even before the letter appeared on the screen. Other examples of motor planning are painting, coloring in lines, writing, dodging opponents in sports, and performing complicated dives and gymnastic skills.

Don't Forget . . .

✔ Motor planning precedes the development of a motor skill.
✔ Motor planning involves the planning, organization, and completion of movements directed toward some purpose (for example, buttoning a shirt, coloring within lines or figures, typing, writing).
✔ Skills become automatic through motor planning and repetitions of the movement.

EVALUATING THE PROPRIOCEPTIVE SYSTEM

In evaluating a proprioceptive problem the major concern is to use the appropriate test items to pinpoint just where the basic problem exists. In other words, what is the *cause* of the child's inability to know where his body parts are in relation to each other and to use them effectively? It can be difficult, however, to determine the exact location of a proprioceptive problem. The cause can lie anywhere along the child's entire sensory motor process.

The proprioceptive and vestibular receptors might not be receiving the initial sensations, the sensations might not progress to the central nervous system, or the sensation might not be associated with past experiences. The youngster's central nervous system might not send the motor impulse to the muscles to act—or the muscles might not be returning feedback to the central nervous system.

Proprioceptive-vestibular evaluations focus on maintaining balance of the body and head in relation to the pull of gravity. They also determine the ability to use the body parts in relation to each other. Children as young as two months are using their proprioceptive, vestibular, and visual systems to hold up their heads. And as you might guess, by using any one test it is almost impossible to separate the proprioceptive, visual, and vestibular systems. Even the simple act of walking involves sensory information gained from all three systems.

Proprioceptive tests evaluate movements of the body and body parts. They involve body schema, coordinating the two sides of the body, and motor planning. Gross and fine motor evaluations of infants and toddlers tend to measure the proprioceptive system. That is, they use the body parts in order to sit, stand, walk, jump, run, kick, or even pick up a toy or object with the thumb and index finger.

As a child moves around the house or performs in the classroom or gymnasium, there are some clues that parents and teachers can use to recognize that he may need evaluation. Does he fall into the "uncoordinated category" and have trouble doing any motor skill such as walking, running, jumping, kicking or throwing a ball? Can he raise one arm without the other arm's moving? Can he walk through a door without hitting the frame? Does he erase the chalkboard by moving his body instead of crossing his midline? These are the children who have trouble learning a skill and frequently try to avoid participation in activities. Each time a skill is introduced, it is almost as if he has never experienced it before. Observe how he grips the pencil or writes. Does he change his grip every time, does he understand the way you asked him to hold the pencils or does he have messy handwriting and seem to write all over the page? Does he have trouble holding his coat and putting his arm in his sleeve, buttoning his coat, carrying his lunch tray or getting on and off furniture?

Angels-in-the-Snow Test

One of the best ways to evaluate the proprioceptive system is to use a modification of Roach and Kephart's Angels-in-the-Snow test (1966). This test evaluates whether or not a child has developed his proprioceptive system enough to progress from the gross body movements of an infant to the cross-lateral skills necessary for walking, running, complex sport activities, and academic tasks. During the administration of this test be sure to place the child on his back so that he can move his arms and legs but cannot visually see them. This position forces him to depend on the proprioceptive system because he cannot *see* his body.

Start by drawing or taping a straight line on a mat. Place the child on his back with his midline (the middle of his body) along the straight line you have already put on a mat. Tell him that you will point to his arms and legs, and that he is to move the limb or limbs you indicate up along the ground as far as he can and then return the limb (or limbs) to the original position. Repeat each movement four times. Here's the progression to use (figure 8.6):

1. Move all four limbs at the same time.
2. Move the two arms.
3. Then move the two legs.
4. Move just the right arm.
5. Move just the left arm.
6. Move the right leg.
7. Move the left leg.
8. Move the right arm and right leg.
9. Move the left arm and left leg.
10. Move the right arm and left leg.
11. Finally, move the left arm and right leg.

Throughout the test, observe whether the child can move the limbs indicated without moving any *other* limbs (associated movement) and whether the movements are coordinated. In addition, see if he can move his limbs without hesitating, looking at them, touching them, or banging them on the floor. These are actions a child often takes to wake up the proprioceptive system. It is not uncommon to see a child hit one of his arms or legs and say, "You mean this arm?" The action of hitting the limb is used to bring both the proprioceptive receptors and sense of touch of that limb into play. Often, after hitting the limb, a child can move it. Each time he returns from a movement, check to be sure that the line on the mat divides his body into two equal halves. The line helps you see if he twists his body or moves one side of his body more than the other when the two limbs are supposed to be doing the same movement at the same time.

The 11 separate test items for Angels in the Snow are arranged in the order in which children progress though the development stages. For

 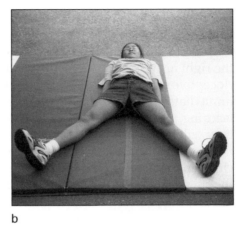

a   b

 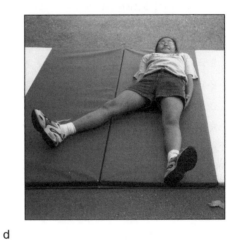

c   d

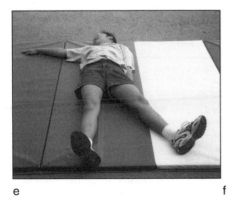 

e   f

Figure 8.6 Angels in the Snow.

this reason, it is to be expected that they will be less successful as the movements progress and become more complex. There is, however, a degree of learning as the test proceeds. When they are asked to move the right arm up and down, bright children, who have an intact proprioceptive system, will finish the test item with their right arm and then immediately perform the movement with their left arm. Children with learning problems will rarely make the connection to the movement they will be asked to perform next.

The results from testing four different groups of elementary school children (see table 8.2), using Angels in the Snow, suggests that some of the children who have learning problems are not as successful with the

Table 8.2
Percent of Students Who Passed the Angels-in-the-Snow Test

Group	A	B	C	D
Both arms and legs	82.2	69.8	86.5	70.5
Both arms	98.4	91.2	95.5	90.9
Both legs	96	87.8	97.8	88.6
Right arm	62.9	91.5	93.3	91.1
Left arm	94.8	89.4	95.5	93
Right leg	74.8	79.1	92.1	63.6
Left leg	76.2	76.6	88.8	62.2
Right arm and leg	57.7	50.6	74.2	44.4
Left arm and leg	69.6	53.8	66.3	48.9
Right arm and left leg	34	22.4	55.1	18.2
Left arm and right leg	34.6	16.1	37.1	16.3
Number	135	395	89	45

A: Third-grade students enrolled in 5 elementary schools in different geographic locations in Arlington, Texas. Students represented different academic-achievement levels based on scores received on state-administered achievement tests.

B: Kindergarten to sixth-grade students enrolled in 2 elementary schools in Kalamazoo, Michigan. Students scored 0–3 on the Iowa Achievement Test in reading or were experiencing learning problems.

C: Third-grade students enrolled in 6 different geographic locations in Kalamazoo, Michigan. Students represented diverse academic achievement.

D: Kindergarten to third-grade students in Parchment, Michigan. Students scored 0–3 on the Iowa Achievement Test (scores range from 0–9 with 4.5 considered average), were recommended by the reading teacher, or had low visual and vestibular scores.

test items as children in the groups with more varied academic achievement scores (Cheatum 1986–1989, 1989, 1993, 1996; Cheatum and Hammond 1992). Surprisingly many elementary schoolchildren have difficulty coordinating the movement of all four limbs at the same time. About 70 percent of the kindergarten through sixth-grade students in group B and kindergarten through third-grade students in group D could perform this test item.

The most dramatic drop in the success rate of various groups occurs when the students are asked to move limbs on the same side of the body (unilateral) and different limbs on opposite sides of the body (crosslateral movements). Only 16.1 percent of group B and 16.3 percent of group D passed the most difficult test item, moving the left arm and right leg at the same time. This particular movement requires the most coordination and integration of the two sides of the body.

Rhomberg Test

The Rhomberg Test is used to evaluate the balance (proprioceptive-vestibular systems) of a child in a standing position. It is appropriate to use with any child over the age of three years. In this test the youngster assumes a standing posture with both feet together, the arms relaxed at her side, and her eyes closed. The vestibular system controls the relationship of the head to the pull of gravity. The proprioceptive system is responsible for controlling the various parts of the body (feet, ankles, legs, trunk, arms) to maintain balance. An observer tries to determine or note loss of balance, weaving back and forth, lifting or moving the feet apart, and lifting one or both arms.

Reciprocal Imitations

In a test of reciprocal imitations, the evaluator asks the child to imitate an evaluator's movements that are the opposite of or different from each other. The evaluator might, for example, open one hand while closing the other, turn one hand palm down while turning the other palm up, and raise one arm while lowering the other. Then he or she would observe whether the child can (a) do the skill, (b) maintain the same rhythm as the evaluator's, (c) separate the two sides of the body, and (d) coordinate the movement.

The reciprocal imitations evaluations usually involve only the upper body but demand more from the child than Angels in the Snow. Instead of your pointing to and telling the child the body part you want her to move, she has to interpret your visual demonstration. Roach and Kephart (1966) have a good example of this in the Purdue Perceptual

Motor Test. As one arm on one side of the evaluator goes up and the arm on the other side goes down, it becomes confusing to the child. Children who still have trouble with laterality and directionality have trouble transferring the movement of the evaluator to the action she should make with her own body.

Index Finger–Nose Test

To do the Index Finger–Nose Test, you demonstrate the movement to the child and then have the youngster perform it, first with the eyes open and then with the eyes closed. The child stands with his arms raised to shoulder level and extended straight out to the side. He touches the index finger of his preferred hand to his nose and then returns his arm to its starting position. He alternates the movement with the arm and hand on the nonpreferred side, touching his nose four times with each index finger.

With the eyes open, the test is basically an evaluation of the proprioceptive system. When the child does the test with the eyes closed, however, additional stress is placed on the sensory systems, and he must use his vestibular system to maintain balance. Observe whether the child brings the hand to the nose, bends the head to the hand, misses or hits the nose, or lowers the arms. Some children will have difficulty in keeping the arms extended at shoulder level. These are children whose muscle tone (vestibular system) has little control over the pull of gravity, so their arms slowly start to lower toward the floor.

Evaluators tested four groups of elementary school children on the index finger–nose action (test item). The results suggest that almost 25 percent of the students evaluated have some proprioceptive problems that could seriously affect their performance in school (Cheatum 1986– 1989, 1989, 1993, 1996; Cheatum and Hammond 1992). Only 46 percent of Group B and 51 percent of Group A were successful by the time they reached the fifth movement (see table 8.3). Students in Group D, kindergarten to third-grade students, were the most successful. They had a 75.6 percent success rate on the first movement and still had 57.8 percent by the final movement. On the other hand, scores for Group A, third-grade children with diverse academic scores, fell from a success rate of 77.7 percent in the first movement to just 42.9 percent in the eighth trial.

Shoulder-Level Arm-Raise Test

The Shoulder-Level Arm-Raise Test item (also used to evaluate body schema) consists of having the child close his eyes and raise his preferred arm to shoulder level, placing it there four times in a row (see

Table 8.3
Percent of Students Who Passed the Index Finger–Nose Test

Movement	Group A	Group B	Group C	Group D
1	77.7	66.2	66.3	75.6
2	62.9	62.5	69.3	73.3
3	57.7	58.4	66.3	71.1
4	57.0	52.1	70.8	64.4
5	51.8	46.5	60.7	60.0
6	45.2	42.6	62.9	57.8
7	39.3	41.2	57.3	57.8
8	42.9	40.2	49.4	57.8
Number	135	395	89	45

A: Third-grade students enrolled in 5 elementary schools in different geographic locations in Arlington, Texas. Students represented different academic-achievement levels based on scores received on state-administered achievement tests.

B: Kindergarten to sixth-grade students enrolled in 2 elementary schools in Kalamazoo, Michigan. Students scored 0–3 on the Iowa Achievement Test in reading or were experiencing learning problems.

C: Third-grade students enrolled in 6 different geographic locations in Kalamazoo, Michigan. Students represented diverse academic achievement.

D: Kindergarten to third-grade students in Parchment, Michigan. Students scored 0–3 on the Iowa Achievement Test (scores range from 0–9 with 4.5 considered average), were recommended by the reading teacher, or had low visual and vestibular scores.

figure 8.7). The evaluator has the child repeat the action with the nonpreferred arm and then with both arms. In order to accurately see how high a level the arm is raised, it helps to have children perform this evaluation in front of a wall that has some horizontal marks you can use as a reference guide. Children who have a learning problem often have little proprioceptive knowledge about the movements involved in this test item. They will, typically, change the level the arm is raised with each separate movement.

In chapter 5 (see table 5.2 on p. 97), you may remember, we discussed the performance of this test by four groups of elementary students, from kindergarten through sixth grade. Amazingly, 39 percent of the students could not successfully perform the test items. Yet elementary schoolchildren have to rely on their proprioceptive system during all of their academic and movement experiences!

Figure 8.7 Shoulder-Level Arm-Raise Test.

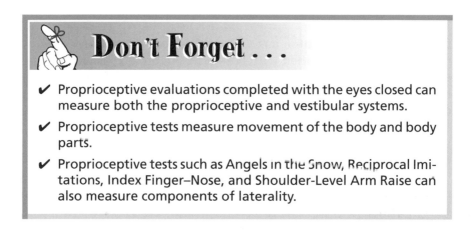

Don't Forget . . .

✔ Proprioceptive evaluations completed with the eyes closed can measure both the proprioceptive and vestibular systems.

✔ Proprioceptive tests measure movement of the body and body parts.

✔ Proprioceptive tests such as Angels in the Snow, Reciprocal Imitations, Index Finger–Nose, and Shoulder-Level Arm Raise can also measure components of laterality.

PROPRIOCEPTIVE SYSTEM PROBLEMS

Teachers are concerned about Yuri. He is failing the second grade. Although he can walk, he is uncoordinated and he continually falls out of his chair and bumps into other students. When the school day is over, he just stands there and looks at his coat, unable to even start a movement toward dressing himself.

Third-grader Consuela still has trouble hopping. It helps when the physical education teacher taps her on the leg that is to be used. But after two or three hops, she forgets which leg she is to use. It is as if she has never heard or does not remember any of the directions that were given.

Mohammed is in the sixth grade but both his arms still move when he is working at his desk. Reading his written work is beyond the ability of any of his teachers.

All of these children have some difficulty with the proprioceptive system. Proprioceptive problems can be very humiliating for children, such as Yuri, Consuela, and Mohammed. They struggle with homework in the classroom and have even more trouble in the gymnasium. All too often, their parents and teachers feel they are not trying. In reality, children who have a blank look on their face may be trying to figure out which hand or arm goes where. Lack of an ability to use the proprioceptive system effectively results in clumsy or uncoordinated movements, as well as in low academic achievement. These children fall a lot, touch other students, run into walls, and cannot participate in even the simplest sport activities. They are shunned or ignored by their peers. Moreover, behind their backs, they are often referred to as clumsy, motor morons, or nerds. It is understandable that their self-esteem is damaged. They may seem depressed or withdrawn and they may even misbehave. Socially, they avoid children of their own age group and instead retreat to computer games, television, or playing with younger children.

Poor Body Awareness and Body Schema

Typically, a proprioceptive problem is related to body awareness, laterality, or directionality, or to some combination of these concepts. A child who cannot identify the parts of his body usually finds it difficult to coordinate his body. If you ask him to move an arm or leg, he may not be able to move the part on command. This lack of body awareness blocks the development of body schema. And without body schema there is little hope that he can progress through the developmental stages of laterality, directionality, and directional discrimination. To determine the right type of corrective program for him, therefore, it is critical to consider and evaluate all of these concepts (you may want to review table 5.1 [p. 93] for a list of developmental stages and problems frequently experienced by children who have proprioceptive problems).

Poor Motor Planning

If a child is unable to "motor-plan," she has a sensory motor problem that prevents her being able to plan and perform a purposeful movement or motor skill. Physicians and physical and occupational therapists commonly call this inability *dyspraxia, apraxia,* or *developmental dyspraxia.* The inability to motor-plan makes a child appear clumsy or uncoordinated, and this is a common symptom in children who have a dysfunction in their proprioceptive-vestibular sensory systems.

One of the most critical problems that goes along with a child's inability to motor-plan is that the neurological system is not developing a file of movements that he or she can use to create additional movements. In other words, each time the child attempts a skill, there is no reference started in the CNS because no sets of connections have been made among neurons. It is as if the motor skill now facing him is a completely new skill that he has never attempted before. Children who lack motor planning remain low on the developmental motor skills assessment charts. Rachel, for example, may want to skip. She really tries, but each time she is asked to skip across the floor, she has no idea which foot to move first or second. Since she cannot plan her movements, she just moves forward using her feet in an uncoordinated series of hops and jumps.

Lack of the ability to motor-plan shows up early in a child's life. Young girls and boys of three and four years may not be able to put clothes on baby dolls or toy animals. Although toddlers start to push cars around— almost as soon as they can lie on their sides and identify a car—children are usually about three years old before they start pushing the car on a make-believe road. Preschool boys and girls who lack the ability to motor-plan become frustrated and just bang the car on the floor; they try to force the car back and forth with no direction in mind. Repeated failure at these kinds of play or tasks causes many a child to become aggravated and resort to inappropriate behaviors that carry over to classroom activities.

A child's inability to motor-plan is frustrating for him as well as for his parents and teachers. However, it does explain why he may fail to catch the ball 20 times in a row when his father is struggling to teach him to play ball. By using much repetition, some of these children can develop a few splinter skills. With a splinter skill, however, there is no transfer to other skills. They are not able to use the splinter skills to help them learn additional or even similar motor skills (see chapter 2).

Each child with a proprioceptive problem is different. If you suspect a child is having proprioceptive problems, make a list of the problems that occur at home and at school. Compare the list to developmental stages and to the general symptoms of proprioceptive problems found in the box titled "General Symptoms of Proprioceptive Problems." Although the list is long, it clearly illustrates the different symptoms that you can expect to observe in children whose proprioceptive systems are not functioning normally.

General Symptoms of Proprioceptive Problems

Poor naming and locating of body parts.

Trouble judging the force needed to throw balls or bounce on a minitrampoline.

Poor balance, both static and dynamic.

Problems with fine motor skills, cutting, writing, and so forth.

Appears not to know when he is touching others.

Uses either hand to write, color, throw, bat, and so forth.

Poor posture and muscle tone.

Uses either foot to kick.

Often hits or moves a body part to "wake it up" before moving it.

Problems with gross motor skills, such as running or jumping.

Difficulty learning to dress himself.

Has splinter skills and cannot transfer them to related skills or activities.

No left and right awareness

Has no memory of past instructions involving motor skills

Cannot coordinate use of his eyes.

Midline problems cause lack of coordination between the two sides of the body.

Cannot use the two hands together for skills.

Retains "constancy"; sees p,d,q,b as the same letters.

Falls often and has more accidents than other children his age.

Cannot tell directions; gets lost easily.

May run into furniture, walls, or other people.

Has no awareness of up and down, before and behind.

Immature locomotor patterns for walking.

Poor awareness of space.

Prefers to play with younger children.

Has trouble finding place in books and on paper.

Classified as learning disabled or attention deficit disordered.

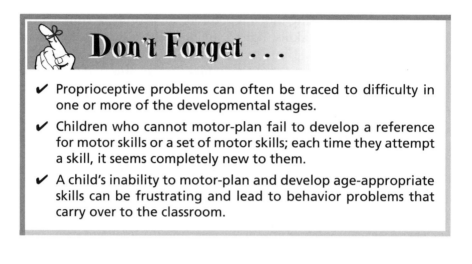

Don't Forget . . .

✔ Proprioceptive problems can often be traced to difficulty in one or more of the developmental stages.

✔ Children who cannot motor-plan fail to develop a reference for motor skills or a set of motor skills; each time they attempt a skill, it seems completely new to them.

✔ A child's inability to motor-plan and develop age-appropriate skills can be frustrating and lead to behavior problems that carry over to the classroom.

CORRECTING PROPRIOCEPTIVE PROBLEMS

When you're trying to develop a motor program to reduce proprioceptive problems, it is important to remember that the cause of the problem is the failure of sensory information to be received from inside the body. Since the proprioceptive system involves the muscles, joints, tendons, and connective tissue, the activities you choose must include the children initiating and completing movements of their bodies. The keys to helping them are *movement* and *different kinds of movement* than they have previously experienced. These are children who have already been using their bodies, but as yet the movements have done nothing for them. For example, if you have already tried to get a child to catch a ball by continually repeating the skill, doing more of the same will do little for him unless there is some different information going into his proprioceptive system.

Children who cannot name the parts of the body often cannot name them because they really do not know that the parts are there. They cannot feel the parts. The body just sort of carries the head around. Barbara, for instance, did everything with one arm and completely ignored the other side of her body. When she was asked to use the other arm, Barbara was shocked to find out it was there. It was as if she never knew she had another arm. Clearly, she could not feel the presence of the arm, even though she could see it. Efforts to help her should include connecting the identification and purpose of the body part to the use of the part.

Applying pressure to a body part or massaging it sometimes helps to wake up that limb or part. For example, rubbing a child's legs may help him realize that they are there. The sensations will also travel to his neurological system and begin to create references for his body schema. Teachers commonly use this technique. For example, when a child cannot move the correct arm, teachers touch the limb and say, "Move this arm." This touch technique should be used in addition to other motor-planning activities and activities that push the joints together and stretch them.

Correcting a Proprioceptive Receptor Problem

There are five techniques that are effective in getting some different feelings (sensations) into the proprioceptive systems of children with problems, and the activities in this chapter include some or all of these techniques:

- Contraction (shortening) and stretching of muscles
- Compression and traction of joints
- Tonic contraction of muscles surrounding a joint
- Increasing the amount of force the muscles must use to perform a movement
- Increasing the length of time a movement is performed

Contraction and stretching of muscles takes in the full range through which a muscle can move. This, of course, also involves the joints that the muscles move. When a child bends his elbow and touches his hand to his shoulder, he is contracting (shortening) some muscles and stretching (lengthening) others. Straightening the elbow reverses those muscles that have been shortening and lengthening. This kind of action may be sufficient for some children with mild problems. Other children may benefit by adding weights to the movement. The additional weight increases the amount of force that the muscles must apply; it also increases the amount of weight that is transferred to the joints. Depending on how old the children are, you might have them add the use of light free weights, size-appropriate medicine balls, or movements (such as push-ups) that involve adding the body's weight. Other muscle contraction and stretching activities are pushing and pulling types of movements, the kinds you use in playing tug-of-war or hopping like a rabbit.

Joint compression and traction also involves the use of the muscles, but the goal is to get the children to feel a difference *in the joint itself.* Activities for joint compression include walking on the hands (which compresses the wrists, elbows, and shoulders), bouncing on a trampoline (which compresses the ankles, knees, hips, and spinal column), and balancing a medicine ball on the head (which compresses the neck, spinal column, hips, knees, and ankles.) Children can even do activities such as lying on a scooter board with the knees bent and the feet flat on the wall, which compresses the ankles, knees, hips, and spine when they forcefully push against the wall.

Some of the best illustrations of joint traction are hanging from parallel bars, handwalking the bars (figure 8.8), and hanging by the knees. Gymnastic activities on the uneven bars are great for pulling on the joints. Sport skills, such as basketball free throws and shots from the floor, also involve joint compression and traction. As the child prepares for the shot, he *bends* the ankle, knee, and hip joints as well as the hand, arm, and shoulder. As he leaves the floor, he then *extends* the joints and shoots.

The tonic contraction of muscles surrounding a joint (cocontraction) refers to contracting all of the muscles surrounding a joint to keep the joint in the desired position. If a child tries to stand and balance on one foot, he will use a tonic contraction of the muscles of that leg. Many of the activities that elementary schoolteachers use in physical education employ tonic contraction. The wheelbarrow walk consists of one child holding the legs of another who is walking on his hands (figure 8.9).

Figure 8.8 Joint traction by hand walking on parallel bars.

Figure 8.9 Cocontraction in a wheelbarrow.

The hands, wrists, elbows, shoulders, and spinal column of the student who is walking on his hands are tonically contracted, while the fingers, hands, wrists, feet, ankles, knees, hips, and trunk of his partner holding onto his legs are contracted.

You can *increase the amount of force* a child uses to perform a motor skill in several ways. For a small child, just adding light weights to the wrist or ankle can increase the amount of force he or she must use to move; this extra weight and force increases the amount of information sent to the proprioceptive system. A weight-training program is great for such a child, as is the use of larger, heavier balls. Using simple everyday physical education skills and stunts consistently is beneficial. Many of these activities are designed to make the limbs feel used. Push-ups, climbing ropes, and pulling oneself across the floor on a scooter board all send positive information to the proprioceptive system.

Increasing the length of time a movement is performed involves repetition. When the objective is to develop a proprioceptive feeling in a particular part of the body, the motor skill must be repeated enough times that sufficient information succeeds in reaching the child's system. If a youngster has not developed lateral preference, for example, a different feeling must be created in his preferred limb. To develop this feeling, it is necessary that he use one side, what he thinks will be his preferred limb or side, more than the other side of the body. He needs to spend several days doing nothing but activities that use the preferred side of his body. Often physical education teachers have students dribble the ball down the length of the court with one hand and return using the other. Although this is good for children who have already developed lateral preference, it isn't helpful for those who have no preference; the constant changing of hands only reinforces the lack of lateral preference.

Correcting a Motor-Planning Problem

Children who cannot motor-plan will often have one or more of the body-awareness problems. To help children develop motor planning, you may first have to evaluate their body identification ability and then use activities that progressively move them through the motor development stages of body awareness, laterality, directionality, and directional discrimination. In this way, children will first learn their body parts and then learn how to use them.

A child's inability to motor-plan can be directly related to body schema. He has no past memories of movement and no knowledge of the position of his body parts or the way the parts work in relation to the rest of his body. He also doesn't know how much force he needs to use to move his body or even to move his hands to manipulate objects. In addition, without the ability to motor-plan, he has trouble in his relationship to gravity and often falls. By designing activities that apply the five techniques we discussed for correcting proprioceptive receptor problems, you can assist him in conquering some of his difficulties with motor planning. He will also need vestibular activities, since the vestibular system is affected.

Physical education and classroom teachers are in a good position to help a child learn to motor-plan. Until a child can motor-plan gross motor movements, he may find it hard to use the fine motor skills required for classroom activities. Physical education teachers have an opportunity to combine movements in the gymnasium with an awareness of the part of the body that is moving or needs to move. Activities should be progressive, starting first with very simple motor-planning skills. Make a tunnel out of a mat and have the child crawl through the mat without touching the sides or top. Then use variations: Ask him to crawl through the tunnel without using his left hand or arm. Have him crawl through on his back, then crawl through feet-first, and later crawl through with the left leg in the air and finally crawl through with the right leg in the air.

For more complicated motor-planning skills, use several pieces of equipment and ask the children to move around them. Chairs work well for this activity. Ask the youngsters to move through the legs of one chair or several in a line trying not to touch any of the chair legs. Add this to other skills, such as balancing on balance boards with both legs, then with one leg or the other. Have them crawl over bolsters, pull a scooter board across the floor using a rope, hang from their arms on parallel bars, and walk across parallel bars.

Don't Forget . . .

- ✔ Success of a sensory motor program depends on locating the exact cause of the proprioceptive problem.
- ✔ Sensory motor activities to correct proprioceptive problems must include a different type of movement than the child has done previously.
- ✔ Various techniques to place additional pressure and force on muscles, joints, and tissues help the child become aware of the various parts of her proprioceptive system.
- ✔ Lack of ability to motor-plan is often related to body schema problems, which classroom and physical education teachers can help children correct through appropriate activities.

Proprioceptive Activities

Children recommended for proprioceptive exercises have trouble knowing where their body parts are or how to use them. Many of them have already been trying various movements, such as walking and playing catch, that have not benefited them. So an exercise program must include using the muscles and body in different ways than their normal routines did. Activities to improve proprioceptive function use the five basic techniques: (1) muscle contraction and stretching, (2) joint compression and traction, (3) tonic contraction, (4) increasing amounts of force, and (5) increasing lengths of time doing a movement. These following activities provide opportunities for children to improve proprioceptive function through all or some of these techniques.

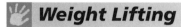 Weight Lifting

Individual

Appropriate Ages

18 months and older.

Preparation

You don't need to buy fancy weights or the machines typically found in fitness centers. Simple light wrist and ankle weights are available commercially. And if you look around the house or classroom, you can find inexpensive household or school objects, such as soup cans or old socks filled with sand, that work quite well. You can give really young children a shoe box or an old purse filled with toys to carry. For children 18 months through five years of age, limit the weight to between 1/2 pound to 2 pounds at the most. Older children can lift 5 to 10 pounds. At first, have children try to lift the weight with the help of an adult. Do not have a child do the following activities with weights that cause strain! Start with light weights and gradually increase the amount of weight.

Activities

Arm exercises. Ask the child to pick up and put down the "weight" 5 to 10 times. Older children can count the repetitions themselves. For a younger child, ask him to pick up a "purse" by the handle and bring it to you again. Once he brings you the "purse," you move to a new place and ask him to bring it to you. Repeat this, using different places, 5 to 10 times.

Leg exercises. Fill two large, long socks with sand (about 1/4 to 1/2 pound of it) and tie them off at the toes so that sand is trapped in them. Put the socks on the child. Seated in a chair, the child straightens his knees to lift the lower legs. He or she should repeat the lifts 5 to 10 times for each leg. Young children will just enjoy walking around with the heavy socks (or maybe adult's shoes) on their feet.

✋ *Muscular Endurance Exercises*
Individual

Appropriate Ages

4 years and older.

Preparation

Place a blanket, mat, or mattress on the ground if a carpeted surface is not available. You will also need a chair for one activity. A horizontal bar is necessary for pull-ups and can be found in sporting goods stores. Commercial horizontal bars expand to fit inside of doorways. Carefully follow the directions that come with them. You might also take the child to a park with climbing bars.

Activity

Abdominal curls. The child lies on his back with the knees bent and arms crossed over his chest. He then lifts only his head and shoulders off the floor while counting to three and returns to the starting position, again counting to three. The counting helps children do the abdominal curl slowly for safety and to increase the benefit of the exercise. See how many curl-ups he can do and then set a goal to increase that number. To motivate a young child, ask her to reach up and ring a bell that you are holding above her.

Push-ups. The child lies on his stomach with his arms bent, hands by his shoulders. He pushes with his arms to lift his whole body off the floor in one rigid piece. Beginning push-ups can be done with the knees on the floor. See how many push-ups he can do in a minute; then set a goal to increase that number. Young children (under four or five years old) may not be able to do push-ups the traditional way. You may ask them to push up into a "bear" position with their bottoms in the air, bending at the hips, their hands and feet on the floor.

Pull-ups. The child hangs from a horizontal bar that is placed at about his height. He may need to flex his knees to keep his feet off the ground. Bending the elbows, he pulls his body up until his chin is above the bar. See how many pull-ups he can do in a minute; then set a goal to increase that number. Even an 18-month-old child can try to hang, with an adult holding him up to a horizontal bar. *Important to note*—children should never hang from horizontal or climbing bars that are higher than they can reach by themselves with their feet on the ground.

Seated leg lifts. The child sits on a chair with her feet flat on the floor. She straightens her knees to lift the lower leg up and then back down. See how many leg lifts she can do in a minute; then set a goal to increase that number. For motivation, ask the child to lift her leg to ring a bell or kick a ball. To add more information going into the proprioceptive system, put light (half- to one-pound) ankles weights on her or use the weighted socks.

Arm circles. With arms straight out from his side, the child circles the arms forward 10 to 15 times and then backward 10 to 15 times. The circles should be small. Have younger children pretend they are birds flapping their wings. You can have the child wear a half-pound or one-pound wrist weight for added stimulation through the muscles and joints. With weights on, children should do the arm circles *slowly.*

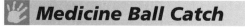 ## Medicine Ball Catch

Two or more people

Appropriate Ages

1 year and older.

Preparation

Medicine balls, which are rather heavy balls used for strength training, are available in a variety of sizes and weights at sporting goods stores. You can make a heavy ball by slitting an old basketball, volleyball, or child's rubber ball and filling it with one to five pounds of sand. Seal the slit with duct tape.

Activity

Play catch using the medicine ball. With children who cannot catch, just hand it back and forth. Try rolling it back and forth with only the dominant hand. You could also have the child dribble the medicine ball with his feet around cones, but do not let him kick it hard. Instead, have him use the feet to push the ball through the cones.

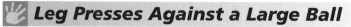 ## Leg Presses Against a Large Ball

Individual

Appropriate Ages

3 years and older.

Preparation

The child sits facing a large ball, with his hands behind him for support. The feet are placed on the ball, and a partner on the other side of the ball holds it still.

Activity

The child presses with his feet against the ball for 10 seconds and then releases. Repeat the press three to five times. For variety, have the child press with just one leg.

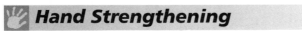 Hand Strengthening

Individual

Appropriate Ages

3 years and older.

Preparation

You will need Play Doh or clay. Some hand exercisers and light wrist weights are available commercially at discount or sporting goods stores. You can also attach a string in the center of a dowel that is 18 to 24 inches long and have a one-half-pound weight hanging from it.

Activity

Here are some simple hand exercises:

- Squeezing Play Doh (see recipe in chapter 9, p. 254), clay, or a hand exerciser
- Holding a dowel straight out from the chest and winding yarn around it, lifting the weight
- Wearing half-pound wrist weights while doing fine motor activities such as writing, cutting, or playing catch

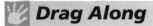 Drag Along

Individual or group

Appropriate Ages

3 years and older.

Preparation

Have the child or children lie facedown on a mat, carpet, or floor.

Activity

The child lies on his stomach and pushes up with his arms until they are straight (figure 8.10). Then, the child pulls his body along the floor with his arms and drags his feet like a sea lion. Children can race each other.

Figure 8.10 Drag Along.

Rabbit Hopping Through Hoops

Individual or group

Appropriate Ages

3 years and older.

Preparation

Lay five or more hoops out on the floor in a straight line or in a random pattern. Number the hoops or put letters in them.

Activity

The child rabbit-hops through the hoops by first placing both hands in the hoop and then hopping with both legs to have all four limbs in the hoop. Have the child rabbit-hop in a certain pattern or on a series of letters.

Body-Part Balance

One or more

Appropriate Ages

4 years and older.

Preparation

Arrange for a CD player and disks or a cassette tape player. Clear a space for play near the music source.

Activity

Play music and have the participants move around the space. They can hop, crawl, walk backward, or whatever. When the music stops, the participants must find a way to balance on three body parts, and only one of the parts can be a foot. Wait about 10 to 15 seconds before starting the music again. For variety, include props such as balls, chairs, or hoops. On the signal to stop, the participants must freeze in a balanced position using a prop.

Wall Headstand or Handstand

Individual or group

Appropriate Ages

4 years and older.

Preparation

Clear a space near a wall. Have music available if possible.

Activity

The child does a headstand or handstand against a wall. With a group, the children can dance, hop, and so forth to music; when the music stops, everyone has to get into a headstand or handstand against a wall.

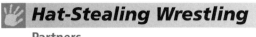

Hat-Stealing Wrestling

Partners

Appropriate Ages

6 years and older.

Preparation

Mark a five-foot-diameter circle on the floor. You'll need to have one hat per participant. Clear the area around the circle of any obstacles. Opponents, wearing hats, stand facing each other and raise their right hands. Each opponent uses his left hand to grasp the right wrist of his opponent.

Activity

On "Go!" each participant tries to steal the hat off his opponent's head without letting his hat be taken (figure 8.11). After a few bouts with the right hand, switch hands. The participants must stay inside the circle. If someone steps out, a foul is called and the bout stops.

Figure 8.11 Hat stealing.

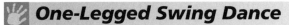

One-Legged Swing Dance

Partners

Appropriate Ages

6 years and older.

Preparation

Partners stand facing each other. Partners each lift the right leg up to the partner's left side, and they each hold the partner's right foot with the left hand.

Activity

On a cue, such as music or "Go!" the partners hop around each other in a circle. When the music stops (or on another cue), the partners switch legs.

Chain Keep-Away

Three or more

Appropriate Ages

8 years and older.

Preparation

Mark a circle on the floor. The size depends on the number of people. Participants stand in a circle and link arms by placing their hands on the shoulders of the people beside them.

Activity

On "Go!" the participants pull each other, trying to get the others to go into the circle on the floor. You can also place a ball in the circle and have the children try to be the person kicking the ball out of the circle. Pulling should occur as the participants try to move their bodies, not jerking the others aggressively.

Chain-Link Soccer

Six or more

Appropriate Ages

6 years and older.

Preparation

Make two parallel goal lines on the floor at least 15 feet apart. Place a soccer ball centered between the lines. Form two teams of at least three people each. Team members stand on their goal line; they form a line by putting their arms around each other's shoulders.

Activity

On a signal, the teams remain linked and move toward the ball. Each team tries to kick the ball across the opposing team's goal line. If a team member becomes unlinked, the team must be rejoined before its members can kick the ball again. Team members should not jerk one another by yanking each other's arms.

 Caterpillar Crawl

Two or more

Appropriate Ages

8 years and older.

Preparation

The participants start out standing in a line. The person at the end of the line sits down in a straddle position with his hands on the floor behind him. The next person sits down close enough for the person behind to wrap his legs around the person's waist. The front person keeps his feet on the floor.

Activity

On "Go!" everyone lifts his bottom off the floor, and the whole "caterpillar" moves forward (see figure 8.12). Children will need to use a lot of arm strength to lift their bottoms, and they must call out which leg is moving forward. Have the children do this activity as a race between caterpillars or against a stopwatch. Just practicing being a caterpillar is a lot of work!

 Tug-of-War

Two or more

Appropriate Ages

8 years and older.

Figure 8.12 The Caterpillar Crawl.

Preparation

Lay a rope out straight. Tie a scarf around the center of the rope. On either side of the scarf make marks on the floor about two feet apart toward each end of the rope. Participants pick up the rope, keeping the scarf between the marks.

Activity

On "Go!" participants try to pull the scarf over the mark on their side of the rope. The first team to do so wins. An adult should supervise this activity to ensure that children do not let go while they are pulling. Participants should not wrap the rope around their bodies.

If you do not have a heavy rope, you can tightly twist a sheet. Do not use any material that might rip when it is pulled—both teams would end up falling backward if the rope broke.

chapter 9
The Tactile System

When people refer to the tactile system, they are talking about the sense of touch. The sense organ for the tactile system is the skin. Therefore, the tactile system receives information when something comes in contact with the skin. Some professionals use the term *haptic* to talk about the tactile system. Haptic is a term that combines the sense of touch that occurs on the skin with movement of the body. The theory is that there is seldom a movement of the body that does not involve some stimulation to the skin, and, most of the time, stimulation to the skin causes some reaction in the body. However, for our purposes in this book and to keep the two types of stimulation separate, references we make to the tactile system will include anything that touches the skin, regardless of any movement of the body.

This chapter, like the last one, presents five major topics. It discusses the tactile receptors, overviews the tactile system and its development, and describes a series of tests that parents and teachers can use to evaluate the tactile system. Then it explains common problems related to the tactile system and suggests movement programs and activities to help children with those tactile problems.

TACTILE SYSTEM RECEPTORS

The receptors or sense organs for the tactile system lie within the various layers of the skin (see figure 9.1). There are seven different types of skin receptors that are stimulated by touch, pressure, temperature, and pain. Scientists used to believe that each type of skin receptor responded to a different stimulus. Recently they have determined that once a stimulus is received, all of the receptors cooperate in a response. The information

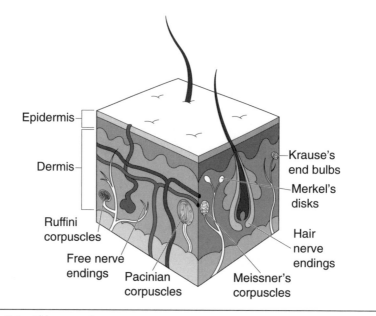

Figure 9.1 Skin receptors.

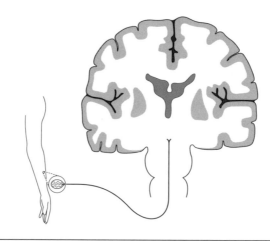

Figure 9.2 Tactile stimulation traveling to the brain.

then travels along nerves to the spinal cord, crosses the spinal cord, and goes on to various parts of the brain (see figure 9.2).

Stimulation of the touch receptors occurs most often as children use their hands, feet, and other parts of their bodies. Both handling objects and moving across a surface involve *active touch*. In contrast, when someone or something (such as an insect) contacts a part of the body, *passive touch* occurs. The skin's touching such items as clothes, equipment, chairs, and all varieties of furniture and objects also results in passive stimulation.

The hands and fingers in humans contain a lot of tactile receptors that makes them highly sensitive to pressure. The fingers are especially adapted for gaining information through touch. The hands and tips of a child's fingers are therefore some of the most important parts of his body for gathering information about the external world.

THE TACTILE SYSTEM AND ITS DEVELOPMENT

Information gained through stimulation of the skin receptors is important for learning about the environment and protecting our bodies. The tactile system is one of the first sensory systems to develop in a baby, functioning in the fetus as early as seven and a half weeks after conception. Sensitivity to touch is greatest in the mouth, lips, tongue, fingers, and hands. During the prenatal period and the first few months of life, the mouth is one of the few ways in which an infant gains information about the world. This is one of the reasons why infants and toddlers put everything in their mouths.

Tactile Discrimination

One of the major responsibilities of a tactile system is to enable a child to tell the difference (to discriminate) between such things as skin moisture and the size, shape, weight, and texture of objects touched or held in his hands. Discrimination is especially important when using the hands to manipulate objects and instruments. When a ball is placed in the hand of a child whose vision is blocked, he can feel the weight of the ball and the texture of the surface touching his hand. However, if he uses his proprioceptive system to close his fingers around the ball, he will be able to add still more to the description.

The child also uses discrimination in evaluating objects or people that touch his or her skin. Does the clothing feel comfortable, scratchy, or too tight? Is the coat heavy or light? When a grandparent tickles a baby, does he seem tense and uncomfortable or does he enjoy it but know when he has had enough? (See figure 9.3).

Development of Body Schema

Children are able to identify where on the body they have been touched, how they were touched, and even how many times they were touched, a phenomenon that is possible because of the *localization of touch*. Some

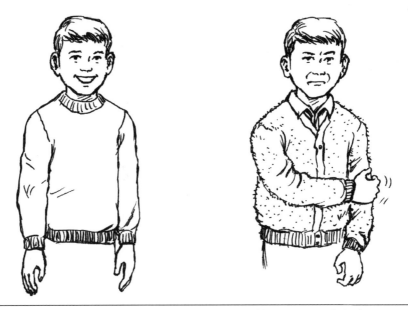

Figure 9.3 Reaction to tactile stimulation caused by texture of clothes.

people call this same ability the *perception of touch*, which is just another term for this phenomenon. The ability to localize touch is directly related to body schema. Children vary greatly in their ability to recognize touch, and they will respond differently according to the area of the body. Newborn infants have little ability to discriminate touch. They may feel that their diapers are wet without knowing exactly where the diapers are on their bodies.

Even before birth, stimulation to various parts of a fetus starts to build an awareness of body schema. This enables a newborn to turn her head toward food when the edge of her mouth is stroked or touches a nipple. The tactile system creates a bond between her and her caregivers. She learns about her body and where it begins and ends, as well as what objects and people are in her surrounding environment. The system supplies the neurological information that establishes a map in her brain of the body parts, and this starts the formation of body schema. In addition, touch enables a child to form a stable foundation for a positive body image, which leads to emotional and social development.

Each area of the body that is touched has a special area in the brain's sensory cortex where the stimulation is recorded and where it creates a map of the skin surface (see figure 9.4). In this way, every touch to the body travels to a specific area in the map and tells the child where contact was made. The fingers, thumbs, and lips are the most sensitive

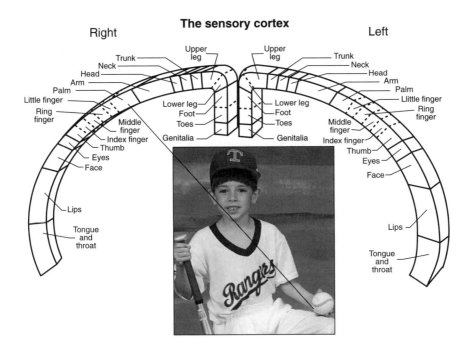

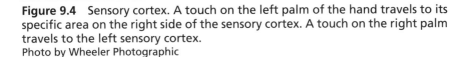

Figure 9.4 Sensory cortex. A touch on the left palm of the hand travels to its specific area on the right side of the sensory cortex. A touch on the right palm travels to the left sensory cortex.
Photo by Wheeler Photographic

parts of the body. Spaces in the sensory cortex created by impulses from these sensitive areas are larger than the combined space reserved for impulses from all of the other body parts!

The Tactile System and Pain

An intact tactile system acts as a warning device, which is essential for the protection of a child's body. The receptors are sensitive to stimulation that has the potential to damage or injure the skin. The tactile system responds to temperature (especially heat), cutting, crushing and piercing injuries, and pain. Other deeper receptors are involved in sending impulses concerning pain to the spinal cord and brain. These are located in blood vessels, muscles, and sheaths that cover bones, internal organs, and other structures.

When a child's skin receptors perceive a stimulus as painful or dangerous enough to cause injury, such as when her hand touches a hot stove, her response must be fast. In this case, the stimulus will activate a *spinal (muscle) reflex*. The stimulus travels along her nerves to her spinal cord, but instead of crossing the cord and going to the brain, a reflex response occurs. This reflex response sends messages to the muscles of her hand and arm, which pull her hand away from the stove. The reflex response lessens the amount of time her hand would be in contact with the stove and perhaps prevents serious injury (see figure 9.5). This is done without any involvement of the brain.

There are several ways for the pain caused by trauma to the skin to be modified (blocked or inhibited). One theory is called the *Gate Control Theory* or *Gating*. According to this theory, which has relevance to children with learning or behavior problems, gating involves stimulation of the skin receptors and revolves around signals sent to the spinal cord by both the large and the small fibers. Tactile information sent through the small fibers excites the neurons in the spinal cord and causes pain. Tactile sensory information sent through the large fibers, on the other hand, acts to block or modify neurons within the spinal cord that cause pain. Children, therefore, experience pain when action through the small fibers is not blocked by action in the large fibers.

Figure 9.5 Spinal cord reflex.

In order to block or modify pain, sensations must be sent through the larger fibers. We do this when we apply deep pressure, by rubbing or pressing, for example, to the area surrounding a painful stimulus. Deep pressure activates both the receptors of the skin and the deep receptors of the muscles, bones, and tissues surrounding the injury. For instance, if a child hits his shin on the coffee table, he feels an immediate sharp, intense pain, which is reduced when he rubs the area. Rubbing activates the larger fibers that reduce the pain (figure 9.6).

Don't Forget . . .

✔ The hand, along with the fingertips, is equipped with many tactile receptors that play an important role in the ability to gather information.

✔ Tactile receptors enable a child to discriminate between size, shape, texture, weight, and more.

✔ When a touch on a part of the skin reaches its specific area in the sensory cortex of the brain, maps of body schema are created.

✔ Early touch and tactile experiences between a child and the people in his environment are the foundations for body image and future emotional and social development.

✔ Receptors in the skin alert a child to possible damage to the skin.

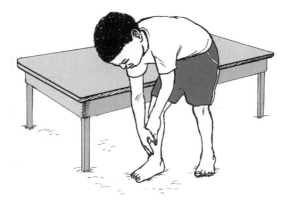

Figure 9.6 Reduction of pain by stimulating the large fibers.

Suppression of Tactile Information

One of the most important functions of the tactile system is to enable the brain to *suppress* or *ignore* a vast amount of the information it receives though the skin. An estimated four or five times more stimulation occurs to the skin than the information about it that actually reaches the brain. Much of this information is not needed to function in the environment, and it is sensory data that does not appear as a danger or a threat to a child.

Consider the amount of tactile stimulation that occurs when a child dresses in the morning. At first, he feels the clothes touching his body and senses whether the clothing is soft, rough, tight, or loose. Eventually, his nervous system ignores or suppresses most of the continuous tactile stimulation. Similarly, other such ordinary stimuli as socks and shoes, chairs or car seats, wind, water, and incidental touches by a relative or friend are best ignored.

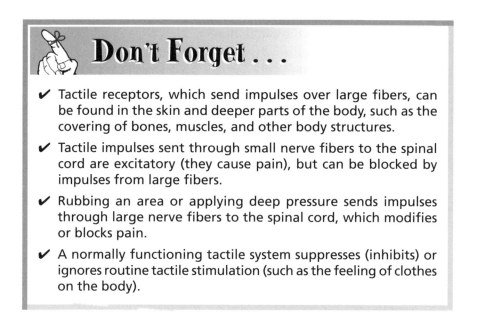

Don't Forget . . .

✔ Tactile receptors, which send impulses over large fibers, can be found in the skin and deeper parts of the body, such as the covering of bones, muscles, and other body structures.

✔ Tactile impulses sent through small nerve fibers to the spinal cord are excitatory (they cause pain), but can be blocked by impulses from large fibers.

✔ Rubbing an area or applying deep pressure sends impulses through large nerve fibers to the spinal cord, which modifies or blocks pain.

✔ A normally functioning tactile system suppresses (inhibits) or ignores routine tactile stimulation (such as the feeling of clothes on the body).

EVALUATING THE TACTILE SYSTEM

Teachers and parents can evaluate the stability of a child's tactile system through formal tests, informal observations, and interviews or questioning. In most cases, you should gather data from all three of these sources before deciding how the tactile system is functioning. When you examine a child's tactile system, you need to observe the child over a period of time. The tactile stimulus should be presented in a random manner so that the youngster isn't able to anticipate the procedure you plan to use.

Tests for Localization of Touch

To evaluate the *localization of touch* you can use the *one-touch method* or *two-touch method*. An example of a one-touch evaluation item is the *Skin-Touch Tactile Awareness Evaluation*. The version of this test presented here is a modification of the tests used by physicians at the Mayo Clinic, material presented in a *Compendium* published by Ciba Pharmaceutical Company (Lucey 1974) and Jean Ayres (1980). The parts of the body to be examined need to be as free as possible from clothes that would interfere with the touches involved in the test. Therefore, a child should be wearing shorts and a short-sleeved shirt. He will be blindfolded during the test. Demonstrate what you plan to do and explain it to the child before you begin the evaluation.

To begin the test, blindfold the child, who is standing in front of an examiner. The examiner takes an object (such as a small piece of cotton or the eraser on a pencil), dips it in powder or chalk dust, and applies a light pressure with it to different parts of the child's body (figure 9.7). Ask the child to place his index finger on the spot marked with the powder. When the child is lightly touched, the chalk mark that remains can be used to determine how close the child came to identifying the area touched. He passes an item when he places his index finger on or within a half inch of the spot the examiner touched.

The order in which the child is touched should be a random sequence that varies from one part of the body to another and from side to side. The top of both forearms, hands, and legs as well as both sides of the face are important parts to evaluate. Information gathered from looking at the test results can tell you not only whether a child has the ability to localize touch but also which parts of the body are sensitive and whether he finds the stimulation uncomfortable. Some children will correctly identify touch on the upper part of the body, but not the lower part. Others may feel nothing on one side of the body.

This test can also indicate signs of a midline problem. Does the child fail to cross the middle of the body with the preferred hand to identify a touch on the opposite side of the body? In this case, he will try to use his right hand to touch all the areas on the right side of his body, and then switch to his left hand when he receives a stimulus on his left side. However, a touch on his forearm forces him to cross his midline, and he

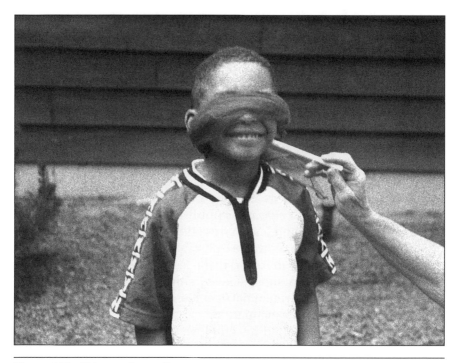

Figure 9.7 Skin touch tactile awareness test.

may hesitate locating that touch. Remember that a child with a midline problem can cross his midline but will try to avoid doing so.

You can see an example in table 9.1 of the difference in the ability of elementary school children to localize touch in the results of the Skin-Touch Tactile Awareness Evaluation completed on four groups of students (Cheatum 1986–1989, 1989, 1993, 1996; Cheatum and Hammond 1992). Within each group, more students could correctly identify tactile stimulation to the left and right sides of their faces than they could on other parts of their bodies. In most cases, examiners obtained the lowest scores when they touched the child's right and left forearms.

One interesting result of comparing the groups of children is that most of the correct scores obtained by the third-grade students in Arlington, Texas (Group A) were higher than those obtained by students in Michigan. These scores may reflect the different climates and types of clothing worn by each group. Children in Texas wear shorts and short-sleeved shirts through most of the year, which results in exposure of the skin to stimuli other than clothes. In contrast, children in the Midwest have longer and colder winters, which requires "bundling up"

Table 9.1
Percent of Students Who Passed the Skin-Touch Tactile Awareness
Evaluation

Body part	Group A	Group B	Group C	Group D
Left forearm	60.7L	60.3	40.4L	51.1L
Right thigh	67.4	59.2L	44.9	60
Left face	85.9*	81*	77.5*	75 *
Right hand	69.6	69.9	60.7	68.9
Right face	93.3*	79.5*	77.5*	75.6*
Left thigh	70.3	60.5	49.4	64.4
Right forearm	57.8L	55.9L	31.5L	57.8L
Left hand	71.1	68.1	55.1	75.6
Number	135	395	89	45

A: Third-grade students enrolled in 5 elementary schools in different geographic locations in Arlington, Texas. Students represented different academic-achievement levels based on scores received on state-administered achievement tests.

B: Kindergarten to sixth-grade students enrolled in 2 elementary schools in Kalamazoo, Michigan. Students scored 0–3 on the Iowa Achievement Test in reading or were experiencing learning problems.

C: Third-grade students enrolled in 6 different geographic locations in Kalamazoo, Michigan. Students represented diverse academic achievement.

D: Kindergarten to third-grade students in Parchment, Michigan. Students scored 0–3 on the Iowa Achievement Test (scores range from 0–9 with 4.5 considered average), were recommended by the reading teacher, or had low visual and vestibular scores.

clothing designed to cover the arms, legs, and head and keep the wind and cold air out.

When recording information on the Skin-Touch Tactile Awareness Evaluation, observe the way children react to the stimulus and whether or not their reactions change as the test progresses. Their reactions may be quite normal at first, but successive touches may become ever more disturbing to them. A typical reaction of children who find touch uncomfortable is to either slap the area with their hand (instead of using the index finger) or scratch or rub the area.

Two-touch tactile awareness evaluations are usually administered by neurologists and other physicians. These tests determine the smallest space between two simultaneous points of touch on the same body part that a child can recognize as two separate touches (instead of one). An individual's ability to identify two separate touches often varies from one part of the body to another. Two touches on the mouth that are very close together still can be identified as two separate sensations. In contrast, those on the back of the hands, shins, and feet have to be much farther apart in distance to be correctly identified as two separate touches.

Practitioners in various fields use other two-touch tests that involve touching the child simultaneously on two different parts of the body. Performing the Two-Touch Tactile Awareness Evaluation requires formal training and practice. Touching someone on separate parts of the body at *exactly* the same time is extremely difficult. Evaluators may think they applied two touches simultaneously; however, the child may correctly feel it as two separate touches because of the speed with which tactile stimulation travels to the brain.

Object-Identification Test

Object identification is the ability of a child to identify an object by feeling it. To test this ability, you blindfold the child and place items that are familiar to him in his hand for identification. You might ask him to identify objects such as keys, combs, and toys (figure 9.8). Some chil-

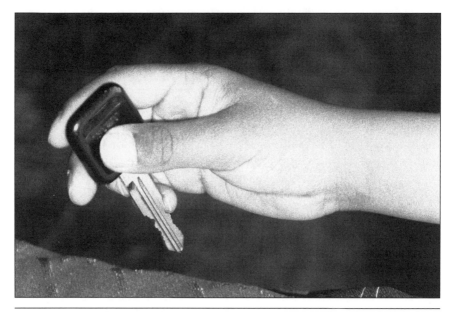

Figure 9.8 Object identification.

dren may have normal ability with one hand and not with the other. A child who has *tactile agnosia* can recognize an object by sight but not by feel alone when the object is placed in his hand.

Tracing Test

Traced-number identification is a test to determine if a child can identity numbers that are traced on various parts of his body. The evaluator first demonstrates and explains the test to the child. Choosing a digit from 0 to 9, the examiner stands and traces the number on the child's palm, fingers, or face. For accuracy, the examiner needs to stand beside the child (facing in the same direction) so that the numbers can be traced as if the child were writing them.

This test is like other tests used to determine *graphesthesia* (the ability to identify figures written on the skin). In some of the other tests, examiners make different diagrams or letters on a child's back or other parts of his body. The ability to identify writing can be a learned experience that also improves with practice. Each time a child experiences the test, he tends to improve.

Informal Observations and Interviews

Parents and teachers should spend time casually observing the behavior of a child if they suspect the youngster might have a tactile problem. The longer you can observe a child informally, the more information you can collect that will help you understand her. Notice the type of clothing she prefers to wear and whether she actually keeps it on. See if she avoids sitting on rough carpet squares, doing activities at the chalkboard, or using Play Doh or clay in art class. Is she uncomfortable standing or playing near other children? Does she become more aggressive as the day progresses?

Interviews are extremely important when a child is suspected of having trouble with his tactile system. The evaluator or teacher should gather information from the parent concerning the child's habits and reactions from the time he was an infant until his present age. Please refer to the Parent Interview Questionnaire. Questions should be directed toward the child's reaction to touch by parents, siblings, and others in his environment. It is equally important to learn about his sleeping habits, clothes, eating habits (preferred foods and those he avoids), crawling techniques, choice or avoidance of toys, emotional control, and how his reactions vary from day to day or according to the part of the body that is touched.

Other caregivers, such as grandparents, can also provide information about a child's reaction to touch. Caregivers sometimes notice the

Tactile Reactions of Children—Parent Interview Questionnaire

Sleeping patterns _____
    Type of clothing _____
    Type of covers _____
    Lights _____
    Music or noise _____
    Type of schedule _____
    Amount of sleep in 24 hours _____

Movement patterns
    Creeps and crawls with fingers curled _____
    Avoids touching carpets with bottom of feet or palms _____
    Likes to be left alone when moving _____
    Does not like others to hold hands when walking _____
    Avoids getting hands, knees, and body parts in dirt _____

Interaction with parents and siblings
    Does not like to be touched _____
    Prefers to be alone in crib _____
    Pulls back when parent tries to hold child _____
    Does not physically interact with others _____
    Avoids combing or cutting hair, washing face, etc. _____
    Avoids use of towels _____
    Responds negatively when touch is not visible
        (pat on back, etc.) _____
    Prefers baths to showers _____
    Complains when he or she has to sit close to others _____

Eating patterns
    Preferred type of food _____
    Preferred textures of food _____
    Order in which food is consumed _____
    Overreacts to food on face, hands, or body _____
    Amount of food consumed _____

Play habits
    Avoids playing with other children _____
    Avoids crayons, paste, glue, etc. _____
    Likes to play alone _____
    Prefers to play on smooth surfaces _____

Clothing
    Prefers soft textures similar to flannel blankets _____
    Prefers loose clothes _____
    Pulls hands into sleeves of shirt, sweatshirt, or coat _____
    Avoids having clothes touch palms _____

little things that a parent may overlook, such as why a child dislikes certain types of food or that he will take a nap only when he is wrapped in flannel blankets. They may also notice unusual ways a child moves, such as avoiding crawling on the carpet or whether she uses her palms on the carpet or avoids touching the rough surface of the rug.

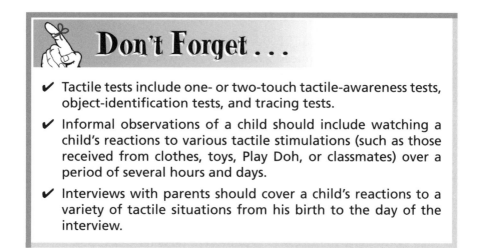

Don't Forget . . .

✔ Tactile tests include one- or two-touch tactile-awareness tests, object-identification tests, and tracing tests.

✔ Informal observations of a child should include watching a child's reactions to various tactile stimulations (such as those received from clothes, toys, Play Doh, or classmates) over a period of several hours and days.

✔ Interviews with parents should cover a child's reactions to a variety of tactile situations from his birth to the day of the interview.

TACTILE SYSTEM PROBLEMS

Jimmy has a negative response every time a classmate touches his back. He reacts by hitting his classmate. His teacher classifies Jimmy as a bully whose behavior pattern is out of control; she suggests transferring him to an alternative school.

Christiana's mother cannot understand her daughter. Every time she touches her arm to help her dress, Christiana cries and says, "You're hurting me!" Robert, on the other hand, has trouble holding his pencil, but when his teacher touches his arm to help him, he is *not aware* that she touched him until he sees her.

These children have different problems with how their tactile systems function. Although Robert's problem is different from Jimmy's and Christiana's, each of them has trouble with *tactile dysfunction,* with the way the tactile system is functioning. Children who have a dysfunctional tactile system have many of the symptoms that hyperactive children and those with learning or behavior problems have, such as restlessness, hyperactivity, a short attention span, poor attitude, and poor academic achievement.

Tactile dysfunction is a broad term, and it covers many complications that occur along the tactile neurological pathways. In this section we concentrate on the inability to localize tactile stimulus, tactile defensiveness, and tactile deprivation, three of the problems most frequently faced by teachers and parents.

Inability to Localize Touch

An inability to localize touch (tactile perception) occurs when a child cannot tell—or has a reduced awareness of—where a part of his body received tactile stimulation. The stimulus occurred but it was not received by his tactile receptors or was not processed correctly by his tactile system. He does not feel the sensation of where his clothes touch him, where someone else touches him, or where he receives an injury. Children with this inability might plow through two playmates and knock them over. Since they did not feel anything, however, they might not even be aware that they have hit their playmates or caused them to fall.

Children who have an inability to localize touch typically have learning problems related to body concept and body schema. Since they are not processing contact to the individual parts of their bodies, the map of their body parts in the brain is poor to nonexistent.

Developing the map is an example of *plasticity.* If a part of a child's body is often touched, that particular part of the sensory cortex of the brain develops and expands. When stimulation does not occur to a part of the body, that part of the brain's sensory cortex is not included in the map. Maintaining the space in the sensory map for a particular body part ceases when touch to that part of the body is missing for an extended period of time.

Children who arrive at school without such an internal map in the brain are not able to identify their body parts; they have no knowledge of the way the body parts work together. Holding a pencil is almost impossible since they simply do not know how to move their fingers around it. Lack of sensitivity from their feet will cause them balance and movement problems. If a teacher asks them to raise the right hand, they may have no idea which hand to raise so they just stare back at the teacher.

Children differ in the ways that they gain knowledge. Most of them have either a visual, auditory, or tactile-proprioceptive learner style. All children retain information when they are actively involved. This is particularly true of those youngsters who cannot localize touch. It also characterizes at-risk students who lean toward the tactile-proprioceptive style of gaining information. If academic subjects are presented to them only through the visual or auditory systems, they might have trouble grasping the information and might fail.

When these children are injured or exposed to cold temperatures they might display a similar lack of sensitivity. As a teacher or parent, you may have noticed that when some children are asked about an injury, they are unaware of when or where it happened. These children also experience temperature differently than children whose tactile systems are intact. They may run outside without a coat even when the temperature is below freezing. Their skin may feel cold to your hand, but they repeatedly insist, "I am not cold." Other children may prefer their bath temperature extremely hot; they must be supervised to avoid severe burns. You can find a summary of the symptoms that children who are insensitive to touch show in the following box.

Symptoms of Children Who Are Insensitive to Touch

Cannot identify body parts	Has poor balance skills
Has poor spatial awareness	Has poor gross motor skills
Lacks body schema	Lacks laterality and directionality
Lacks desire to participate	Has poor awareness of right and left
Has poor body image	Has trouble finding way around school
Exhibits poor posture	
Appears clumsy	Shows poor motor skills
Is unable to adjust body to the tasks it faces	Has trouble in art class using scissors
Doesn't show refined movements	Has trouble in writing
Seeks physical contact	Lacks ability to discern shapes, textures, and weights
Has poor motor planning	

Tactile Defensiveness

Tactile defensiveness is a disorder of the tactile nervous system. A child with this problem has a tactile system that is not functioning properly and is not in balance. Tactile sensations (impulses) sent through the large nerve fibers, which are supposed to the block painful stimuli from the small nerve fibers, are not working. With tactile defensiveness, therefore, even normal touches to the surface of a child's skin, such as the feeling of clothes on the body, produce a negative and often painful reaction.

Children who are tactile defensive perceive touch as irritating and painful. They attempt to avoid contact with other people or objects. Small babies who are tactile defensive will cry when touched or held by family members but remain calm when left alone. Parents soon learn that these children prefer to sleep tightly wrapped in a soft blanket or without any clothes or blankets. Interestingly, they frequently have a similar aversion to lights and noise. At night, they can sleep only without clothes, without noise of any kind, and in a dark room.

When something touches tactile-defensive children, they cannot control what happens within their tactile system. This restricts the control they have over their reactions. Rewards and reasoning do not help. In most circumstances the children will automatically respond with a fight-or-flight reaction. The thought of being touched is almost as painful as an actual touch. Just standing in line is extremely painful for them. As a result, these children prefer to play alone; they resort to solitary activities, such as reading. When forced into contact with others, they are typically labeled as uncooperative or aggressive.

Not all children who are tactile defensive respond immediately with a negative reaction to being touched. An *accumulation factor* causes a buildup of irritations. They may be able to control their reactions and respond normally for a while, but as the day progresses, the tactile sensations build up and become too much for them (figure 9.9). A child who doesn't mind clothes in the morning might by late afternoon want to disrobe—and sometimes does take his clothes off. He might tolerate his hair being combed in the morning, but by the afternoon a teacher patting his head could trigger a fight-or-flight reaction. People with a normal functioning tactile system can also experience the accumulation effect when they try to wear a rough wool sweater next to their skin. Add to this a stressful day, poor lighting, the phone ringing, and noisy traffic, and the overall effect on their nervous system can be terrible.

Children with tactile defensiveness have difficulty concentrating on academic activities or even behaving normally. Normal tactile stimuli found in classroom activities can be overpowering for them. Sensations that are ignored by the teacher and other children cause these children to be distracted. These may include all of the things that a child touches or interacts with in the classroom. They find particularly annoying the sensations from wearing clothes, sitting at their desks, touching their desks, and handling objects such as paints, crayons, and paste.

Figure 9.9 Accumulation effect of tactile stimulation.

When 135 third-grade students in Arlington, Texas, took the Skin-Touch Tactile Awareness Evaluation, results suggested that some of the students were tactile defensive (Cheatum 1993). Thirty-eight of the 135 students placed their hands over at least one area stimulated instead of using their index finger. Twenty students actually rubbed the area touched, trying to reduce the painful or itchy effects of the stimulus. Many of these students did not have a reaction until the last few touches. However, one child was so tactile defensive that he vigorously rubbed his skin after each of the eight touches.

When possible, these children try to avoid situations that are disturbing to them. When mothers wash their faces, teachers move their hands across the page, or fathers roughhouse them, they cry or become distraught. They detest physical education activities such as sitting on carpet squares, standing in line, and handling balls that have rough surfaces. Other children bumping into them rouses their anger. Fighting is a typical reaction. Look at the list of behaviors the box titled "Common Tactile-Defensive Symptoms Seen in the Gymnasium" for occurrences teachers might observe in physical education situations. Fighting is a typical reaction for these children.

Common Tactile-Defensive Symptoms Seen in the Gymnasium

Dislikes tag games	Hates having dirt on body or hands
Avoids somersaults	Avoids standing in line
Hates being hit or tagged with a ball	Avoids back-to-back activities
Avoids most stunts with other students	Does not like logrolls
	Prefers loose-fitting clothes
Avoids sitting on rough carpet squares	Responds with fighting when touched from behind
Prefers to be alone	Responds to someone's touch by hitting
Cries when made to get into the water for swimming	Dislikes contact sports such as soccer and football
Does not like to towel dry	
Dislikes tug-of-war games	Complains about gym clothes
Socks always feel uncomfortable	Considered a troublemaker
Tries to stay back in the line	Aggressive

Tactile Deprivation

In a condition of *tactile deprivation* a child's tactile system has not received the necessary amount of stimulation for normal growth and development, which results in tactile defensiveness. This is not uncommon in children who have been raised in situations where they were not held or were left alone for long periods of time. Even in large families, younger siblings may not receive the same amount of touching, cuddling, and care given to the firstborn.

An infant receiving touch affects her ability to handle stress. The touching does not have to be done by the mother, but receiving adequate tactile stimulation is essential. This became evident in a study of Rumanian orphans and caretakers in the ratio of 20:1 (that is, with one caretaker for each 20 orphans; see Carlson et al. 1997). The orphans who had the least interaction with a caretaker had the highest levels of stress hormones and the lowest cognitive test scores. In addition, they were inactive and weighed less than children raised by parents.

Children who do not receive sufficient stimulation to the skin have a disorganized tactile system. The receptors responsible for blocking painful or dangerous stimuli are not functioning. Their symptoms are similar to those of tactile-defensive children. Every touch on a child's skin by another person, every passive stimulation from clothes, sheets, towel, and furniture is uncomfortable to the point of being painful. This can lead the child to a fight-or-flight reaction.

Don't Forget . . .

✔ Children who cannot locate tactile stimulation do not know how to hold objects and they lose their balance and fall into other people and objects.

✔ Negative responses to tactile stimulation can accumulate (build up) over time, affecting children more as the day goes on.

✔ Children who cannot suppress normal tactile stimulation received from their clothes, desk, chairs, and other objects have difficulty concentrating on schoolwork.

✔ Tactile deprivation causes an extreme aversion to touch; it occurs when a child has not received a normal amount of tactile stimulation.

CORRECTING A TACTILE PROBLEM

Developing a program of activities that will benefit children who are tactile defensive involves using a variety of activities that bring their systems into balance. Both tactile defensiveness and the inability to localize touch involve some problem with the way the tactile information is processed. Tactile deprivation happens when children do not receive a normal amount of touch, which, in turn, interferes with their ability to process the information coming into their systems when they are touched.

Activities for correcting tactile problems usually fall under the categories of indirect and direct. Indirect activities are those in which the child, almost without knowledge that she is receiving therapy, applies pressure or touch to her own body (figure 9.10). Some children may be so tactile defensive or deprived of touch that they cannot tolerate anyone touching their skin, and in some severe cases they may avoid touching themselves. The therapy program for these children should start with indirect activities. For example, encourage them to do logrolls, forward rolls, roll themselves up in a blanket, and practice swimming on a mat. As the weight of the body presses against the mat, they will receive a considerable amount of stimulation.

Direct tactile activities are those administered by someone other than the child. These include applying stimulation to a part of the child's body. The stimulus could be rubbing a child down after a bath, massage, painting a clown's face on her, or rolling balls over his body (figure 9.11). A child can tolerate touch on certain parts of the body more than on others. The top of the hands and forearms are least sensitive, followed by the top of the legs and feet. The back, back of the legs, and areas around the face and mouth are the most sensitive to touch. Leave these areas until later in an intervention program.

Creating the right environment prior to initiating a program of activities is critical. Many children apparently have an "overloaded" nervous system. They may receive an amount of information that is overwhelming to them, through their ears and eyes as well as through their tactile system.

You should direct your attention toward reducing negative or excessive stimulation. This includes having (a) neutral colors on the wall, (b) few pieces of equipment in sight of the child, (c) lights adjusted down to a level that is not irritating, (d) space suited to the temperament of the child (often a youngster prefers a small space, and you may need to use several different ones), (e) no excessive noise, and (f) only those people in the room who are directly involved in the activity.

Changing the environment also refers to changing the actions of individuals in the child's living situations. Provide activities and stimulation that organize the tactile system, but also avoid activities or actions that cause the fight-or-flight reaction. Allow the children to sit in

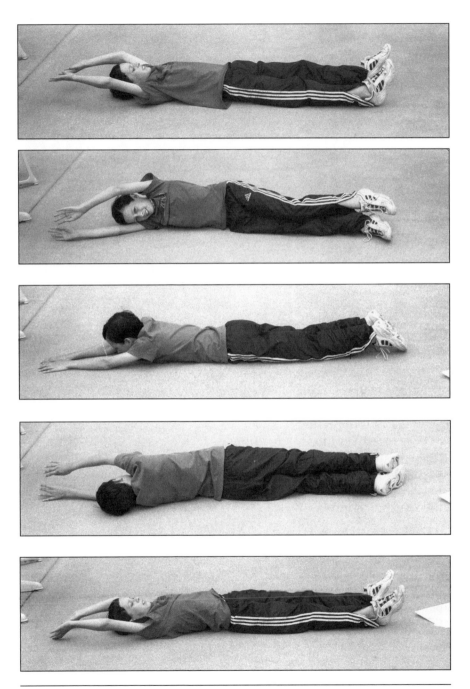

Figure 9.10 Indirect activity.

Figure 9.11 Direct activity.

the back row of the class, stand at the end of the line, and skip erasing the chalkboard. Let them wear loose clothing, and try not to touch them from behind if they can't see you.

The most successful way to bring the tactile system into balance is to stimulate the pain-blocking receptors through *deep pressure.* Pressure applied to any part of the body or to the body as a whole is helpful. This application also helps prepare the individual parts of his body for other types of stimulation. Deep pressure activities should be done before administering other types of tactile stimulation. For example, if you wish to reduce the tactile defensiveness of a child's forearms, it is helpful to apply deep pressure as you move your hands back and forth over his arms several times. If you can, avoid going against the direction that the hair is growing. The skin receptors at the base of the hairs are highly sensitive and cause further irritation.

Two easy and fun techniques to use for applying deep pressure to the whole body include rolling a heavy ball over his body and making a "hamburger." To build a hamburger, place a heavy mat on the floor (this is the bottom piece of bread). The child lies down on the mat (acting as the meat). You then cover him by another mat (the top piece of bread). Instead of just meat in the center, other children can be the

a

b

c

Figure 9.12 Making a "hamburger."

mustard, lettuce, and tomato, with each child atop the other (figure 9.12). Children should be told not to "jump" on the hamburger but to quietly lie down in the order called out. Another alternative is to have the teacher or parent lie down on the top crust, which adds more weight and thus more deep pressure to the child. This, of course, depends on the size and weight of the children and teacher.

You can also use massage to apply deep pressure. In addition to giving neurological benefits, massage has the physiological advantages of increasing blood circulation to all parts of the body, slowing down breathing, relaxing the muscles, and encouraging sleep. Many parents have found that rubbing the back of a baby helps him fall asleep. Use something such as oil to put on your hands, which allows them to glide smoothly over the child's skin. Start with the area on his body that is least defensive, such as the forearms, top of his hand, and front of his legs.

Massage is not just for babies but it can also be used to apply deep pressure to elementary schoolchildren who are tactile defensive. Use a moderately deep pressure to stimulate the skin receptors and the underlying tissues, muscles, and bones. Gradually increase the pressure. When you feel this area of the child's body relaxing, move to another site. There are a variety of books available on massage techniques for infants and older persons. Numerous types of professionals also provide massages for a fee. Some professionals are more tuned in to the muscle structure of the body, including nationally certified athletic trainers, physical therapists, and nationally certified sport masseuses.

Vibrating massagers are useful for applying deep pressure to the skin and deep structures of children. These are often called therapeutic vibrators, and you can find them in the drugstore under equipment for sore muscles. It is wise to have different varieties of massagers so that the children can have a choice among them. At first they will probably prefer to handle the vibrator themselves, since they are usually afraid of being touched. Children generally have a sixth sense about which part of their body needs or can tolerate the stimulation. Usually they will start on their forearms or the tops of their hands. Let them determine where they want the vibrator and how long to continue the stimulation. Initially, large vibrators that apply stimulation over a big area seem to be more easily tolerated. Encourage the children to move the vibrator to different sites but do not force them. It may take days or weeks for a child to feel comfortable enough to move the vibrator to other parts of the body.

Correcting an Inability to Localize Touch

Children who cannot locate tactile stimulation on their bodies benefit from therapy directed toward the tactile, proprioceptive, and vestibular systems. These children do not respond correctly to touch sensations and have trouble in the areas of body concept, body schema, laterality, and directionality. Use some activities from chapter 5 under the body-awareness section. If the child has performed poorly in body-concept test items, direct the activities toward combining movement and tactile stimulation with identification of the body parts. It is particularly important to apply deep pressure to stimulate the tactile receptors while also moving the various parts of the body.

Start therapy sessions with some of the vestibular activities found in chapter 7 to organize the sensory system. You can also add the activities suggested in chapter 8 for proprioceptive problems; these can also benefit a child who is insensitive to touch. Any movement that is used to contract, shorten, or stretch the muscles or that applies joint compression or traction will stimulate some of the deep skin receptors. Even putting weights on different parts of the body helps to involve the proprioceptive and tactile systems. Unless there is some special medical problem, impulses that travel to the brain will gradually begin to form a map of the body and body parts. Many of the activities in this chapter under "Correcting Tactile Defensiveness" provide beneficial stimulation to the skin and deep tactile receptors.

Let's return to an example of how a sensory motor program influenced the tactile awareness of elementary schoolchildren. In one study, kindergartners through third-grade students took pretests and posttests of the Skin-Touch Tactile Awareness Evaluation (see table 9.2; Cheatum and Hammond 1992; Cheatum 1986–1989). After taking the pretest, these children received a daily, 30-minute sensory motor program for 10 weeks. The first 15 minutes of the sensory motor program was devoted to vestibular activities, with the remainder of the period devoted to other activities. No effort was made to apply tactile stimulation. At the end of the 10-week program, the children again took the tactile-awareness test. Gains of more than 10 percent occurred for the left and right forearms as well as for the left and right thighs. There was a slight gain of 3.3 percent for the right face and 3.4 for the right hand.

Discrimination activities also help youngsters with problems of touch localization. Since their neurological pathways have not experienced much tactile sensation, the youngsters have no basis for telling

Table 9.2
Percent of K–3rd-Grade Students Who Passed the Skin-Touch Tactile Awareness Evaluation Before and After a 10-Week Sensory Motor Program

Body part	Pretest	Posttest	Change
Left forearm	51.1	61.7	+10.6
Right thigh	60	70.2	+10.2
Left face	75	72.3	–2.7
Right hand	68.9	72.3	+3.4
Right face	75.6	72.3	+3.3
Left thigh	64.4	74.4	+10.0
Right forearm	57.8	68	+10.2
Left hand	75.6	72.3	–3.3
Number	45	47	

the difference between objects. The games and activities you can use to teach children to discriminate are unlimited. Blindfold the child, for example, so that he has to rely on his tactile system; see the Touchy-Feely Bags Game and Blindfolded Treasure Hunt in Rice Bowl later in this chapter.

Don't Forget . . .

- ✔ Direct activities involve the child or someone else applying tactile stimulation to his skin.
- ✔ Changes in the environment (for example, using neutral room colors, reducing noise, dimming or repositioning lighting) are necessary for a tactile-defensive child to improve.
- ✔ Children who cannot localize touch will need tactile stimulation as well as activities that focus on the proprioceptive system and body concept, body schema, laterality, and directionality.
- ✔ Children who cannot localize touch benefit from vestibular, proprioceptive, and discrimination activities.

Activities for the Localization of Touch

Activities that develop the localization of touch stimulate various body parts. These also help children learn the names of the various parts. For example, while massaging a nine-month-old infant's feet, you might say, "These are your feet, and here are your toes." Eventually, ask the child to tell you what part of the body you are touching. Or while a child is using whipped cream to "body-paint" her face, you might ask her to tell you which part she will paint next.

Massage

Individual or partners

Appropriate Ages

Infants and older.

Preparation

Various baby oils, lotions, and massage oils are available commercially. Be sure to read the bottle for any precautions. Oils that have fragrances or other additives may not be safe for infant's delicate skin.

Libraries and bookstores have books on basic massage techniques for infants and children. These will give you more information about how to give a massage.

Activity

Children may want to massage themselves first before another person does. The best time to do a massage is just before or after bath time. Children can rub down with their towels or washcloths. Some children will benefit from massage before they participate in activities with others. The massage helps their tactile systems prepare for interactions that may include touch. You should also quietly name or have the child name which body parts are being massaged.

These are some good items to use for massage:

Small balls	Vibrating massagers
Rolling pins	Soft cloths

Whenever you massage a child, you should progress in the following order, which is from least to most sensitive:

1. Back of the forearms and hands
2. Front of the legs
3. Back
4. Stomach
5. Face

As you massage a child or the child massages himself, your hands should move slowly and firmly (ask the child if you are pressing too hard). Light, fluttery touches are irritating. Your hands should also be warm. Hand movements can be long strokes about the length of the limb or back. Circle motions that are slow and cover a large surface of the skin are also good.

Body Painting

Individual or group

Appropriate Ages

18 months and older.

Preparation

This is a great outdoor or bath-time activity. Use a small amount of food coloring to dye a container of prepared whipped cream or use chocolate and vanilla pudding. Place the "paints" in containers, such as small plastic bowls.

Activity

Let the children paint themselves using their hands with the "paint." Encourage them to paint lots of body parts—a face on their knees, dots on their faces, and so forth. Ask the children which part of the body they are painting. If they know and trust each other, you might also have them paint each other, especially on their backs. For clean up, just hose everyone down.

This activity is also good for children who are tactile defensive and who may have difficulty getting started because the "paint" feels awful to them. You may need to have these children start painting with a clean paintbrush or a spoon. Be careful when you hose them down afterward, because the water hitting them is a new sensation and may cause a negative reaction.

Mud Pies

Individual or group

Appropriate Ages

3 years and older.

Preparation

Do this activity outside or inside over plastic drop cloths or thick newspapers. Use mud you find outside or mix water with potting soil. Give each child a small pile of the mixture in a plastic bowl or on a plate.

Activity

Spread the mud around the bowl and then mix it into balls or other shapes. Encourage the children to use their hands in the mud, rather than using utensils such as spoons or shovels.

Body-Part Naming Songs

Individual or group

Appropriate Ages

3 years and older (or check the recommended age on the recording).

Preparation

Look for commercially recorded songs in which children not only name body parts but also use them in different ways, such as stamping their feet, clapping their knees, and patting their faces. A good example is "What a Miracle," published by Hap Palmer Records of Educational Activities.

Activity

Play the recordings and help the children understand that they should follow the words' directions or what the singer says. The songs need to do more than just having the children pointing. They must direct the children providing touch stimulation to their body parts. You may need to alter some of the movements to provide tactile stimulation (i.e., tap your head rather than point to your head.)

Sand Castles

Individual or group

Appropriate Ages

18 months and older.

Preparation

Sandboxes should be part of the life of all children. In the summer, playing in an outdoor sandbox is ideal. Indoors, a new, clean cat's litter box or other large flat containers work well as a substitute sandbox. Have large kitchen spoons and plastic bowls on hand for the children to use.

Activity

The children can use the large kitchen spoons and plastic bowls to build sandcastles. Use a small spray bottle filled with water to wet the sand. When children are playing in an outdoor sandbox, encourage them to sit in the sand and be barefoot for maximum tactile experience.

Play Dough

Individual or group

Appropriate Ages

3 years and older.

Preparation

You can purchase Play Doh or make your own. Here is a simple homemade recipe for the dough from Liza Wolfe's book *The Best for Kids* (1990):

1 cup water	1/2 cup salt
1 tablespoon cooking oil	1 tablespoon alum (available
Food coloring	in the spice section at the
1 cup flour	grocery store)

Combine water and oil in a saucepan and bring it to a boil (add the food coloring now if you like). Remove liquid from the heat and add the dry ingredients. Mix well and dump onto a floured surface. After the dough cools a bit, knead it to remove all the lumps.

If you did not add the food coloring before, you can knead it in now. This part of making the play dough can be fun.

Activity

Once the dough is colored and kneaded, it is ready to be molded, cut, and rolled into anything your child chooses. When she is through with the play dough, store it in an airtight container. Or you can let her creations dry.

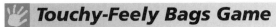

Touchy-Feely Bags Game

Individual or group

Appropriate Ages

4 years and older.

Preparation

Fill several small paper bags with a variety of textured items. Place a different textured item in each bag. For example, one bag could have an apple, and another, a fuzzy slipper. Write a number on each bag, from one to however many bags there are. Give each child a pencil and a piece of paper with a number for each bag listed.

Activity

Each child gets a bag and *without looking* in the bag feels inside for its contents. He or she writes down what he thinks is in the bag by the number on the list that corresponds to the number on the bag. Then, the bag is passed to the next child. Continue until each child has had a chance to identify the contents of all the bags. At that point, see who named the most items correctly. For children who cannot write, a partner or adult can be assigned to write down the answers. Little children can whisper what they think is in each bag to an adult.

Blindfolded Treasure Hunt in Rice Bowl

Individual

Appropriate Ages

4 years and older.

Preparation

Fill a four- or five-quart plastic bowl with rice. Mix buttons, pennies, marbles, or other "treasures" into the rice. Place the bowl on a cookie sheet or large piece of paper. You'll also need a stopwatch or clock with a second hand.

Activity

Blindfold the child and have him carefully search through the rice for the treasures. Use a stopwatch to see how quickly he can find all of the treasures. Larger items are easier to find. As he improves his ability to feel the treasures, try using paper clips or macaroni as the treasure.

Blindfolded Touch-and-Say

Partners

Appropriate Ages

5 years and older.

Preparation

One of the partners puts on a blindfold and stands facing the other partner.

Activity

The partner without the blindfold gently touches the other on a body part. The blindfolded partner must touch the spot where he was touched and say the name of the part. Children who are tactile defensive may be fearful of being blindfolded. You might ask these children to shut their eyes instead.

Blindfolded Scavenger Hunt

Partners

Appropriate Ages

5 years and older.

Preparation

Set up an obstacle course of boxes, chairs, cones, and so forth. Place five or six objects that have various textures throughout the obstacle course. Be sure that all of the obstacles are secure and that extra objects are removed from the hunting area.

Activity

One partner is blindfolded and begins to walk or crawl through the obstacle course. Using hands and feet to go through the obstacle course, he tries to find and identify all the objects. The partner may tell the blindfolded person how to move. For example, the partner may tell the blindfolded person to get in a crawling position and go straight to pass through a box.

Correcting Tactile Defensiveness

There are three considerations to keep in mind when you work with children who are tactile defensive: (a) how long it takes for activities to start making a difference in the child's tactile system; (b) how long the change lasts that day; and (c) how many days, weeks, and months it takes to make a permanent change in the individual's tactile system. At the beginning of an activity program to correct tactile defensiveness, it usually takes 10 to 15 minutes before the tactile system begins to come into balance. Following the activity session, the change may last from 30 to 60 minutes. However, be assured that with each session the time the change in his tactile system lasts will lengthen.

Certainly, the time it takes to bring the tactile system into balance depends upon the severity of the problem, the age of the child, and the number of days a week he or she receives therapy. One seven-year-old child enrolled in the Special Physical Education Learning Laboratory at Western Michigan University often complained that a slight touch on her arm hurt her. The pain of touch was so intense that she avoided contact with her parents. Although she participated in activities twice a week, it was a year before her mother could sit beside her on the couch and put her arm around her. Wilbarger and Royeen (1987) suggest that parents of a tactile-defensive infant use massage and joint compression each time the child has a diaper change or a bath. This provides approximately six or seven therapy sessions a day and greatly reduces the time before positive results occur.

Pay attention to erratic behavior. Does a child like to be hugged sometimes and but cry at other times? What type of hug started the crying? What type of hug was tolerated? A tactile-defensive child usually likes long bear hugs that apply deep pressure (balancing the tactile system) but will pull away from short, jerky hugs or patting. Does he resist certain type of clothes or socks? If so, change them. Dress him in clothes that do not disturb his system. Gradually—and this may take years— move him toward other types of clothes.

Don't Forget . . .

✔ Depending on the severity of the problem, changes in a child's ability to process tactile information may take months or years.

✔ Tactile-defensive children enjoy deep pressure contact, such as bear hugs.

Activities for Children With Tactile Defensiveness

Activities using deep pressure help the body learn to trigger the neurons that inhibit pain. In addition, deep pressure sends messages through the touch receptors that help strengthen the internal map of the body, which increases body awareness. The activities in this section provide deep pressure. As you invite children who are tactile defensive to join in, you must carefully watch for signs of stress. Is the child becoming withdrawn or aggressive? Is he trying to control the situation by being silly (so that the game cannot continue)? Give the children a way to let you know when they have had enough. For example, the child could say, "I need a break."

Massage

Use the massage tips found in the earlier section on Activities for the Localization of Touch. Children who are extremely tactile defensive may first need to learn to self-massage as a start. They can rub their hands, feet, legs, and arms.

Roll Out the Pizza Dough

Individual or partner

Appropriate Ages

3 years and older.

Preparation

A child pretends she is a piece of dough and lies on her stomach on a mat or blanket. The "pizza chef" can use a large ball or bolster (tube-shaped) pillow to roll out the "dough."

Activity

Roll the child's back, legs, and arms or have the partner do this. Then have the partners switch places. For deeper pressure, you can gently use a real rolling pin. Be sure that the child who is the dough is comfortable being rolled. This may be an advanced activity for a child with tactile defensiveness. It may be best to let him or her start as the "pizza chef."

Musical Chairs Pile-On

Group

Appropriate Ages

5 years and older.

Preparation

Place five or six children in each group. Set as many chairs as there are children in a circle. Each child sits on a chair to start.

Activity

When the music plays, the participants walk, hop, or crawl (but do not run) around the inside of the chair circle. When the music stops, each participant finds a chair. The next time the music plays, one chair is removed as the participants move around the circle. When the music stops, everyone finds a chair and, as necessary, sits on another child's lap. Repeat the game until only one chair is left and all participants are trying to sit on one chair (figure 9.13). Then start adding the chairs back to the circle. A child who is tactile defensive may not enjoy this game unless he is familiar with the other participants. This would be a game for children who have either

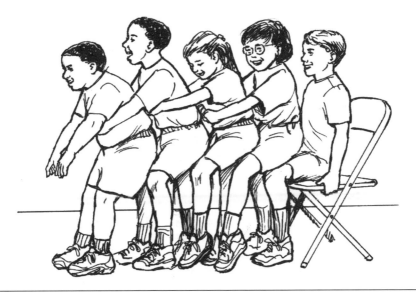

Figure 9.13 Musical Chairs Pile-On.

had individual massage before participating or who are becoming more tolerant to touch.

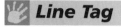 Line Tag

Group

Appropriate Ages

6 years and older.

Preparation

Activity

Use a small, defined space rather than a large outdoor area or gymnasium. One person is "It." When It tags another child, the two hook arms and both become a new It. Continue the game until all children have been tagged and have joined the line. You may need to limit the number of children who attach together before changing who is It. A child who is tactile defensive may need to break from the group before everyone has been caught.

Centipede Relay

Group

Appropriate Ages

6 years and older.

Preparation

Mark start and finish lines on the floor. Divide the group into teams of four or five children. Have the teams line up behind a starting line. If you have only four or five children, have them race against a stopwatch.

Activity

On "Go!" the first team member runs to the finish line and back. Then, the second team member holds the shoulders of the first, and both run to the finish line and back. Continue this process until all team members are joined at the shoulder, looking like centipedes, and have them run to the finish line and back. Then, the team must sit down, still holding shoulders to indicate the team is done.

 *Changing Clothes Relay*

Group

Appropriate Ages

8 years and older.

Preparation

You will need one extra-large T-shirt and extra-large shorts per team of four or six people. For added fun, you could also have a hat, coat, and mittens. (Do not use socks—they are too slippery to run on.) Mark both a start and finish line, and place each set of clothes in a pile on the finish line opposite each team. If you don't have enough children for teams, you can have the children race against a stopwatch.

Activity

On the "Go!" signal, the first child runs to the pile of clothing and puts them on (over his own clothing). He returns to his team at the start line and takes the clothes off. The next team member in line puts the clothes on and runs to the finish line. He then removes the clothes and runs back to his team at the start line. Then the next child runs to put on the clothing. Continue the process until all team members have had a chance to put on and take off the clothing.

chapter 10
The Visual System

Mary thinks it is normal for the words on the page to be blurry. Jacob constantly blinks his eyes and cannot seem to locate his place in his book. His teachers believe he is not paying attention. Jill can read for about 10 minutes before she rapidly loses her concentration and begins to squirm and look out the window. These children all have problems with their visual system.

Visual problems, particularly in elementary schoolchildren, often go undetected. They have earned the name *hidden disabilities.* The national organization Parents Active for Vision Education states that about 25 percent of children and 70 percent of juvenile delinquents have visual problems. Children who have been labeled with *attention deficit hyperactive disorder* often have some symptoms that can be traced to learning-related visual problems.

The eyes are a window that connects the world to the brain. Visual images received through the eyes provide 80 to 90 percent of the information that a brain receives. Children who are having problems with their vision are getting distorted views of most of the information going to their brains. When these distorted images are combined with information from the vestibular, tactile, proprioceptive, and auditory systems, the information can be mildly or severely disorganized.

Visual problems interfere with a child's ability to learn. Generally speaking, the youngster tries to do her lessons. However, the visual demands are too much for her system. You may observe a child putting a hand over one eye, using the fingers to follow a line in reading, or moving the head instead of her eyes.

If the problems continue to go undetected and untreated, an undue amount of stress is placed on the child's nervous systems, triggering fight-or-flight responses. Then he resorts to behaviors such as dropping a pencil, talking to the person next to him, pretending he doesn't care, or claiming that he doesn't like to play sports. The result is that the child is not learning to read but is instead developing a series of behavior patterns that can isolate him from classmates and follow him throughout the school years.

This chapter covers five major topics: (1) the visual system's receptors, (2) the relationship between the visual system and motor development, (3) techniques for evaluating the visual system, (4) visual problems, and (5) activities that are useful for children who have visual problems.

VISUAL SYSTEM RECEPTORS

The eyes are the receptors for the visual system. They are spherical in shape and approximately one inch in length. Each eye rests in a hole called an *orbit* (socket), which protects the sides of the eyeball from injury. There are three layers to the eye. The outer layer consists of the cornea and the firm white skin of the eyeball called the *sclera* (see figure 10.1). Six tiny muscles, located externally on each eye, are connected to the top, bottom, and sides of the sclera.

The *iris* is the colored part of the eye, and it has an opening in the middle called the *pupil.* The iris is actually a muscle that controls the size of the pupil based on the amount of light in the environment. When there

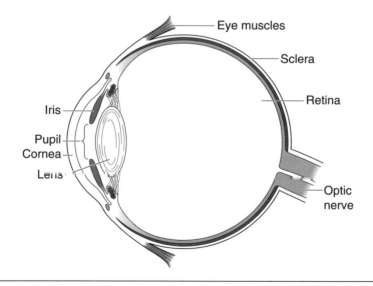

Figure 10.1 Structures of the eye.

is a large amount of light entering the eye, the iris contracts; when the light is dim, it expands. The *lens,* which separates the anterior part of the eye from the posterior, lies behind the pupil. Within the inner part of the eye is the *retina,* which fills almost 60 percent of the space occupied by the eye and forms the posterior part of the eyeball. At the back of the retina a group of nerve cells mesh together to become the *optic nerve.*

The eyelids function like shutters on cameras. When they are open, light rays can enter the eyes. *Sight* is the process by which the light rays are changed into visual images. Light passes through the cornea and the pupil to the lens (see figure 10.2). The lens brings the images into focus and then onto the retina. As the images are passed through the retina, they are changed into *nerve* (electrical) *impulses* and passed through the optic nerve to the brain.

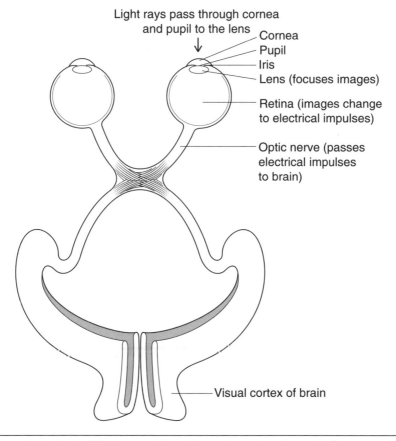

Figure 10.2 Path of light rays (visual image) passing through the cornea and the pupil to the lens, retina, optic nerve, and brain.

THE VISUAL SYSTEM
AND MOTOR DEVELOPMENT

Information gained through the eyes enables children to distinguish between people, events, and objects close by, across the room, or even miles away in the sky. They are able to tell the approximate size, shape, and color of objects and to see them in three dimensions. Children use their eyes to guide them in almost every action they take, including crawling, walking, eating, reading, writing, playing, and participating in motor skill development.

In discussing and understanding the visual process, it is helpful to first define the difference between acuity and vision. *Acuity,* often referred to as sight or *visual acuity,* is the ability to see clearly. In other words, acuity refers to the acuteness or sharpness of the image striking the retina. The nervous system that is destined to become the visual system starts to develop as early as three weeks after conception. By the time a baby is born, his or her visual system is ready for use. A newborn baby sees clearly up to a distance of about eight inches—or the distance between the infant and his or her mother's face.

Vision (*visual perception*) is a learned process that involves changing the images gained through acuity into *useful* information. At first, when a child sees his blanket it has no meaning for him. Later he learns to match the visual information with information from the other sensory systems. This total perception tells him that what he sees is his blanket. Children need still more complex visual perception in order to read. They must link the letters and words they see with how they sound and what they represent.

Vision applies to situations such as Lee's ability to determine the speed and direction of the baseball as it approaches him. It also includes understanding the differences between shapes and forms, knowing where to put the answers to the math questions, and understanding which images in the visual field suggest danger.

Acuity and vision are only part of the ability to use the eyes for physical activities and class work. Images gained through the eyes depend on a pathway known as the *vestibular-ocular reflex arc* (VOR). The purpose of the VOR is to combine images received from the eyes with information received from the rest of the sensory systems. When there is interference with sensory information received from the vestibular system, it reduces functioning of the vestibular-ocular reflex arc, and function may even be lost. This results in blurred vision, when a child moves his head or body, for example. Damage to any one of the semicircular canals of the vestibular system results in distorted vision. Visual perception also depends on several visual skills: binocular fusion, accommodation (convergence and divergence) fixation, visual pursuit (pursuit fixation), depth perception (stereopsis), visual memory, and visual sequential memory. Let's take a look at each of these skills.

Binocular fusion is the ability of the visual system to blend the images received from the two eyes into a single image. Since the eyes are located a few inches apart on the face, they have different visual fields. These fields overlap somewhat with each other. The brain then gathers the information from each eye and changes it into a single image. For example, if a child is looking at the word *balloon* from the phrase *the red balloon floated*, the visual field of one eye could include letters to the left of the word and the visual field of the other eye could include letters to the right of the word. Through binocular fusion, his brain merges the images, and he sees only "balloon," and not the letters to the left or right of the word. If not, he would see something like *edba onfl*, which would make no sense to him.

Accommodation is the ability of the visual system to adjust to a change in distance. The eyes remain in focus when objects move toward or away from them or when they shift their gaze from objects close to the face to those at a distance. Accommodation allows children to shift their eyes and clearly see the printed material in a book held at reading distance, the teacher across the room, or the words or mathematical problems written on the chalkboard.

Convergent accommodation (convergence) occurs when someone is called upon to focus on an object near his face or one that is moving toward his face (figure 10.3). As the object gets near his face, there is an increased amount of stress placed on his two eyes to maintain a single image, with the result that his eyes start to move toward his nose (to "cross") to help maintain focus. Children at school, completing work at their desks, depend on this convergence skill.

Divergent accommodation (divergence) is a term used to describe a person's ability to focus on an object *at a distance* or as it moves *away* from her face. When a child is reading and must suddenly look up at the teacher, her eyes will diverge to enable her to focus on the teacher.

Fixation (direct fixation) is a person's ability to look at and focus on an object for a length of time. The object might be a block, word, picture, or teacher. A newborn infant in even the first few days can fixate for a few seconds on large objects, such as a mother's face, that are within a few inches of his face. By the time he is two to three months old, fixation should be fully developed. At five or six years old, a child should be able to fixate for 10 seconds.

Visual pursuit or *visual tracking* (also called *pursuit fixation* or *ocular-motor tracking*) is used for reading a line in a book. As a child's eyes

Figure 10.3 Convergent and divergent accommodation.

move across the page, he must maintain visual attention on the printed words while gaining and losing fixation. Visual pursuit also occurs as a child follows or tracks moving objects, such as his parents walking across the room, the cars driving by, or balls in the air. Tracking requires more effort from the child's visual system than direct fixation does, since his visual system has to continually adjust the focus as the distance of the object changes.

Depth perception is the ability to tell the distance between two objects. Driving a car, walking down the aisle, driving a basketball between two opponents, and running out the door all demand good depth perception. Binocular fusion aids depth perception. If a child can fuse the objects he sees into one image, then his depth perception is good.

Visual memory (recall) is the ability to remember what you have seen when the image is removed. It depends upon visual perception (the internal recognition of the image) and being able to focus the eyes. Most babies begin to develop visual memory when they are between the ages of four and eight months. At this stage the ability is often referred to as *visual constancy*. When an object is placed in front of a baby and covered, the baby tries to remove the blanket to find the object, rather than simply thinking the object is gone once it is out of sight.

Visual sequential memory is the ability to remember a series of visual images *in correct order*. A toddler's being able to see and comprehend a series of images presented to him depends on many of the other visual functions mentioned previously in this chapter.

Visual figure-ground is the ability to separate the desired object from the rest of the information in the viewing field. We know that many newborn infants have demonstrated figure-ground skills, yet some older children may not be able to separate the assigned words or letters from the background material on the printed page. In some cases, children may reverse the process, viewing the background but not the significant object.

Professionals use the phrase *ocular motor control* to describe the ability a child develops to use the six eye muscles. The muscles connect to the top, sides, and bottom of each eye, and they allow the eyes to move in all directions for tracking. These muscles also hold the eyes steady for fixation on a target. In order for children to be able to focus both eyes on a target, they must coordinate movements of the eye muscles. If the muscles of the two eyes are not coordinated, the child receives a blurred image (or two visual images).

Don't Forget . . .

✔ Vision is the individual's ability to understand or make sense of what he sees.

✔ The vestibular-ocular reflex arc (VOR) is a pathway in the brain that combines images received from the eyes with information from the other sensory systems.

✔ Binocular fusion occurs when the visual system blends the images received from both eyes into a single image.

✔ Accommodation is the ability to focus on an object as it moves toward or away from the person.

✔ Fixation is the ability to look at and focus on an object for a length of time.

✔ Visual tracking enables a child to keep her eyes focused on a line in a book, and this ability is necessary for success in the classroom and movement activities.

EVALUATING THE VISUAL SYSTEM

Optometrists and ophthalmologists are two kinds of professionals that specialize in problems relating to the visual system. Doctors of optometry are trained to examine children for visual problems and recommend corrective glasses, contact lenses, vision therapy, and low-vision aids. Ophthalmologists are physicians who specialize in the treatment of eye diseases and are qualified to perform surgery. Selecting a professional depends on the problems and needs of the individual children.

Visual examinations should be learning related. That is, the chosen specialist should be someone who is knowledgeable in the area of developmental vision care and who believes in vision therapy. Before agreeing to an appointment, check to see if the evaluation includes these skills: (a) acuity, both near and far, (b) eye tracking, (c) fixation, (d) accommodation, (e) binocular focus, (f) depth perception, (g) visual memory, and (h) visual sequential memory. Also ask about the availability of vision therapy services in the professional's office or the local area.

Recommendations for when children should have their first professional evaluations vary from three months to three years. However, almost all professionals prefer to see them by the age of three and again before they enter elementary school. Please refer to the Preschool Visual-Maturity Evaluation. This checklist includes a few simple tasks that are useful in determining whether a child's visual system is mature enough for school. In addition to beginning to focus their eyes on objects and people in their surroundings, very young children begin to develop other reading skills. As early as 18 months, they look intently at pictures and start turning pages and pointing to pictures a few months later. When they are four and a half they like to sit close to a parent, follow the pictures and words with their eyes and recite the book by memory. At the end of a long day, weary parents often are "caught" by a child who realizes a page of the book was skipped.

After children enter school, professional examinations should be repeated annually, because vision tends to change dramatically from one year to the next. Children should also be referred for professional examinations when they are (a) performing in the lower one-third of their class, (b) performing below their potential, or (c) showing symptoms of behavior problems.

Periodically talk to children who are having academic problems. Ask them a series of questions (see the Visual Interview Questionnaire) to learn more about whether they can actually see. Do they have frequent

Preschool Visual-Maturity Evaluation

Can the child clearly see words in his book? _____

Can he look at an object for an extended period of time? _____

Can he change focus from objects near his face to those at a distance? _____

Can he tell the distance between objects? _____

Can he tell the distance between objects and himself? _____

Can he coordinate the use of his two eyes so that he receives one image? _____

Can he coordinate the use of both eyes while reading a line in a book? _____

Can he coordinate the use of both eyes while following a moving target? _____

Can he make sense of what he sees? _____

Can he see an image and remember what it is after it is removed? _____

Can he remember the sequence of objects after they have been removed? _____

---

headaches or are the words blurry? Most of these questions can be answered by children as young as those in kindergarten. Since most children think they look with both eyes, you may need to teach them the difference between looking out of one eye and using both. Do they have symptoms of visual problems, such as squinting or rubbing their eyes? If you move them from the back row to the front row because they cannot clearly see the material on the board, be sure that you again check their ability to see from the front row.

These interview questionnaires were used to test 395 kindergarten through sixth-grade students in Kalamazoo, Michigan, and you can see the results in the tables that follow (Cheatum 1986–1989). Their answers had a lot of value in identifying children who needed help. These children had learning problems or were recommended for evaluation by the reading teacher. Those who wore glasses kept them on for the evaluation. Nevertheless, more than one-fourth of the children indicated that the printing in books appeared blurred. In addition, 9 percent said material on the chalkboard was blurred, and 37.2 percent said that they frequently lost their place when reading. Twenty-eight percent also blinked when catching a ball, and 38.7 percent got tears in their eyes during reading and writing. Children who have learning problems also have trouble catching balls, particularly those thrown to the middle of the body. They usually blink or turn their head away when the ball gets close to them.

Visual Interview Questionnaire

Can you clearly see the writing on the chalkboard? yes _____ no _____

Is the writing on the chalkboard ever blurred? yes _____ no _____

Can you clearly see the printing in your textbook? yes _____ no _____

Is the printing in your textbook ever blurred? yes _____ no _____

When you are looking at something, do you see two images or one? two _____ one _____

Do you blink a lot when you're reading? yes _____ no _____

What happens when you blink your eyes? _____

When you catch a ball, do you have to blink? yes _____ no _____

Do your eyes ever water or get tears in them? yes _____ no _____

Do you use one eye or two when reading? yes _____ no _____

Do you lose your place a lot when reading? yes _____ no _____

How do you find your place again? _____

Do you read or write with your head on your desk? yes _____ no _____

Do you find it easier to read when you put your hand over one eye? yes _____ no _____

Do you rub your eyes a lot during the school day? yes _____ no _____

Do you get a headache after reading or writing tasks? yes _____ no _____

Do you get tired after reading or writing assignments? yes _____ no _____

Follow-up questions may be necessary. For example, children who are having reading problems may be under such stress visually that their eyes water, but there are other causes that make the eyes water. One child who answered "yes" to her eyes' watering, for example, said it happened when she got something in her eye. Another child said her eyes watered when the wind was cold.

Children who lose their place only periodically when they are reading seem to be able to find their place again with no help. Those who have more serious learning problems and lose their place frequently report that they have to have assistance from another student or the teacher to find their place.

Far and Near Vision

The ability to see clearly (acuity) is influenced by the way the light rays enter and land on or near the retina. *Refractive* errors occur when the light rays do not land where they should for normal vision. This results in *farsightedness* (hyperopia), *nearsightedness* (myopia) and *astigmatism*. The Snellen test is the most common test used to assess far-vision acuity for children entering school and for adults applying for a driver's license. An eye chart that contains different-sized letters on several lines is located 20 feet from the child (figure 10.4). He reads the letters on various lines and should be able to clearly read the 11/32-inch-high letters on the line that indicates sharpness of vision at 20 feet. If he can do this, he is said to have 20/20 vision, which is considered normal. It is the second score of 20 that indicates his acuity. If he cannot clearly see the letters on the line designated 20 feet, but can see letters that are twice as large on another line, he has what is called 20/40 vision. In other words, he can see at 20 feet what other people see at 40 feet. Each eye is tested separately and then both eyes are evaluated together.

The Snellen test is fast and simple to use, and a large number of children can be examined in a short period of time. This test gives an accurate view of the sharpness of vision at 20 feet (far-point vision)—and that is all it measures. Most of the demands placed on a child's visual system at school involve deskwork. Passing the Snellen test does not give any indication of the ability a child has to see clearly at reading and writing distance (near-point vision).

To measure near vision many professionals use the American Medical Association reading card. The card is placed 14 inches in front of the child, who is asked to read the line of the smallest letters that he can. Usually these letters are on line 14 and he is said to have 14/14 near-point vision. The child should have both eyes tested separately and then together.

Some children have blurred vision at 20 feet but have perfect near-point vision; they are said to be nearsighted. About one in four people in the United States is nearsighted. Students who are nearsighted and assigned seats toward the back of the classroom can clearly see material in their workbooks but have trouble accurately seeing and copying material from the chalkboard. The symptoms of nearsightedness include headaches, dizziness, squinting, covering one eye, and having trouble copying material. However, if a child with nearsighted vision is fitted with corrective lenses for distance vision and told to keep them on at all times, she is likely to have blurred vision as well as headaches and stress when doing work at her desk. A summary of the symptoms of astigmatism and near- and farsightedness is included in the box titled Symptoms of Refractive Errors.

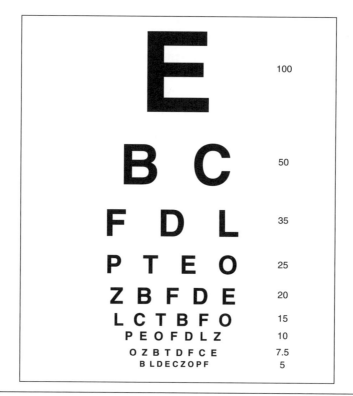

Figure 10.4 Snellen test.

Symptoms of Refractive Errors

Squinting and blinking to clearly see close work (farsightedness)

Squinting to see distance (near-sightedness)

Eyes are red

Headaches

Dizziness

Overly frequent blinking

Blinking to get vision to clear up (clarity does not last)

Covering one eye

Teary eyes

Trouble copying from material on desk to paper

Rubbing the eyes after only a short time of visual activities

Avoiding nearsighted or farsighted tasks

Declining comprehension as a task continues

Bringing book close to the face

Tiring easily

Trouble copying material from chalkboard to paper

In recent years, a growing body of information suggests that nearsightedness is brought about by doing an excessive amount of near-vision tasks and activities. Many vision problems seem to be country-specific, with nearsightedness being a good example of this phenomenon. One third of a group of Eskimos was found to be nearsighted whereas it is estimated that over two-thirds of the people in China are nearsighted.

Astigmatism is a vision problem that frequently occurs in combination with near- or farsightedness and interferes with acuity. With an astigmatism, the horizontal and vertical lines of words or letters do not come into focus at the same time, causing the word to be distorted. Children with an astigmatism will have difficulty telling the difference between letters and words. While they may see some blurring of letters, the most common symptom is an increased amount of stress when they try to get their two eyes to focus together. Merging the images from the two eyes into one is extremely difficult. To counteract this problem, children may start to use only one eye. Astigmatisms that are not corrected can lead to lazy eyes (*amblyopia*), which is a condition in which the eye muscles are weakened, causing one eye to be out of alignment with the other.

Bringing books and classroom materials excessively close to the face is a common symptom of students who have learning disabilities and learning problems. This technique is used to enlarge the letters or to compensate for other visual problems. If the youngsters continue close work for a long period of time, however, there is the strong possibility that permanent nearsightedness will result. Additional conditions that lead to nearsightedness are spending less time playing outdoors or having long study periods and poor light in the study areas. Often children who are nearsighted will have other problems, such as astigmatism or problems of convergence and visual tracking.

Visual Fixation

You can check for fixation by holding a penlight (or a pencil with a clown or other ornament on top of its eraser) about 18 to 24 inches in front of a child's nose (figure 10.5). Ask him to look at the penlight with both eyes and to continue to focus on the penlight for at least 10 seconds. A five- or six-year-old child should be able to maintain fixation for at least 10 seconds. During the 10 seconds, he may blink his eyes but not excessively. Note the number of seconds he maintains fixation and also notice if he keeps his head in a normal position. Does he need to turn his body or does he turn his head to change focus to only one eye or the other? Some children will experience so much stress during this test that their eyes water or they rub them. Other children may start

Figure 10.5 Fixation tests.

their hyperactive behavior by wrinkling their faces, shifting around in their chairs, scratching parts of their bodies, or becoming defiant.

Fixation ability can have a profound effect on how well children succeed in school, especially in reading and writing activities. If a child cannot hold her eyes steady on a reading assignment, writing activity, or even on the teacher, the information will be lost, distorted, and misunderstood. To evaluate how well children with reading and learning problems could fixate or focus their eyes, evaluators gave four groups of elementary schoolchildren a fixation test (Cheatum 1986 1989, 1989, 1993, 1996; Cheatum and Hammond 1992). Although most of these students could look at an object on the end of an eraser for 10 seconds, students in Groups B and D who had reading or learning problems were less successful than that. Maturity might have been a factor. Groups A and C consisted of third-grade students, whereas some of the students in Groups B and D were in kindergarten and the first and second grades. However, 25 percent of Group B, which also contained fifth- and sixth-grade students, could not sustain fixation for 10 seconds (see table 10.1).

Table 10.1
Number and Percent of Students Who Passed Fixation Test

Group	Number	Percent
A	130	96.3
B	293	74.2
C	83	93.2
D	37	82.2

A: Third-grade students enrolled in 5 elementary schools in different geographic locations in Arlington, Texas. Students represented different academic-achievement levels based on scores received on state-administered achievement tests.

B: Kindergarten–sixth-grade students enrolled in 2 elementary schools in Kalamazoo, Michigan. Students scored 0–3 on the Iowa Achievement Test in reading or were experiencing learning problems.

C: Third-grade students enrolled in 6 different geographic locations in Kalamazoo, Michigan. Students represented diverse academic achievement.

D: Kindergarten to third-grade students in Parchment, Michigan. Students scored 0.3 on the Iowa Achievement Test (scores range from 0–9 with 4.5 considered average), were recommended by the reading teacher, or had low visual and vestibular scores.

Accommodation and Convergence

Convergence and divergence are measured by holding a penlight or toy-topped pencil about 18 inches in front of a child's nose. He is asked to follow the path of the pencil with his eyes as it moves slowly toward the tip of his nose and then returns to its starting position. As the pencil moves in, his eyes will slowly move toward the nose (converge). Stop the pencil approximately two inches in front of his nose. If he has good accommodation, both eyes will remain focused on the penlight. However, in a number of cases, one or both eyes will break (lose focus with the penlight) and turn outward away from the nose. Indicate which eye shifted away and about when that occurred.

Divergence is observed as the penlight moves back to the starting position. Look for smooth movement of his eyes. If the eyes water or the movement is jerky, there may be a problem with muscle control. Some children need to be reminded to keep their eyes looking at the pencil. Often they will focus their eyes on the evaluator, and when the penlight moves toward their nose, their eyes do not move.

Binocular Fusion

You can easily measure binocular fusion at the beginning and end of the fixation test by asking the children how many pencils they see. They should see only one, which means that the images received from their two eyes are being merged into a single picture. Some will answer that they see two or more pencils, which suggests that their visual system cannot fuse the two images into one and they have what is called *double vision*.

Professionals measure binocular fusion with a variety of instruments. An optometrist or ophthalmologist can distinguish among different levels of fusion. Some lay people can learn to use a simple telebinocular instrument in which children are asked questions about what they see. One item used with a telebinocular instrument is a card with a dog on the left side and a pig on the right side. If the child is visually coordinating the image with the two eyes together, he would see a dog jumping over a pig (rather than seeing the pig out of one eye and the dog out of the other).

The ability to achieve binocular fusion is critical for success in either academic activities or sports. If a child cannot blend the images from the two eyes into one, he must constantly shift his vision from one eye to the other, often losing his place. He may otherwise, as an alternative, use just one eye. Four groups of elementary school students took a binocular fusion test (Cheatum 1986–1989, 1989, 1993, 1996; Cheatum and Hammond 1992). The test consisted of a telebinocular machine and a card with four balls (two on each side of the card). As the students looked through the machine at the card and focused their eyes, the four balls should have merged into three, which would indicate that the two eyes were working together. At least one-third of the students in Groups B, C, and D were unable to achieve binocular fusion (see table 10.2). Almost half of Group B could not fuse the four balls into three, whereas 87.4 percent of Group A passed the test. This result might have been influenced by the weather among the different geographic locations of the test cities. Students in Group A were living in Texas, where they could spend more time outdoors and, perhaps, less time indoors doing close-vision activities.

Visual Tracking

Eye-tracking skills are not fully developed until a child reaches the age of seven. Younger children need to be told to move their eyes but not their head. Five-year-olds can visually track an object and pay attention to the material, but their actions are not smooth or sustained for any length of time. They also tend to move their eyes past the target (to overshoot it) and move their head instead of their eyes.

People have developed many variations of eye-tracking or pursuit tests. Some suggest tracking a penlight during a *single* movement in

Table 10.2
Number and Percent of Students Who Passed Binocular Fusion

Group	Number	Percent
A	118	87.4
B	205	51.9
C	53	59.5
D	28	62.2

A: Third-grade students enrolled in 5 elementary schools in different geographic locations in Arlington, Texas. Students represented different academic-achievement levels based on scores received on state-administered achievement tests.

B: Kindergarten–sixth-grade students enrolled in 2 elementary schools in Kalamazoo, Michigan. Students scored 0–3 on the Iowa Achievement Test in reading or were experiencing learning problems.

C: Third-grade students enrolled in 6 different geographic locations in Kalamazoo, Michigan. Students represented diverse academic achievement.

D: Kindergarten to third-grade students in Parchment, Michigan. Students scored 0–3 on the Iowa Achievement Test (scores range from 0–9, with 4.5 considered average), were recommended by the reading teacher, or had low visual and vestibular scores.

horizontal, vertical, peripheral, and diagonal directions. If you want to duplicate the amount of stress a child experiences during reading, however, it is recommended that the following evaluations for horizontal, vertical, and peripheral visual tracking be repeated 15 times.

The examiner and the child sit facing each other. The examiner instructs the child to look at the penlight or toy on an eraser, hold his head still, and follow the object with only his eyes. He may blink as he normally does. Start with the object at eye level on one side of his nose but approximately 16 to 18 inches away from the child's face. Move the object horizontally across his nose to the other side of his face making a semicircular path. This path keeps the object 16 to 18 inches from his eyes *throughout the movement* (figure 10.6). On each side of his face, there is a point at which vision of the opposite eye is blocked by the nose. Avoid going that far, since the child would be forced to shift all of his vision to the eye that can see the target. Repeat the movement back and forth horizontally in front of his face some 15 times.

Each time that you move the object to the left and back to the right counts as one. Observe whether his eyes move smoothly or if they water, jump ahead, or lose the target. Also notice if he moves his head instead of his eyes or if he blinks excessively. He may blink when you cross his midline or he follows the target to his midline with one eye

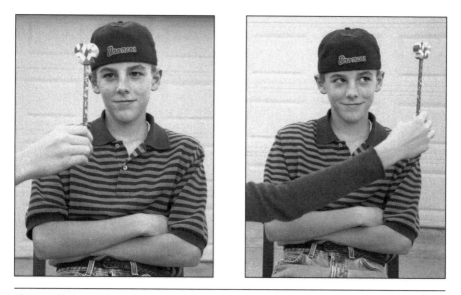

Figure 10.6 Horizontal ocular pursuit.

and then shifts to the other. A young child may need to rest his head in his hands to keep his head from moving. Some children tilt or turn the head or move the body in order to put one eye at an advantage.

When you use the vertical pursuit test, be sure to start at a child's midline, keep the penlight or eraser toy at 16 to 18 inches in front of his eyes, and move it about 10 to 12 inches up and down in line with his nose. Repeat this procedure 15 times. Observe the same difficulties mentioned above but also look for what is called the *S-syndrome*. The S-syndrome occurs when the child shifts his vision from one eye to the other. For example, as you move the object up or down, the right eye (on one side of the penlight) focuses on the object. As the object continues, however, the left eye on the other side focuses on the object. One eye or both may actually turn in toward the nose and out as they follow the object up and down while the vision shifts back and forth between the eyes resembling an "S."

A third ocular-pursuit test involves a peripheral evaluation, which puts an additional stress on the muscles of the eyes. The objective in this evaluation is to move the penlight or eraser toy in a small circle around the face of the child. Keep the object 16 to 18 inches in front of her face and use her nose as the center of a circle. Rotate the circle counterclockwise as you face the child, from the right side of her face down to her chin, up the left side of her face, across her forehead, and then down toward her chin. Make a circle that is about 8 inches in diameter, that is, a small enough circle that it moves along the outside of her face. Repeat each circle 15 times. The reverse circle may also be used, moving clockwise from the left down to the right side of the child as you face her. See if you observe the difficulties mentioned above, and also look for her to blink or change eyes each time you pass midline (see figure 10.7).

In a test of visual tracking that evaluated four groups of elementary school students, the results (see table 10.3) suggest that many youngsters have trouble using their two eyes to track reading or writing material (Cheatum 1986–1989, 1989, 1993; Cheatum and Hammond 1992). Less than one-third of the students in each group passed all of the visual-tracking tests. Only 15 percent of the third-grade students, those in Group C who had quite diverse academic achievements, could track vertically. Yet this ability is crucial for shifting the eyes from one line of reading to the next. The results may suggest that only those students who were more successful academically could visually track. Group A made the highest scores in horizontal tracking (28.8 percent) and peripheral tracking (22.3 percent), and Group D did better in vertical tracking (28.8 percent).

While the objective of tracking is to have smooth, easy movements of the eyes, tracking actually involves very small movements of a child's eyes from one fixation point to another. These are known as *saccadic eye movement skills* or *saccadic fixations*. Reading a line in a book involves several saccadic fixations. As the eyes move across the page, each time

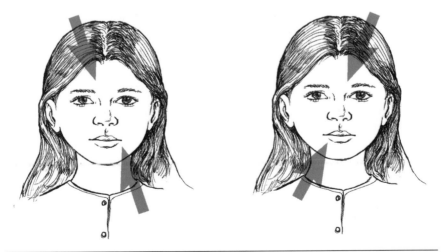

Figure 10.7 Places to anticipate child changing eyes during counter-clockwise occular pursuit.

Table 10.3
Number and Percent of Students Who Passed Visual-Tracking Test

Group	Number & % Horizontal		Number & % Vertical		Number & % Peripheral	
A	39	28.8	32	23.7	30	22.3
B	99	25	78	19.7	71	17.9
C	16	17.9	14	15.7	17	19.1
D	12	26.6	13	28.8	9	20

A: Third-grade students enrolled in 5 elementary schools in different geographic locations in Arlington, Texas. Students represented different academic-achievement levels based on scores received on state-administered achievement tests.

B: Kindergarten–sixth-grade students enrolled in 2 elementary schools in Kalamazoo, Michigan. Students scored 0–3 on the Iowa Achievement Test in reading or were experiencing learning problems.

C: Third-grade students enrolled in 6 different geographic locations in Kalamazoo, Michigan. Students represented diverse academic achievement.

D: Kindergarten to third-grade students in Parchment, Michigan. Students scored 0–3 on the Iowa Achievement Test (scores range from 0–9, with 4.5 considered average), were recommended by the reading teacher, or had low visual and vestibular scores.

the reader sees a letter or a word, he must stop and fixate briefly on the target, then lose the fixation and move to the next letter or word. Vogel (1995) found that a first-grade student reading 100 words would need to make some 230 fixations! By the time that student graduates from high school, having matured and gained better control over tracking and fixation, the number of his saccadic eye movements across 100 words will average only 90.

Determining Eye Preference

Determining a child's eye preference is not difficult. You can easily accomplish this by standing beside the child and having her use a tube to look at some object in the room or to look through a small hole that you have cut in about a 12-inch-square sheet of paper. The eye she chooses (that is, uses) to look through the tube or the hole is her dominant eye.

You can also evaluate eye preference by handing a child a sheet of paper and asking him to roll it into a tube, then hold it in both hands, and look at an object on the far wall (figure 10.8). Let the tube flow back into a sheet of paper, roll it up again, and then hold the tube in the right hand and look at the object. Have him repeat the action with the left hand. Having the child roll the sheet of paper into a tube eliminates the

a

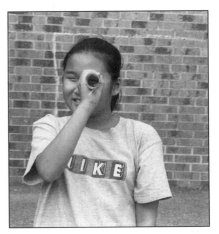

b

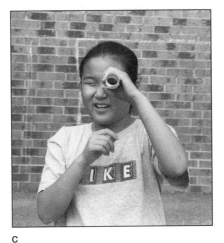

c

Figure 10.8 Eye preference evaluation.

possibility that the examiner influenced his eye preference by handing the tube to the right or left hand. Letting the tube flow back into a sheet of paper between each time he looks through the tube helps to break the pattern of moving the tube to one eye or the other. With a child who is too young to roll the paper, place a tube (such as those that come with paper towels) on a table front of him. Be sure to set the tube in the midline so that he can reach it easily with each hand.

In an examination of 386 kindergarten to sixth-grade students, the majority of the students looked through the tube with the right eye

Table 10.4
Student's Eye Preference

Hand	Left eye	Right eye	Middle
Both hands	148	222	16
Right hand	99	259	27
Left hand	216	139	31

when they held the tube in the right hand, and the left eye when they held the tube in the left hand (see table 10.4; Cheatum 1986–1989). Fifty-seven percent of the students preferred the right eye when holding the tube in both hands. One interesting note from observing this test is that a number of the children, particularly when using the left hand, placed the tube in the middle of their forehead. This suggests that they still have some trouble with their midline and have not fully developed laterality.

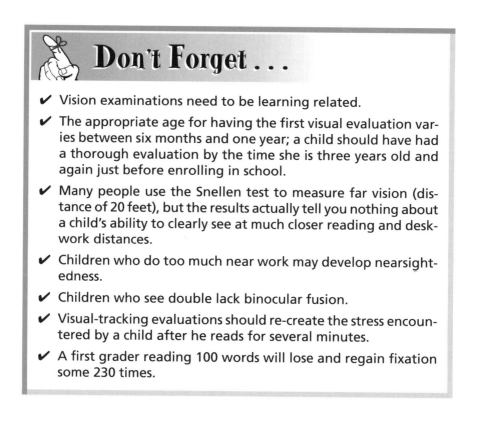

Don't Forget . . .

✔ Vision examinations need to be learning related.

✔ The appropriate age for having the first visual evaluation varies between six months and one year; a child should have had a thorough evaluation by the time she is three years old and again just before enrolling in school.

✔ Many people use the Snellen test to measure far vision (distance of 20 feet), but the results actually tell you nothing about a child's ability to clearly see at much closer reading and desk-work distances.

✔ Children who do too much near work may develop nearsightedness.

✔ Children who see double lack binocular fusion.

✔ Visual-tracking evaluations should re-create the stress encountered by a child after he reads for several minutes.

✔ A first grader reading 100 words will lose and regain fixation some 230 times.

VISUAL SYSTEM PROBLEMS AND DEVELOPMENT

Approximately 20 percent of children entering schools have visual problems. Seventy percent of the children who have specific reading problems, however, have been found to have problems in their visual system that relate to movements of the eyes, depth perception, and finding targets. Almost every family has a TV, and most families have computers. Youngsters in these families spend countless hours viewing images a few inches from their faces. Rarely are they involved in games, sports, and family activities that encourage visual development. Five- and six-year-old children who are still visually immature nevertheless enter schools. There they face reading and writing tasks that can excessively stress their visual systems. Children now get more reading assignments than past generations did. Moreover, they are encouraged to join reading programs, with recognition going to those who read hundreds of books.

Children do not have the benefit of knowing what something should look like. After being fitted with glasses, one child was amazed that a brick house consisted of many bricks rather than one large brick. Another child commented that she did not know there were spaces between words and numbers in books. She could finally see that trees were not large green structures but had separate leaves, some of them at different depths from the others. Many elementary schoolchildren believe it is normal for the words at the bottom of the TV to be blurred, for words in books to move around, or for material on the chalkboard to be fuzzy. They do not know otherwise because they have never seen clearly. This is why testing is so important.

Many children have vision problems that are related to seeing clearly at near or far distances. We discussed nearsighted and farsighted problems already in the evaluation section of this chapter. Vision problems, however, are not restricted to the ability to see clearly. Some children who have academic problems may, in fact, have better-than-average visual acuity. They pass the Snellen test and go to school with their visual problems undetected. In a very short time, they present symptoms that suggest some sort of learning problem, such as *not* paying attention or learning to read or getting along with classmates. These behaviors, really symptoms, often become a part of their progress report and follow them throughout their school years.

Success in school demands not only acuity but also vision. Unfortunately, each problem with accommodation, fixation, binocular fusion, perception, or visual tracking can provide a stumbling block to children trying to see accurately or *understand* their classroom materials and assignments.

Inability to Accommodate

Accommodation, the ability to shift the focus of the eyes to view objects at different distances, changes with age. At approximately four months of age, children begin to use both eyes together to visually track and explore people and objects moving toward and away from them. Accommodation becomes more firmly established during the next two months and continues to develop until it reaches maturity during the teenage years.

Accommodation depends on muscles of the eyes and on the autonomic nervous system. Preadolescent children have no control over this ability. Elementary schoolchildren can, therefore, be expected to have immature visual systems and to have trouble moving their focus from one target to another. Looking quickly from the chalkboard to the desk creates stressful situations. These are the children who are always trying to get caught up, to get their eyes to focus on what the teacher is talking about. When they finally locate the image, even if it is not blurred, nonetheless their stress level might limit their ability to process the visual information. They also may overshoot their target and have to readjust their eyes, which takes valuable time away from what the teacher is saying or the material written on the chalkboard.

Symptoms of Accommodation Problems

Loses target at near point	Sometimes alternates use of eyes
Over- or undershoots target with eyes	Gets headache after doing close-vision work
Has trouble relaxing the near vision after doing deskwork	
	Double vision
Has trouble shifting from looking at the chalkboard to deskwork	Eye strain
	Drowsiness
Blurring sometimes occurs	
	Lack of concentration
Sometimes shifts to using only one eye at near point	

An insufficiency in convergence can often result in double vision. Being unable to focus on or clearly see only one object as it comes near the body is particularly disturbing for children during motor skill activities, play, and sports. As the baseball, Frisbee, volleyball, or football approaches the face, they lose the ability to use both eyes, and instead shift the focus to just one eye. This causes them to momentarily lose sight of the ball. Thus, their ability to judge when and where the ball will land will be disrupted. If the single image of the ball turns into double vision, they will see two balls. So these children must then decide which ball is the real ball! Some children use the technique of swinging at whatever ball they cannot see through. Batting in baseball is almost impossible for them since the ball is traveling toward them at such high speeds.

Eventually, everyone experiences some problems with accommodation. From the teenage years on, the ability to change focus from far to near is gradually lost. By the age of 40, readers find that small print in telephone books and newspapers becomes blurred; most middle-aged people then resort to reading glasses.

Inability to Fixate

Fixation is one of the basic visual skills. Direct fixation means focusing on one target for a period of time. Fixation ability varies according to the time of day, amount of stress, and amount of time the eyes are used.

At the beginning of the day or at the beginning of the reading assignment, children may be able to focus on the material for some time. However, as the reading lesson continues, the stress of trying to keep the eyes focused on the material increases rapidly and comprehension is reduced.

Some children experience great discomfort when they try to look at something even for a few seconds. They have difficulty reading and writing, as well as doing activities and sports. These "split-second children" have to gather all the information they can in the short amount of time they have before they lose fixation. Therefore, the overall ability to see the work or objects in front of them is greatly reduced. Within this short time they manage to fix their vision, they may get only a fraction of the material in the visual field. Anytime a child shifts his vision from one fixation target to another, he has to change accommodation. Without this ability, he does not receive the necessary visual information to help him make perceptual decisions, such as understanding the meanings of letters and words.

When youngsters must fixate beyond their ability, they will show signs of stress. Their eyes might start watering, they feel fatigued, they grip their hands and move the head. One of the most noticeable symptoms is their eyes constantly shifting. Their eyes dart from one target to the next with their concentration and body following. Although it seems as if they are not paying attention and are just being inattentive, this is the only action they can take. They do not have the muscle and visual control needed to sustain fixation.

Symptoms of Fixation Problems

Cannot sustain focus on target	Not getting classroom information
Eyes tear	Short attention span
Appears fatigued	Losing the place in reading
Stress	Reversing letters or words
Trouble in sports and motor activities	Behavior problems
Constant shifting of eyes from target to target	

Inability to Maintain Binocular Focus

When a child's visual system cannot merge the images received from the two eyes into one, she may see two or more different images or blurred images. This is referred to as an inability to maintain binocular focus, or *binocular fusion*. One of the possible causes of poor binocular fusion is an imbalance in the eye muscles. To compensate for this, the visual system may automatically block or suppress one eye when trying to bring the object into focus or it may shift the focus from one eye to the other. This causes the child to lose her place, skip words and lines in reading, and function below potential.

One eight-year-old child at Western Michigan University's Special Physical Education Learning Laboratory said that he saw four images of the pencil, a monumental problem of binocular fusion! This provided good insight into why the youngster was having serious trouble in school and had little interest in sports. His scores on various vision tests were clues to the severity of his problem. When he was asked to sit in a chair, since he was seeing four chairs he put his hands on each side and then moved his hips against his arms and hands to locate the "real" seat. He was referred to an optometrist, and within a year was performing at grade level in academics—and participating in sports.

An easy way to find out if older children have problems with binocular focus is to ask them if they have trouble looking through binoculars, microscopes, or the games in video arcades in which you look through two lenses at once. Usually, they say it is stressful trying to see what everyone else is seeing, and that they find it necessary to either alternate eyes or block out one eye. The strain causes the eyes to become fatigued, and they will appear tired or sleepy. Headaches and other symptoms of eyestrain such as tears and rubbing of the eyes appear. These children may even adopt a typical fight-or-flight attitude: they try to avoid classroom activities that put them under stress or, if that does not work, they resort to disruptive behavior.

Binocular fusion has an enormous effect on the learning potential of children in elementary schools. As early as 1967 Metzger and Schur found a significant relationship between third-grade students and their ability to maintain binocular vision and performance in academics. Children who (a) did *not* suppress one eye read above grade level, (b) who shifted vision from one eye to the other read at grade level and (c) who consistently suppressed the same eye read below grade level.

Symptoms of Binocular Focusing Problems

Seeing double

Alternating eyes

Assuming strange postures at the desk

Squinting

Skipping words

Misplacing numbers in rows or columns

Feeling fatigued from trying to focus

Avoiding tasks that cause trouble

Covering one eye

Tilting the head

Getting irritations in the eyes (particularly if only one is used)

Having problems in reading and writing

Repeating letters

Tensing the body

Forming crusts in the corners of the eyes

Leaning the head over onto the desk to read and write

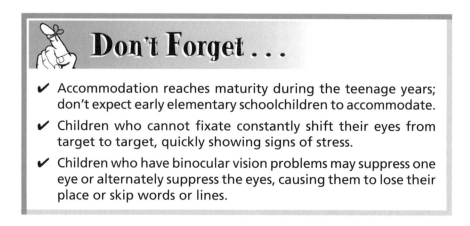

Don't Forget...

✔ Accommodation reaches maturity during the teenage years; don't expect early elementary schoolchildren to accommodate.

✔ Children who cannot fixate constantly shift their eyes from target to target, quickly showing signs of stress.

✔ Children who have binocular vision problems may suppress one eye or alternately suppress the eyes, causing them to lose their place or skip words or lines.

Inability to Track Objects

What seems to be the simple act of reading actually depends on the successful functioning of several different visual skills. One of the major skills is the ability to visually track (using ocular motor pursuit) material in books and objects or people moving through space. The ability to track enables a child to keep attention on the task. This is important in reading since it keeps the individual from losing his or her place or reversing letters or words.

Tracking, or reading across a line, involves several fixations, and children in the early elementary school grades take longer to read because of the time it takes them to fixate. This amount decreases with the age of the students. First-grade students take about a third longer to fixate than adults. In physical activities, this increased fixation time causes children to have trouble tracking balls from one player to another; it also interferes with their ability to catch balls.

Koslowe (1995) found visual tracking problems to be the major visual deficit in a group of 100 elementary schoolchildren referred to a center for reading disabilities. All of the children were in a regular classroom and supposedly all those who needed glasses had them. Examinations found that 41 percent of the children had trouble tracking, 6 percent had refractive errors, and 4 percent had strabismus.

To examine the relationship of visual difficulties to academic success, Johnson, Nottingham, Stratton, and Zaba (1996) evaluated 81 at-risk students who were between the ages of 8 and 18. Thirty-three of the students were enrolled in alternative schools as a result of their behavior problems. Almost all (85 percent) of the students failed at least one of the visual tests. The greatest areas of difficulty were in tracking, visual acuity for both distant and near objects, and binocular depth perception.

In 1994 Johnson and Zaba investigated the visual differences between graduate students and illiterate adults. The most dramatic difference occurred in the area of visual tracking. All of the graduate students passed the visual tracking tests, but only 39 percent of the illiterate adults passed. While this is dramatic, it should not be surprising since for someone to read he must be able to move the eyes across a line of print and from one line to another. The major question is how many young children who now have visual tracking problems will grow up to join the ranks of the next generation's illiterate adults.

Symptoms of Visual Tracking Problems

Losing one's place	Reversing letters or words
Omitting words	Skipping lines in reading or rereading lines
Moving head but not the eyes	
Placing drawings on the page poorly	Not fully comprehending material
Crossed eyes or one eye that turns inward or outward	Alternating use of the eyes
	Having a midline problem
Reacting slowly	Having trouble catching
Having trouble tracking in sports	Performing below potential in class

Children who have a midline problem have additional trouble in tracking. They have not been able to unify the two sides of their bodies. The left side of their body is used for doing tasks on the left side, and the right side for activities on the right side. It also occurs with the eyes. When tracking across a line in a book, a child with both a midline and tracking problem will use the left eye for material to the left of the midline and then switch to the right eye for material on the right side. This causes the child to shift vision back and forth between the two eyes. A major problem occurs when he finishes reading a line with the right eye. Then he must shift his vision to the left eye to begin reading on the next line. However, since the eyes are not communicating with each other, one eye does not know where the other has been. In this case, the child often skips a line, rereads the same line, or goes back and lands on the preceding line.

Midline problems also interfere with the ability to write legibly. A child with these kinds of problems may have trouble even writing her name across the midline of vision. As she crosses the midline, she shifts vision from the left to the right eye. To compensate for this problem, she might move the paper until it is only visible to one eye. Another child might turn his head to block out one eye, lower his head toward the desk, or even put a hand over one eye.

Strabismus

Strabismus, known as crossed eyes, is a condition in which the two eyes are not aligned. One or both eyes may turn in toward or away from the nose (see figure 10.9). A common condition occurs when an imbalance in the strength of the eye muscles causes one or both eyes to turn in toward the nose. If the condition remains uncorrected, some of the pathways saved for the visual system in the brain can get lost.

The change in the alignment of the two eyes interferes with binocular vision. The two eyes see different images, with one eye clearly seeing the intended target and the other eye receiving an image that is unrelated to what the child is wanting to see. As a result, the brain suppresses (or ignores) information from one of the eyes, and the child is actually relying on only one eye. A child who has an uncorrected cross-eyed condition and consistently suppresses one eye is said to be one-eyed. One-eyed children have neither good binocular coordination nor fusion between the eyes.

Strabismus occurs in about four percent of the population. It is not present at birth but usually begins to appear when children are between two and five years old. Infants who are born prematurely have a greater than average (10 to 14 percent) chance of having strabismus. In some cases, the condition can be detected as early as three months.

Figure 10.9 Strabismus.

Symptoms of Strabismus

Headaches	Covering one eye physically
Blurring of vision in one eye	Unaligned eyes
Double vision	One or both eyes turn in
Blocking out one eye subconsciously	

Problems With Eye Preference

When children do not have a preference for one eye, it usually means they have not fully developed laterality. They are at the stage in which they use the left side of the body for activities on the left side, and the right side for activities on the right side. These children will have difficulty reading and writing since they have no internal awareness of right and left. They will experience some of the symptoms and problems mentioned in chapter 5 (see discussion of midline) and earlier in this chapter (see discussion of inability to visually track).

Problems With Visual Memory

There is a strong relationship between reading ability and visual memory. A child's visual memory skills start to develop during the early days of his life. He first becomes familiar with the faces of his parents and objects used to care for and play with him. By the time he is 9 or 10 months old, he has the ability to look for an object when it is removed from his sight. Simple reading-related tasks, such as learning the alphabet, depend on the working of visual memory. If a child cannot remember the letter B after he can no longer see it, for example, there is no chance that he can learn to use the letter in words.

Reading a small word such as *eat* depends on visual sequential memory, which is the ability of the child to register and remember the letters and the sequence of E and A by the time his eyes reach T. If he does not, he may think the word is *tea*, for instance, or he may not make any meaning at all out of the word. Visual sequential memory learning exercises can include different objects, such as lettered or numbered blocks (figure 10.10), varying sizes of blocks, stuffed animals, beads, or toy cars. Visual sequential memory is more complicated when it involves phrases such as directions in workbooks ("Take out your pencil, go to lines 5 and 6, and circle the words that are similar.").

Figure 10.10 Visual sequential memory exercise.

Problems With Figure-Ground Discrimination

A young child's inability to separate the main target from background images can seriously impede his learning. For example, if his teacher tells him to color one of five pictures on a page, he may start out focusing on and coloring the correct assigned picture. However, he may unconsciously shift his focus to the background, in which case his motor system will follow his visual system and send the crayon all over the page. Children who have a "figure-ground" problem will often move their classroom activities closer to their face in order to block out the background and reduce the stress on the visual system. Many of them also are unable to use their two eyes together. They shift their vision from one eye to the other, which causes them to lose their places.

Visual-Motor Problems

Some children have trouble being able to use the information they gain through the visual system. The brain does not receive the information, process it correctly, or transfer it to the other sensory systems that need it for doing the particular action. You might say that these children operate in two different worlds, the *visual world* and the *motor world*. The best example of this is a child who often walks into a wall. He sees the wall, but it has no relationship to where he is walking. Some children with problems of separated visual and motor worlds trip every time they walk onto a mat on the floor. They appear to see the mat each time they cross it, but for some reason the visual or proprioceptive system does not process the correct information. There is no connection between what they see and what their legs consequently do.

Visual-motor problems are not always so severe as these examples, but they are similarly traumatic to children. The youngsters cannot hit or catch most balls. Tracking balls between bases or down the field is extremely difficult. A delay in visually fixating on targets, such as the catcher, can easily result in a scored run before the ball is even released. Relays and games in which the children must move between and around pylons or other players can end in disaster.

It is no wonder that eventually many of these children with visual-motor problems will attempt to skip gym, hide out in the bathroom, stand on the sidelines pretending to be hurt, or stay home on days that they have gym class.

Common Visual Problems Seen in Physical Education

Seeing double, particularly near the face

Double vision causes trouble figuring out which ball to catch or hit

Cannot track balls from one person to another

Cannot focus on the teacher long enough to get directions

Not paying attention, looking away, inability to bring eyes back to focus on desired target

Catching on the right or left side but having trouble catching in middle of body

Blinking or turning head away when trying to catch ball

Delays (waits to run in baseball, for example, because he can't tell if the batted ball is in or out)

Clumsiness; being uncoordinated

Trouble moving around and between players

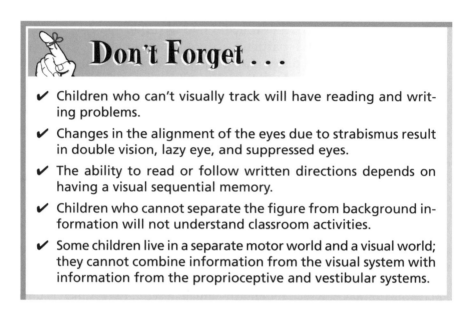

CORRECTING VISUAL PROBLEMS

Prevention, lens therapy, and visual therapy activities form the core interventions for correcting visual problems. But it also takes the coordinated efforts of parents, teachers, and visual professionals to design and monitor programs to help children see well. A lot of responsibility falls on the shoulders of teachers, since they have more opportunity to see the children reading and writing and in other activities that could indicate a visual problem. If a child is having trouble academically, one of the first considerations should be to evaluate his ability to see. Many children with undetected visual problems are bright but simply cannot cope with the academic demands placed on them.

Prevention

Prevention of visual problems involves knowing the potential visual ability children have at various ages and providing them with a variety of age-appropriate visual opportunities. There is clear evidence that elementary schoolchildren who do an excessive amount of work or leisure activity at close range may become nearsighted. This, of course, includes sitting too close to the TV and viewing computer programs or playing computer games.

Doctors may recommend glasses, either *learning lenses* or *reading glasses,* for the prevention of certain kinds of eye problems. Some first and second graders are visually immature and have difficulty focusing on reading and writing activities at their desks for any length of time. These children have good vision but close deskwork causes them an undue amount of stress. They often benefit from preventive lens therapy, with reading glasses to magnify the material. The glasses reduce eye stress and help them to concentrate on their deskwork for longer periods of time. However, using the glasses for distance (or far) vision may cause material on the chalkboard to look blurred. The solution may be to use bifocals or to allow them to remove the glasses for far-point tasks.

Without the assistance of glasses, overachieving children tend to force themselves to continue working on near-point tasks. This causes them to eventually become nearsighted and lose the ability to see the chalkboard. If a child has seen a professional, does not have a vision problem, but still has trouble reading, ask a visual professional about the benefits of using learning lenses.

Lens Therapy

Lens therapy usually includes glasses or contacts designed to reduce the stress caused by reading or other activities performed close to the face or at a distance. Glasses also correct the refractive errors of nearsightedness, farsightedness, and astigmatism. However, lenses can cause problems. Children who are nearsighted have 20/20 near-point vision but cannot see distances. If they are prescribed glasses to correct distance vision, they may need to remove them in order to focus on deskwork and reading. If they do not remove the glasses, there is a strong likelihood for the near-point vision to deteriorate. Wearing glasses, the children have difficulty in some motor skills since a ball, Frisbee, or other object may get increasingly out of focus as it nears their faces.

Children who are farsighted have the reverse problem. They often need corrective lenses for close work but have to remove their glasses to focus clearly on material on the chalkboard. Some children who are farsighted can converge the eyes for near-point vision; consequently, they may not be prescribed lens therapy. However, this in an individual decision to make, which should be considered only on the advice of a vision professional. Ask your doctor about the appropriate use of glasses.

Vision Therapy

Vision therapy involves using lenses, prisms, or a series of exercises to improve the skills necessary for learning. Vision therapy enhances efficiency and processing. It also includes techniques for functional problems such as fixation, eye tracking, convergence, binocular fusion, visual memory, and visual sequential memory. A relatively new kind of therapy called *advanced vision therapy* uses equipment (such as computer programs) designed to improve vision.

Vision therapy is used either by itself or combined with lens therapy for functional visual problems. Through it, children have been able to attend to subject matter for longer periods of time. They can read and write with better comprehension, which ultimately improves their overall academic performance. In addition, vision therapy benefits self-esteem and improves motor skills and behavior.

Coordination problems with the two eyes are at the root of disorders in the use of the two eyes for convergence. Since these disorders often cause children to suppress or block one eye or to alternately suppress their eyes, vision therapy has been found to be the treatment of choice. It has a good success rate: more than two-thirds of the children and adults who have had vision therapy for convergence deficits have successfully corrected their reading problems. One kind of therapy for binocular problems involves using felt patches over the strong eye or alternately over both eyes. Patches are not worn all day; the amount of time depends on the child's age and visual deficit.

Visual tracking is a learned skill, and children can improve in their skill. For improvement to occur, however, the children must have developed the ability to fixate, focus, and converge the two eyes. Therapy for the tracking deficiency should start with large targets that a child can easily follow. Even though tracking involves both eyes, some professionals recommend tracking techniques with each eye separately and then with both eyes. With a young child, you should emphasize his keeping the head still and using only the eyes. If he is having a lot of trouble following the target, the proprioceptive and tactile systems can be added: have him put his finger on the target as it moves. Another technique is to have him hold his head still and track with his eyes while he pushes a car across his desk.

One effective vision therapy activity for improving fixation, binocular focus, and convergence is variously called the Convergence Rod, Block String or just String Thing. A 10-foot-long string is attached to a doorknob or bedpost (see figure 10.11). Three different colored beads are placed on the string, with one near the face, one in the middle, and

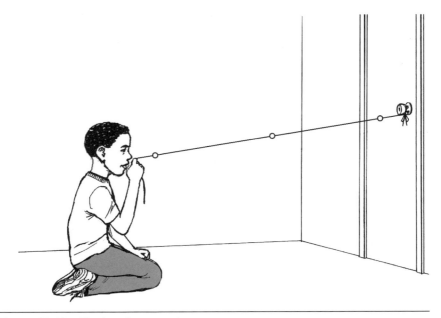

Figure 10.11 Block string exercise.

one at the far end of the string. A child holds the other end of the string to his nose and adjusts the beads so that he can focus clearly on each one. He is then told to shift his eyes from one bead to the next, concentrating on seeing only one bead at each location. Two beads would indicate that he is not merging the two eyes together.

A combination of glasses, visual therapy, and sometimes surgery can correct strabismus. For at least a hundred years, however, vision therapy has been the treatment of choice for strabismus, and it is considered the first line of defense. Visual therapy has a high rate of success, particularly if children begin the treatment when they are young. Professionals used to tell parents of children with strabismus that the youngsters would outgrow it. This does not happen. If vision therapy is started too late, even though the muscles are corrected and the children have their eyes aligned through exercises, the pattern of using only one eye has become too firmly established in the visual system and brain.

Some conditions of strabismus require surgery. Fortunately, most cases can be treated with exercises for the eye muscles. Patches may be used over the strong eye or alternately over each eye to force the use of muscles in the opposite eye. Eventually, both eyes are exercised at the same time.

Don't Forget . . .

✔ Correction of vision problems involves prevention and lens or vision therapy.

✔ Reading glasses enlarge material and can alleviate some kinds of eye problems.

✔ Lens therapy is usually prescribed for nearsightedness, farsightedness, and astigmatism.

✔ Functional problems such as visual tracking, accommodation, and fixation respond to vision therapy.

These are some places to contact for additional information:

American Foundation for Vision Awareness (AFVA)
243 N. Lindbergh Boulevard
St. Louis, Missouri 63141
314-991-4100
Web site: http://www.ioa.org/afva.htm

Optometric Extension Program Foundation (OEP)
2912 S. Dalmier Street
Santa Ana, California 92705
714-250-8070
Web site: http://www.healthy.net/pan/pa/oep/annual.htm

Parents Active for Vision Education (PAVE)
   National Headquarters
9620 Chesapeake Drive, Suite 105
San Diego, California 92123\619-467-9620
Web site: http://www.pave-eye.com/~vision/

 **Visual-System Activities**

The following visual-motor activities allow children to practice fixation and tracking of the eyes. They will be most effective if you use them *after* vigorous activities, which stimulate the vestibular system and prepare the children to successfully use their visual-motor system. The vestibular system holds the eye muscles steady during fixation and controls the movement of the eyes during tracking. In addition, it provides tonic muscle control to the neck muscles, which allows the head to be balanced on the neck.

We begin with fixation activities. If a child cannot fixate for a few seconds, tracking activities will put too much stress on the visual system; they should be avoided until a reasonable amount of fixation is accomplished. As your child practices these exercises, it is important that you watch his or her eyes to be sure that they are actually fixating or tracking—and not jumping from one target to another.

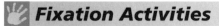

Fixation Activities

Individual

Appropriate Ages

6 months and older.

Preparation

Activities in which the eyes must focus on an object without moving for a prolonged amount of time will help the child work on fixation. Decide on some objects to have around. They can be toys, faces, beanbags, puzzles, and other games.

Activity

An infant can fixate on toys, a face, or other objects that you hold about 18 inches from the face. Objects that have interesting patterns or colors may keep their baby's attention for longer periods. However, some children are overwhelmed by objects or faces that are overstimulating. If a child becomes distressed, simply have her look at something plain, such as a ball.

Some children may not be able to fixate for even one second. These activities should not be forced until children can fixate for a few seconds. Have a preschool-age child fixate on targets that are 5 to 10 feet away. While fixating, the child throws balls or beanbags at the target.

Fixating on objects nearer to the face can be practiced when children color in a coloring book or put puzzles together. Try to extend the amount of time children can fixate by using a stopwatch or clock to time them.

✋ *Tracking Activities*

Individual

Appropriate Ages

6 months and older.

Preparation

Activities in which the eyes must follow an object will work on tracking. You'll need a pencil, toy, mobile, ball, toy car, balloon, soapy bubbles, or a punchball, depending on the child's age.

Activity

Have the child visually follow a pencil, toy, or other object. However, notice how long he can do these activities without undue stress. Start with the number of repetitions the youngster *can* do, trying it for a few sessions before adding difficulty. Children younger than five years old may not be able to track without turning their heads, but the practice of tracking for a few seconds can be done at very early ages. Mobiles in cribs are great objects for infants to start tracking and fixating.

For toddlers, rolling a ball back and forth (or even a toy car) helps them practice tracking. At about three years of age, children can try catching balloons, balls, or bubbles that you blow. Starting with a large balloon or a punchball (without the rubber band attached) makes catching easier for them. When a child can successfully catch large balls, begin to use 8- or 10-inch balls, and then gradually shift to playing catch with smaller balls.

✋ *Punchball Wall Volleying*

Individual or partner

Appropriate Ages

4 years and older.

Preparation

Pair up the children with partners. Have a punchball for each pair, *without* the rubber band attached to it.

Activity

The children volley a punchball against a wall by tapping it with their hands. For an added challenge, the children sit down or lie on their backs with their knees bent and toes touching the wall. Count the number of volleys before the punchball goes out of control.

Two children can sit or lie down, with their knees bent and toes touching together. Then, they can volley the punchball back and forth. See if the children can increase the number of volleys each time.

Punchball Catch

Partners

Appropriate Ages

4 years and older.

Preparation

You'll need a balloon or punchball and an open area indoors or outside.

Activity

Play catch with a balloon or punchball. Count the number of times the children catch the ball before it hits the floor. Children can also practice tossing the balloon up and catching it themselves.

Scarf Catch

Individual or partners

Appropriate Ages

4 years and older.

Preparation

You'll need at least one or two scarves for each child. Place hoops or carpet squares on the floor at least two feet apart. Each child stands in a hoop or on a carpet square.

Activity

Children toss their scarves up in the air and catch them without stepping out of the circle. They can also toss their scarves up with one hand and catch them with the other. Then the children put one scarf in each hand, toss them up, and catch them.

Seated Circle Soccer

Group

Appropriate Ages

4 years and older.

Preparation

Set chairs in a circle with about two feet between each chair. You'll need an 8- to 10-inch ball. You can crush wastepaper into a ball and wrap it in masking tape for a homemade ball.

Activity

Participants sit in the chairs with the ball in the middle. While they remain seated, they try to kick the ball out of the circle. When a child kicks the ball out of the circle, he gets a point, retrieves the ball, and then returns to his seat for the next round. For added challenge, use two or three balls.

Punchball Tennis

Partners

Appropriate Ages

5 years and older.

Preparation

Mark a line on the floor or use a rope tied and stretched between two chairs to function as a net. Each child will need a Ping Pong paddle. Foam paddles are available that also work well.

Activity

Bounce and hit the punchball over the net. Younger children can try to increase the number of volleys. Older children can keep score as in a regular tennis match.

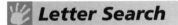 *Ball Bail-Out*

Three or more children

Appropriate Ages

5 years and older.

Preparation

Fill a large laundry basket or box with balls of various sizes. One child is the "bailer" and stands next to the ball-filled container. The others stand in a circle around the container and the bailer.

Activity

On "Go!" the bailer begins to toss balls out of the container. The other participants pick up the balls and toss them back in the container. As balls go back in the container, the bailer continues to toss them out. If and when the bailer empties the container, he lifts it upside down over his head. A new bailer is then chosen. As a variation, set an amount of time for the bailer. See how many balls remain in the container after 30 seconds and then change bailers. This may be easier and less frustrating for less skilled bailers.

Letter Search

Individual

Appropriate Ages

6 years and older.

Preparation

Use masking tape to make the patterns on the floor as illustrated in figure 10.12.

Activity

Assign the child a letter and have him walk, jump, and so forth on the lines that form "his" or "her" letter. You can also do this activity with numbers or have a child spell words. For math practice, give the child an equation, such as 1 + 3 = ?, and have him trace the number that is the answer.

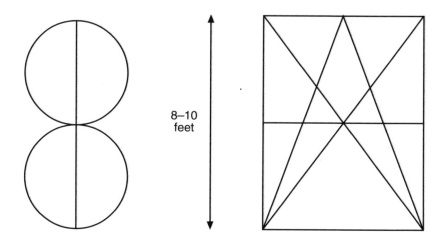

Figure 10.12 Lines on floor for Letter Search.

Jog and Pass

Ten or more

Appropriate Ages

6 years and older.

Preparation

Children find partners and stand in a circle. One partner is inside the circle facing out, and the other stands outside facing in. Each set of partners has an 8- to 10-inch ball. Small balls made of waste-paper and covered with masking tape also are fine for this activity.

Activity

On "Go!" the partners begin to jog in place and pass the ball back and forth by gently tossing it (figure 10.13). If partners drop the ball they must leave the circle and run around the outside. Then, they return to their places and start jogging in place again.

Figure 10.13 Jog and Pass.

 ## *Jog and Kick 1*

Ten or more

Appropriate Ages

6 years and older.

Preparation

Children find partners and stand in a circle. One partner is inside the circle facing out, and the other stands outside facing in. Each set of partners has an 8- to 10-inch ball. Again, small balls made of waste-paper and covered with masking tape are fine for this activity.

Activity

Do this activity the same way as Jog and Pass, except that as the partners jog in place, they gently kick their ball back and forth. They must run around the outside of the circle if they lose control of the ball.

Word Unscramble Relay

Six or more

Appropriate Ages

8 years and older.

Preparation

Choose a word of five letters or more—water, chair, friend, and so on. Using index cards, make a set of cards, 4.25 inches by 5.5 inches, with one letter of the word on each card. You will need as many sets of letter cards that spell the word as there are teams. Mark a start and finish line about 8 to 10 feet apart. At the finish line, place the letter cards in a row face up but out of order, using a set for each team. Space each set at least 2 feet apart.

Activity

On "Go!" the first person of the team runs to the finish line and looks at the letter cards. He then picks up two letter cards and switches their places, trying to put the letters in the correct order to spell the word. Then, he returns to start. The next team member runs and switches two cards. This continues as the teams change only two cards at a time until the letters are in the correct order to spell the word. This game is more challenging if team members are not allowed to help each other figure out which cards to switch or what the word says.

chapter 11
The Auditory System

Hearing problems are often overlooked in children, even when the youngsters have motor development, learning, or behavior problems. Surprisingly, even parents are not likely to suspect a hearing problem in an infant or young child. The *Journal of the American Medical Association* in 1998 published findings (Niskar, Kieszak, Holmes, Esteban, Rubin, and Brody) that only 11 percent of the parents of children who had a hearing loss had recognized the problem. Parents often, unconsciously, accommodate to a hearing problem and do not realize that they have changed their behavior around their child's hearing difficulties. For example, parents may give a child a snack before he asks for it, not realizing the child rarely speaks (a symptom of hearing loss). At other times they may react to him by pointing to what he wants, rather than asking him verbally.

Parents and teachers tend to focus on the delayed speech or language development that these children often experience. Unknowingly, they may not consider that a hearing disorder is delaying the development of speech and language. Many times relatives and teachers suspect a disturbance in a child's ability to hear long before parents ask a medical professional to refer their child for auditory testing.

This chapter describes the auditory system receptors and how sound sensations are processed. It provides some simple screening tests that a parent or teacher can use to evaluate children's auditory systems and gives brief information about formal auditory testing. You can read about the effects that auditory problems have on motor development, learning ability, and behavior. And you'll find some strategies to manage a child's auditory problems, as well as some activities to improve a child's auditory processing.

AUDITORY SYSTEM RECEPTORS

Receiving and processing sound include a stimulation being received through the peripheral receptors and then transmitted to the *central auditory nervous system* (CANS). The visible parts of the peripheral auditory receptors are the outer ears, which resemble satellite dishes on either side of the head. Auditory canals and the tympanic membranes (eardrums) lead into the head from the outer ears. Next, three small bones called the *hammer, anvil,* and *stapes* form the middle ear. The inner ear comes after these bones, and includes the cochlea as well as the various parts of the vestibular apparatus (see chapter 7). Another important component of the auditory system is the *eustachian tube,* which maintains the appropriate air pressure surrounding the eardrum. The auditory nerve transmits sounds to the central auditory nervous system (see figure 11.1) to complete the system's components.

Receptors in the central auditory nervous system are complex structures, and we have only recently begun to understand them. Although

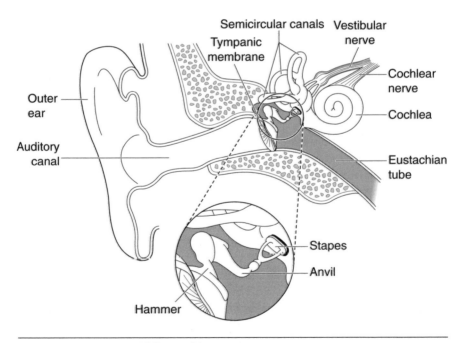

Figure 11.1 Outer, middle, and inner ear.

some of these structures are found on both the right and left sides of the brain, other auditory pathways cross from right to left and vice versa. Tracking the pathways of auditory stimulation is difficult, which is why central auditory processing, not yet fully understood, is hard to research.

Peripheral Receptors

Once sounds enter and pass through the peripheral auditory receptors, they are not simply transmitted "as is" to the central auditory nervous system. In the auditory canal, the eardrum detects vibrations caused by sound waves. Then a response called the *acoustic reflex* is created by the hammer, anvil, and stapes bones. Muscles around these small bones begin to pulse (move). These muscular movements begin the transformation of sound waves into electrical impulses that are sent to the cochlea.

The pitch and loudness characteristics of sounds are determined as the auditory system processes the frequency and intensity of the sound waves. High-pitched sounds, for example, have greater frequencies than lower pitched sounds. Sound waves of a bird singing have a higher frequency than sound waves from thunder. Our auditory systems normally do not detect extremely high or low frequencies. A dog whistle is an example of a sound that has a frequency or pitch too high for human hearing to detect.

The intensity of sound waves determines the loudness that enters the ear and strikes the eardrum at the same time. In other words, the sound wave's level of force striking the eardrum determines loudness. Sound waves of a lawn mower in your yard strike your eardrum with more intensity than do the sound waves of a lawn mower a block away. High-intensity sounds (see figure 11.2 for examples of these intensities) can cause the muscles of the middle ear to contract with such force that humans will experience pain. In fact, extremely loud noises can injure the delicate structures of the auditory system. Recently, health professionals have been advising parents of infants to avoid toys that make noise because of possible damage to their developing auditory systems.

Another critical function of the peripheral auditory system is to locate sounds. A human determines location in several ways. First, the individual discerns whether the sound is coming in more strongly through the right or left ear. Second, it detects that sound waves are subtly changed by the direction in which they pass by the outer ear (see figure 11.3). This happens because sounds coming from behind the body

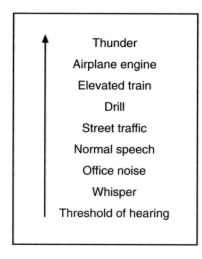

Figure 11.2   Thresholds of sound.

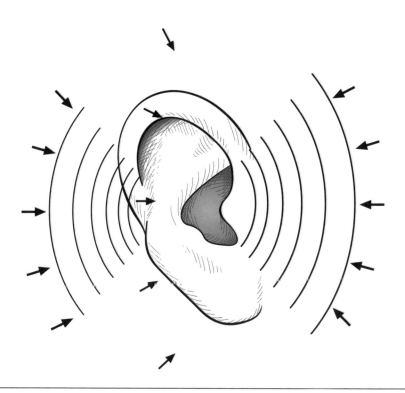

Figure 11.3   Sound waves passing over parts of the outer ear.

are transmitted into the inner ear differently than those coming from directly in front of the body.

Central Auditory Nervous System

The brain interprets sound sensations in the central auditory nervous system through several simultaneous processes that seem to occur throughout it. Auditory information is integrated with information from the other senses. Think of a child as he is hearing sound. Does the sound go with what the child sees? How fast is the body moving toward or away from the sound? Does the child need to react to the sound or is it better to ignore the sound?

An infant matches the pitch of her mother's voice with other senses, such as smell and touch, to form a complete perception of "mama." In the classroom, a child knows which sounds to ignore because he has already learned through experience that seeing and hearing the teacher is important to successful class work.

Fluctuations in the frequency and intensity of sound waves create patterns, which the central auditory nervous system begins to sort into *familiar* patterns. The sounds in the word *mama* or *bottle* begin to be matched with visual and other sensations to create an entire sensory and motor perception of these objects. Organization of the patterns of human speech contribute to the development of language. These patterns are critical for rhythmic movement, such as using music for dance or hearing the water's splash while swimming.

Other processes occur in the central auditory nervous system to create meaning out of sounds. *Pattern matching,* for instance, occurs as children begin to recognize familiar series of sounds that are related to certain voices, words, music, or objects (such as bells). *Intensity encoding,* on the other hand, occurs as the central auditory system learns which sounds need to be attended to, depending on the loudness of the sound.

The Reticular Formation

The reticular formation is at the core of the brain stem. It contributes to the level of attention the auditory system gives to various sounds. Certain sounds make a child more alert and focused. Other sounds, such as lullabies, calm a child and make him drowsy. The reticular formation can be trained to react to or ignore certain sounds. From birth, an infant learns to recognize and attend to her mother's voice. And an example of learning to dismiss a familiar sound is when a youngster ignores that first call to come in the house or an infant falls asleep while her parents talk. We initially respond to the sound of the furnace turning on, but eventually we tune out the noise, as we dismiss many sounds.

Arousal of the reticular formation prepares the brain to act on sensory input in an appropriate manner. A well-rested child may be better prepared to process spoken instructions than a tired tyke because the reticular system has prepared the brain to listen. Sleep deprivation or a general state of drowsiness greatly decreases the nervous system's ability to process auditory sensations. Hearing tests will be highly inaccurate if a child is sleepy. For these reasons, you cannot expect children to listen or pay attention if they are tired.

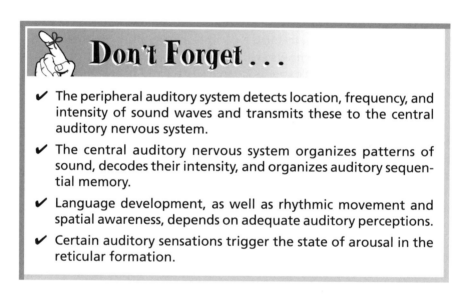

Don't Forget . . .

✔ The peripheral auditory system detects location, frequency, and intensity of sound waves and transmits these to the central auditory nervous system.

✔ The central auditory nervous system organizes patterns of sound, decodes their intensity, and organizes auditory sequential memory.

✔ Language development, as well as rhythmic movement and spatial awareness, depends on adequate auditory perceptions.

✔ Certain auditory sensations trigger the state of arousal in the reticular formation.

THE AUDITORY SYSTEM AND MOTOR DEVELOPMENT

Sound is often a critical cue to initiate or time movements. In addition to hearing sound, a child must learn to judge the characteristics of various sounds in order to decide whether or not to react to them. Auditory processing influences many components of motor development, including the following:

- Location of the source of sound
- Patterns or rhythms of sounds
- Auditory discrimination

- Auditory separation of foreground-background
- Auditory sequential memory

Location of Sound

Through ultrasound images, people have observed that a fetus turns its head toward sounds. A very young infant will turn his head and eyes toward familiar sounds, such as his mother's voice. And he will also turn toward new sounds, such as a jingling bell or whistle. These head movements are the first ways that a baby relates sound to movements.

As children develop, they use the location of sound to develop spatial awareness. Locating sound gives them a sense of where they are in relationship to objects and people. Children begin to determine the distance of a sound source as well as the direction the sound is traveling. For example, Tommy stands in his driveway looking left as he waits for the fire engine to pass his house. He knows to look left because that is the direction from which the sound of the siren is coming.

When children participate in more complex activities, such as basketball or dance, they use sound to help them with their timing and body position. Developing this component of auditory awareness is critical for playing a sport that requires anticipation of an opponent's reaction. By adulthood and before, good tennis players, for instance, automatically use the sound of the ball coming off the racquet and then bouncing on the ground to know how hard and fast it is coming. Dancers in the front row can stay in their places without turning to look backward because they can sense the sounds of the dancers behind them.

Patterns and Rhythms of Sounds

How many of us have seen a young infant begin to rock back and forth when she hears music? Before some children can sit without support, they will rock while propped up on their forearms. This is the beginning of trying to use the body to react to patterns of sound from the environment. Often these rhythmic movements are influenced by the detection of vibrations in the vestibular-auditory system.

As children begin to develop more complex movement patterns, they often learn more quickly if they hear a rhythmic phrase rather than a description of the movement they are attempting. If you teach a young child to cross-country ski, for example, you can say a simple phrase that imitates the rhythm of each glide: Try "swish and glide, swish and glide" rather than "First move this foot, then pick up that foot." At professional athletic events, in fact, you might often hear athletes on the sidelines talking to themselves in a rhythmic pattern as they visualize their next performance.

Children must be able to follow rhythmic patterns to clap to music, write with a pencil, or hit a ball. Being able to follow rhythm in music may not develop in some children before they are eight years old. Young children often do not have the ability before then to inhibit internal rhythmic patterns. Until the ability to follow an external pattern develops, children may either speed up or slow down, regardless of an audible rhythmic pattern.

Auditory Discrimination

Recognizing familiar patterns and rhythms is part of auditory discrimination. From birth, an infant appears to distinguish between environmental sounds and the voice of his mother. When children play on a noisy playground, for instance, through auditory discrimination they can hear their parents or teachers call them. As a toddler or child, being able to discriminate between sounds affects reaction time during physical activity. During a game, players discriminate between a whistle signal for a time-out and their many cheering fans in the stadium.

Auditory Figure-Ground

The flip side of being able to attend more closely to certain sounds is the ability to *ignore* the auditory sensations that are unimportant. This ability to ignore background noise is called auditory figure-ground. Children must first be able to discriminate among sounds and have some knowledge of what or who is making the sound. Once they are able to discriminate sounds, they begin to choose the individual sounds on which to focus. A baby who is younger than one year old can pick out from the busy environment not only the voice of his mother, but can also choose whether or not to attend to her voice for any length of time. An infant can ignore his mother's voice, for instance, if he finds a jingling bell more interesting.

Auditory Sequential Memory

Auditory sequential memory is the ability to hear and recall sounds in the order in which they occur. This ability is critical for language development, following directions, and ultimately, reading. Children learn to say words in a certain order to make a sentence. They know to say, "The ball is blue," not "Ball blue is." Children also learn to follow instructions in the order in which they were given. When the teacher says, "Take out your reading book, turn to page 10, and start reading," children have to do these items in that order or they may be reading in the wrong place, assuming they get out the correct book at all.

Auditory sequential memory seems to be dependent on the ability to recognize and understand sounds. The order in which sounds are perceived is more important than the order in which they occurred. For example, if a child hears and recognizes the following sounds—his mother's voice, a bell, and a siren—he will remember them in that order. If he does not recognize the bell, his central auditory nervous system may ignore that sound altogether. However, a different reaction may be becoming stuck in trying to identify the novel sound of the bell and therefore ignoring the other two sounds.

Don't Forget . . .

✔ *Auditory discrimination* is the ability to identify specific sounds related to certain objects or people.

✔ *Auditory figure-ground* is the ability to attend to important sounds in the environment and ignore other sounds.

✔ *Auditory sequential memory* is remembering sounds or messages in the order in which they were given, an important skill for language development, following directions, and reading.

EVALUATING THE AUDITORY SYSTEM

Although only about one percent of children have a *severe* hearing loss, an estimated 15 percent of them have some hearing loss. Many children considered to have an attention disorder, learning problem, or both have hearing problems, including a central auditory processing disorder. Parents, teachers, and other professionals may not be aware of these problems. Children with autism have been reported to be oversensitive or undersensitive to sounds. Any child who is experiencing behavior or learning problems should be recommended for comprehensive auditory tests.

Informal Auditory Screening

It isn't difficult to do an informal auditory screening. Parents and teachers often start by noticing certain behaviors that would indicate an auditory problem. Speaking poorly, ignoring directions, or usually playing alone are signs of possible hearing problems. See page 320, Symptoms of Auditory Problems, for a checklist of items that may indicate that further evaluation of auditory function should occur. If you think your child is experiencing problems with hearing or if you find yourself constantly saying, "He just doesn't listen," do not hesitate to have a professional follow up your screening by evaluating the child for possible auditory problems.

There are three good examples of simple, informal screening procedures: watch ticking, clapping, and auditory memory games. If your child has trouble with two or more of the screening methods, you should consider requesting a complete auditory evaluation.

For the *watch-ticking test,* stand behind the child. Hold a watch that ticks about three feet from his right ear. Slowly bring the watch toward the ear, and ask him to tell you when he hears it. Repeat for the left ear. If the child never hears the watch or does not hear it until it is a few inches from the ear, you may suspect a hearing problem.

The *clapping test* should be done more than once, and you should do it in a different setting each time. When the child does not suspect it, enter a room quietly and clap loudly. See if the child shows any reaction, such as flinching, turning, or jumping. Try this test while the child is watching TV, playing with a group of friends, or reading a book. If the child has a delayed reaction or no reaction, she may have a hearing problem.

Auditory-memory games require a child to listen to a sequence of words or instructions. For a sequence of words, simply say three to seven words that are unrelated, such as *ball, tree, sock, blue, car.* Base the number of words on a child's age. Three-year-old children should remember three words, whereas seven-year-old children through adults should remember at least seven words. Try three or five sets of words. Some children can focus enough on the first set to remember the words, but lose their ability after a couple of sets.

If a child who is 5 years old or older can repeat a sequence of words, try asking her to do a series of three to five simple tasks. For example, (1) walk to the door, (2) open the door, (3) close the door, (4) walk to the chair, and (5) sit down. See if she can do the tasks in order. Repeat the test three to five times using different tasks. If the child consistently has difficulty, you may suspect an auditory memory problem.

Formal Auditory Testing

In the United States, health and educational professionals are beginning to recommend that all newborn babies receive formal auditory testing. Hearing problems are 20 times more common than hypothyroidism and sickle-cell anemia, for which newborns are commonly tested. Early detection of an auditory problem is critical. Children identified before the age of six have a better chance for developing normal speech and language skills than do children who are not identified until elementary school.

Most children are screened for low-frequency hearing problems when they enter school. The teacher, school nurse, or doctor who suspects a child might have a hearing loss then refers the youngster to an *audiologist* for testing of the peripheral system. If the audiologist finds no peripheral hearing loss, a child is usually identified as having hearing that is in a normal range. There is a growing concern, however, that the screening tests performed in most schools test only for low-frequency hearing loss and do not even begin to determine difficulty with auditory discrimination or "figure-ground."

If your child's peripheral auditory test appears normal and you still suspect a problem, you may request central auditory processing tests. Do not be surprised if you need to search for an audiologist who is qualified to do this type of testing. Many teachers, audiologists, speech pathologists, and pediatricians are still unfamiliar with these tests.

You should have experienced audiologists or neurologists conduct formal testing of the auditory system, such as testing the *auditory brainstem response* (ABR) and *late auditory-evoked response*. We give only highly simplified descriptions of these procedures here to give parents and teachers a general sense of what the tests involve and what they can indicate. Audiological assessments should also include evaluations of academic performance and behavior. Assessments of speech and language are also valuable in determining just what and how a child hears.

Both the ABR and the late auditory-evoked response tests involve electrodes being placed at special sites on the scalp. The ABR, which can be performed as early as at birth, detects and measures the strength of electrical impulses that pass through the auditory brainstem pathway. The late auditory-evoked response test detects and measures the strength of electrical impulses that actually travel to central auditory processing sites in the brain. The absence, delay, or weakness of these impulses in the brainstem or the brain may indicate a problem with central auditory processing.

Some children who have had frequent ear infections may have abnormal ABR results. Excess fluid in the ear can impair the ability of the peripheral auditory systems to transmit sound into the central auditory nervous system. The resulting lack of sound sensations and experiences may have impaired the creation of neurological pathways needed for auditory processing.

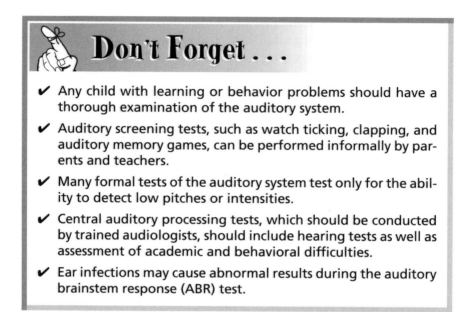

Don't Forget . . .

✔ Any child with learning or behavior problems should have a thorough examination of the auditory system.

✔ Auditory screening tests, such as watch ticking, clapping, and auditory memory games, can be performed informally by parents and teachers.

✔ Many formal tests of the auditory system test only for the ability to detect low pitches or intensities.

✔ Central auditory processing tests, which should be conducted by trained audiologists, should include hearing tests as well as assessment of academic and behavioral difficulties.

✔ Ear infections may cause abnormal results during the auditory brainstem response (ABR) test.

AUDITORY PROBLEMS AND DEVELOPMENT

Problems with the auditory system can adversely affect some components of efficient movement. The following is a list of problems commonly found in children with a hearing loss or central auditory processing problem:

Symptoms of Auditory Problems

Poor attention span	Delayed reactions to sounds or instructions
Not following directions	
Frequently asks "What?"	Poor balance
Overly sensitive to loud or sudden noises	Not knowing where to look to find sounds or to listen
Difficulty in changing activities	Always speaking loudly
Not following directions in the order in which they were given	Poor speech and language ability

Central auditory processing disorders are not completely understood. Some possible disorders have been identified, however, which we can discuss briefly. In *Central Auditory Processing: a Transdisciplinary Approach* Katz (1992) proposed three categories of disorders in central auditory processing: (1) decoding, (2) tolerance-fading memory, and (3) integration.

Decoding Problems

A child who has decoding problems finds it difficult to make sense out of the sounds he is hearing. He has difficulty matching the auditory stimuli to past experience or knowledge. For example, he might be unable to match written letters to their sounds or to match words to objects. These kinds of difficulties stem from decoding problems. Children who have trouble learning sounds that go with letters, as in phonics, have decoding problems. These children may have trouble learning the new words that accompany learning a new skill or activity. For instance, football players make *touchdowns*, basketball players make *baskets*, and soccer players make *goals*. These three terms sound quite different, but they all are means of scoring in their respective games.

Tolerance-Fading Memory (TFM)

Tolerance-fading memory (TFM) is a disorder that really encompasses two problems. First, children with TFM have problems with auditory figure-ground. In fact, these children become stressed in noisy environments. In a mall or on a playground, these children often try to get away (flight reactions) or become aggressive (fight reactions). TFM is related, second, to poor auditory sequential memory; the youngsters are unable to process and remember instructions *when they are irritated by background noise.* If you ask a child with TFM to do three things while he is overwhelmed by other noise, she may only process the first and third items. Although the words entered through her peripheral auditory receptors, it is as if you hadn't even said the second item.

Auditory Integration Problems

The last category, auditory integration, includes problems with mixing auditory information and sensations from the other sensory systems. These children may test normal on hearing evaluations, but still have trouble matching the location of sound with proprioceptive information. Brian may hear Jeff approaching him from behind, for instance, but he still doesn't know which way to move to get out of the way.

Auditory Deprivation

Central auditory processing problems may arise if a child goes for a prolonged time with a condition that disturbs his ability to experience sound. Children who have experienced auditory deprivation may not have had enough interaction with auditory stimulation. Being deprived of opportunities to hear sounds may delay the development of auditory discrimination, auditory figure-ground, and sequential memory. An estimated 50 percent of children who had frequent ear infections in the first year of life have experienced enough auditory deprivation to delay their speech-language development, along with the development of other central auditory nervous system structures and functions. Therefore, any hearing loss attributed to peripheral auditory structures and functions needs to be treated early.

Don't Forget . . .

✔ An auditory-decoding problem is an inability to match auditory stimuli to past experience; this difficulty limits a child's ability to match letters to sounds or words to objects.

✔ Tolerance-fading memory problems include low tolerance to noisy environments, which limits the child's ability to process and remember instructions.

✔ A child who has experienced prolonged hearing loss or deprivation may also suffer a delayed development of central auditory processing.

MANAGING AN AUDITORY PROBLEM

Auditory problems can be treated and managed in several ways. Medications or surgery can correct structural and functional problems caused by illness, deformities, or injuries. Two external strategies also benefit children with hearing difficulties: amplification and environmental changes.

Amplification

Hearing devices (hearing aids) are useful for amplifying the intensity and pitch of sounds from the peripheral auditory components to the central auditory nervous system. Professionals prescribe hearing devices for children with hearing losses at certain levels, based on the findings of audiological tests. New technology has made devices available that are more sensitive to certain pitches and tones. Some hearing devices can help filter background noise. However, amplification does not always improve central auditory processing problems. Have you ever seen an elderly relative with a hearing aid turn the device off, complaining that it is too noisy? This occurs because the devices amplify *all* sounds, not just voices.

Microphones and speakers are other sources for amplification. You can place the speakers around the room at the ear level of the listeners. This multiple location is the theory behind "surround sound" in movie theaters to "enhance the film-viewing experience." In one school classroom, speakers for two students with hearing losses were placed at their ear level when seated. The teacher found with these extra speakers in the classroom that not only these two children functioned better—so did several other students who had been causing behavior problems.

Environmental Changes

Some children who have auditory problems may not hear certain pitches, be able to discriminate between sounds, or attend to important sounds. They must learn to cope in a variety of sound environments—from a quiet classroom to a noisy gymnasium. You may not be able to help a child manage every setting, but you can start by looking at home or classroom settings to optimize her ability to hear and focus. By eliminating distracting sounds or amplifying your voice, you may immediately see some difference in her ability to attend to or follow instructions and have appropriate social behavior.

At home, sit quietly and listen to the sounds in your house. Is there a refrigerator running, a fan blowing, a dishwasher whizzing, or a TV blaring? Try to eliminate or minimize some of these sounds when you want your child to hear and respond. This may mean turning off the TV or stereo when you are instructing everyone about chores for the day or playing games with the family. For important conversations, take children to a quiet room. It may help to avoid running the dishwasher after dinner when a child is doing homework.

In the classroom, teachers also should take a few moments to listen to all of the environmental sounds that are present. Is there background noise while the students are quietly doing their work? Do the fluorescent lights buzz? Or are students laughing on the playground outside your classroom window? Is the quiet reading period at the same time that several other classes of students are walking past your room on the way to lunch? Physical education classes are often held in gymnasiums with terrible acoustics that echo. Once you have identified all of the possible noisy distractions, think of how you might help children with auditory problems cope with them. Have all of the students face you as you speak, for instance. Stand close to students with auditory problems. This will enable them to focus not only on the sound of your voice but also on visual cues. If noise distracts some children, move them away from a door or window.

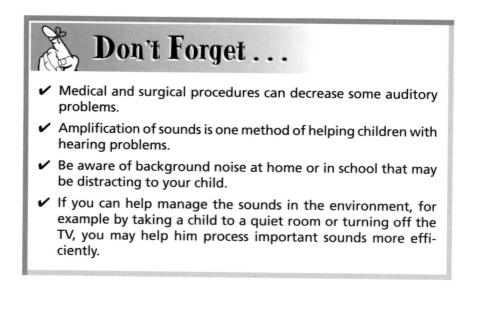

Don't Forget . . .

✔ Medical and surgical procedures can decrease some auditory problems.

✔ Amplification of sounds is one method of helping children with hearing problems.

✔ Be aware of background noise at home or in school that may be distracting to your child.

✔ If you can help manage the sounds in the environment, for example by taking a child to a quiet room or turning off the TV, you may help him process important sounds more efficiently.

Auditory Activities

You can help children reduce auditory problems in two ways. First, you can provide activities that help children learn to cope with an auditory problem, and, second, you can provide opportunities for them to practice listening. Teaching children to repeat instructions before doing an activity gives them a strategy to avoid misunderstanding directions and then incorrectly completing the task. Using activities in which children must listen for a signal to stop or change movements can help some children develop auditory discrimination and figure-ground.

Recognizing Sound Rhythms and Patterns
Individual or group

Appropriate Ages

Birth through adulthood.

Activity

Singing, dancing, or playing rhythm instruments help children learn to hear patterns. Singing is especially useful for learning sound patterns related to speech and language. Performing movements to rhythmic patterns provides an opportunity to integrate auditory information with vestibular and proprioceptive sensations. This integration is critical to the development of smooth motor patterns for such actions as running, skipping, or throwing.

Musical Games
Individual or group

Appropriate Ages

1 year and older.

Activity

Try a variety of prerecorded children's exercises or activities such as Disney's Mousercise. These activities require the children to learn to distinguish between the musical sounds, verbal sounds, and any other sounds in the room.

Auditory Discrimination or Figure-Ground Activities
Individual or group

Appropriate Ages

3 years and older.

Activity

For a child to develop auditory discrimination or figure-ground, she needs opportunities to listen to and select specific sounds to hear when general background noise is present. A simple game is for the child to move to music and freeze when the music turns off. You can also play a tape of animal sounds and have the child identify which animals made the sounds—*while* another tape of music is being played in the background.

Go—Stop

Individual or group

Appropriate Ages

3 years and older.

Preparation

Gather a collection of noisemakers, such as whistles and various kinds of bells.

Activity

Any activity that uses sounds as signals for going and stopping requires children to use the auditory system to hear the commands. Have the children practice going and stopping to various sounds, such as bells, whistles, and hands clapping. Some children respond better to sounds than to the human voice.

Musical Chairs

Group

Appropriate Ages

4 years and older.

Preparation

Use chairs or carpet squares for this activity, and place them in a circle with one for each child.

Activity

When the music starts, the children march, walk, hop, or otherwise move around the chairs. When the music stops, everyone finds a place. For the next round, remove one chair. When the music stops, one person will not have a place to sit. Instead of having the children who cannot find a seat sit out the rest of the game, however, have them march around the entire group and start a parade as each new "odd person out" joins them. This parade must also stop marching when the music stops.

Say, Do, Say

Individual

Appropriate Ages

4 years and older.

Activity

Whenever you are giving instructions to a child with an auditory problem, you can have them practice "say, do, say." Ask the child to do three or four tasks in a sequence. The child then repeats what you said, does the tasks in order, and then tells you what he did. By practicing this activity, a child learns to listen and repeat instructions out loud as a way to ensure that he successfully follows directions. Eventually, the child may be able to repeat the instructions silently to himself (which is what many of us do to remember what we are supposed to be doing).

Simon Says

Group

Appropriate Ages

4 years and older.

Activity

This old standby game, Simon Says, requires children to listen for specific words. One child is the leader called Simon, and stands in front of the others. Simon gives instructions, such as, "Simon says hop on one foot," or "Simon says flap your arms like a bird." As long as the leader says, "Simon says," before each instruction, the others do the movement. If Simon doesn't say "Simon says touch the floor," but instead just says, "Touch the floor," any child who moves is "out." Being out does not mean sitting down. All the children can continue playing, but you keep track of the last person who has not made a mistake. This child becomes the new Simon.

Driving Miss Daisy

Group

Appropriate Ages

5 years and older.

Preparation

Participants find a partner. One partner is the "Driver," and the other is "Miss Daisy" who stands behind the driver with hands on his shoulders (figure 11.4). One person needs to be the "Traffic Controller" and should have a pad of make-believe traffic tickets.

Figure 11.4 Traffic controller.

Activity

The Traffic Controller can give the following commands:

Command	Meaning
Red	Stop
Green	Go
Slow	Partners walk
Fast	Jog
Highway	Run
Switch partners	Change places

If partners do not follow the commands, the driver receives a ticket. The first driver with three tickets becomes the Traffic Controller. Since other children are participating, there will be background noise that needs to be ignored to hear the commands.

Go Where I Say

Individual or group

Appropriate Ages

8 and older.

Preparation

Write letters on colored squares or cards and spread these out around the floor.

Activity

Ask the child to jump on, step over, hop on (and so forth) a series of letters or colors (figure 11.5). For example, "Jump on the letters *C A T*." After the child repeats the letters you want him to jump on, he actually does jump on them. Then, he says the word he spelled. Listening to instructions and repeating them helps a child remember the sequence. He also evaluates his success when he tells you where he jumped.

We hope that the material in this book has provided you with some insight into the underlying causes of learning and behavior problems. We also hope that by using the suggestions for activities, your children

Figure 11.5 Go Where I Say.

will have more success in their academic programs and physical education. Activity and movement benefits your children's health and neurological fitness in ways that cannot be overly stressed. Children who have learning or behavior problems need support from parents and teachers like you to succeed in this complex world. No matter where, when, how, or what the physical activity or game the children do with you, remember to have fun and enjoy your children. We hope that you find the activities in this book a valuable resource. Get these children moving and see how far they can go!

Bibliography

An asterisk (*) denotes a source referred to in the text.

*American Alliance for Health, Physical Education, Recreation and Dance. 1989. *Physical best: the AAHPERD guide to physical fitness education and assessment.* Reston, VA: AAHPERD.

Apell, R., and R. Lowry. 1959. *Preschool vision.* New Haven, CN: Gesell Institute of Child Development.

*Auxter, D., J. Pyfer, and C. Huettig. 1996. *Adapted physical education and recreation.* St. Louis, MO: McGraw-Hill.

*Ayres, A. J., 1976. *Southern California sensory integrative test.* Los Angeles, CA: Western Psychological Services.

*Ayres, A. J. 1975. *Southern California postrotary nystagmus test.* Los Angeles, CA: Western Psychological Services.

*Bárány, R. 1906. Über die vom ohrlabyrinth ausgeloste Gegenrollung der Augen bei Normalhorenden, Ohrenkranken und Taubstümmen. *Archiv für Klinische und Experimentelle Ohren-Nasen und Kehlh Kopfheilkunde, 68:* 1–30.

Bowe, F. 1995. *Birth to five: Early childhood special education..* New York: Delmar.

*Brazelton, T. 1988. The infant as an individual. Symposium: The roots of creativity in infancy. Baltimore, MD.

Brown, C. ed. 1984. *The many facets of touch.* Johnson and Johnson Baby Products.

Buschner, C. 1994. *Teaching children movement concepts and skills: Becoming a master teacher.* Champaign, IL: Human Kinetics.

*Canfield, J. and M. Hansen. 1993. *Chicken soup for the soul.* Deerfield Beach, FL: Health Communications.

*Carlson, M., C. Dragomir, F. Paris, M. Parrell, O. Macovei, P. Nystrom., and J. Sparling. October, 1997. Cortisol regulation in family-reared and institutionalized Rumanian children. New Orleans: Presentation at the 27th Annual Meeting of the Society for Neuroscience.

*Cheatum 1986-1989. Special project to prepare elementary teachers to enhance students education. Federal Grant # G008630044.

Cheatum, B. 1988. Assessment and Program Implementation of low achieving children. Spring Valley Elementary School Teachers (December).

*Cheatum, B. 1989. The effects of sensory-motor activities on classroom behavior of children who exhibit symptoms of learning disabilities. Presentation at 18th National Conference on Physical Activity for Handicapped Individuals, Riverside , CA. (November).

Cheatum, B. 1989. Implications for proprioceptive screening tests for learning disabled children. 7th International Symposium of Adaptive Physical Activity, Berlin, Germany (June).

Cheatum, B. 1990. Sensory motor activities and academic success. Presentation to Michigan Special Education Department and selected members of the State of Michigan House of Representatives (April).

*Cheatum, B. 1993. Relationship between sensory motor development and evaluation of third grade students. Presentation to Elementary school teachers in Arlington, Texas (May). Supported by Faculty Research Grant from Western Michigan University.

*Cheatum, B. 1996. Study of the relationship between sensory regulatory disorders and children with ADD and LD. Supported by Faculty Research Grant from Western Michigan University Relationship between Sensory Motor Development and Children with ADD and LD. Unpublished data.

Cheatum, B. and A. Hammond. 1990. Influence of Sensory integration programs on teacher observation of low achieving children. Research Convocation, Western Michigan University, College of Education (March).

*Cheatum, B., and A. Hammond. 1991. Model sensory-motor developmental program for children who are learning disabled. Presentation at the International Symposium on Adapted Physical Activity. Miami, FL.

*Cheatum, B. and A. Hammond. 1992. A Developmental Sensory Motor Intervention Program for Children who have learning problems/disabilities. International Early Childhood Conference on Children with Special Needs. Council for Exceptional Children Division for Early Childhood. Washington, D.C., (December).

Cook, J., T. Mausbach, L. Burd, G. Gascon, H. Slotnick, B. Patterson, R. Johnson, B. Hankey, and B. Reynolds. 1993. A preliminary study of the relationship between central auditory processing disorder and attention deficit disorder. *Journal of Psychiatry and Neuroscience* 18(3): 130–137.

Cratty, B.J. 1975. *Remedial motor activity for children.* Philadelphia, PA: Lea & Febiger.

Cratty, B J. 1985. *Active learning: Games to enhance academic abilities.* 2nd ed. Englewood Cliffs, NJ: Prentice-Hall.

*de Quiros, J. 1976. Diagnosis of vestibular disorders in the learning disabled. *Journal of Learning Disabilities* 9: 39–47.

de Quiros, J. B. and O. Schrager. 1979. *Neuropsychological fundumentals in learning disabilities.* Rev. ed. Novato, CA: Academic Therapy.

Delcomyn, F. 1997. *Foundations of neurobiology.* New York: W. H. Freeman.

Fisher, A., E. Murray, and A. Bundy. 1991. *Sensory integration: Theory and practice.* Philadelphia, PA: F.A. Davis.

*Friend, T. November 30, 1993. A new school of thought on nurturing a better brain. *USA Today,* 7D.

Gallagher, W. 1990. Touch balance: A tribute to the forgotten senses. *American Health.* January-February.

Getman, G. 1992. *Developmental optometry*. Santa Ana, CA: Optometric Extension Program.

*Greenspan, S. 1994. *Infancy and early childhood: The practice of clinical assessment and intervention with emotional and developmental challenges*. Madison, CN: International Universities Press.

*Hammond, A. 1992. Sensory motor activities to improve balance in students with learning disabilities. Presented at the North American Federation of Adapted Physical Education Symposium. Montreal.

Hasbrouck, J. 1989. Auditory perceptual problems in non-organic hearing disorder. *Laryngoscope 99:* 855–860.

Haywood, K. 1993. *Lifespan motor development*. Champaign, IL: Human Kinetics.

Houde, J. and M. Jordan. 1998. Sensorimotor adaptation in speech production. *Science 279*(5354): 1213–1216.

Hurlock, E. 1972. *Child development*. St. Louis, MO: McGraw-Hill.

Johnson, B. and J. Pyfer. Undated. *Perceptual motor skills*. Topeka, KA: Kansas State Department of Education.

*Johnson, R., D. Nottingham, R. Stratton, and J. Zaba. 1996. The vision screening of academically and behaviorally at-risk pupils. *Journal of Behavioral Optometry 7:* 39–42.

*Johnson, R. and J. Zaba. 1994. Examining the link between vision and literacy. *Journal of Behavioral Optometry 5*(2): 41–43.

Kaplan, R. 1990. *Seeing beyond 20/20*. Kingsport, TN: Arcata Graphics.

Kasser, S. 1995. *Inclusive games: movement fun for everyone*. Champaign, IL: Human Kinetics.

*Katz, J., N. Stecker, and D. Henderson. 1992. *Central auditory processing: A transdisciplinary approach*. St. Louis: Mosby.

Kavner, R. 1986. *Your child's vision: A parent's guide to seeing, growing, and developing*. New York: Simon & Schuster.

*Kempermann, G., E. Brandon, and F. Gage. 1998. Environmental stimulation of 129/SvJ mice causes increased cell proliferation and neurogenesis in the adult dentate gyrus. *Current Biology 9*:16 (July 30-August 13) 939–42.

*Kempermann, G., H. Kuhn, and F. Gage. 1997. More hippocampal neurons in adult mice living in an enriched environment. *Nature 386*:6624 (April 3) 493–5.

Keogh, J. and D. Sugden. 1984. *Movement skill development*. New York: Macmillan.

Knapp, R. 1985. Educational evaluation: The first step toward understanding and remediation of central auditory disorders. *Otolaryngology Clinic of North America 18*(2): 345–352.

Kolb, B. and Q. Whishaw. 1997. "Brain I" and "Brain II." *Grolier Multimedia Encyclopedia*. Macintosh version 9.0.

*Koslowe, K. C. 1995. Optometric services in a reading disability clinic: Initial results. *Journal of Behavioral Optometry. 6:* 67–68.

Kravitz, H., D. Goldenberg, and A. Neyhaus. 1978. Tactual exploration by normal infants. *Developmental Medicine and Child Neurology 20:* 720–726.

Kumai, M. and K. Sugai. 1997. Relation between synchronized and self-paced response in preschoolers' rhythmic movement. *Perceptual Motor Skills 85*(3):1327–1337.

Kuntzleman, C., B. Kuntzleman, M. McGlynn, and G. McGlynn. 1984. *Aerobics with fun: principles of exercise leadership.* Spring Arbor, MI: Fitness Finders.

Leach, P. 1978. *Your baby and children: From birth to age five.* New York: Knopf.

Long, J.G., J.F. Lucey, and A.G. Philip. 1980. Noise and hypoxemia in the intensive care nursery. *Pediatrics* 65:143.

Lucey, J.F. 1981. Clinical uses of transcutaneous monitoring. *Advances in Pediatrics* 28: 27.

*_____. 1974. *MBD Compendium.* Vols. 1 and 2. CIBA Pharmaceutical.

Mayo Clinic. 1976. *Clinical Examinations in Neurology.* Philadelphia, PA: W. B. Saunders.

Mayo Clinic Department of Neurology. 1998. *Mayo Clinic Examinations in Neurology.* St. Louis, MO: Mosby.

*Metzer, D.A. and D.L. Schur. 1967. *Suppressions, academic performance, and near optometric findings: a correlation study.* Unpublished 5th-year thesis. Forest Grove, OR: Pacific University,

Morris, L., and L. Schulz. 1989. *Creative play activities for children with disabilities.* 2nd ed. Champaign, IL: Human Kinetics.

Murray, L., A. Holland, and P. Beeson. 1997. Auditory processing in individuals with mild aphasia: A study of resource allocation. *Journal of Speech Language and Hearing Research* 40(4): 792–808.

Nelsen, J., L. Lott, and S. Glenn. 1993. *Positive discipline A to Z: 1001 solutions to everyday parenting problems.* Rocklin, CA: Prima.

Niclollis, M. 1992. *From neuron to brain.* Funderland, MA: Sinauer.

Niskar, A., S. Kieszak, A. Holmes, E. Esteban, C. Rubin, and D. Brody. 1998. Prevalence of hearing loss among children 6 to 19 years of age: Third National Health and Nutrition Examination Survey. *Journal of the American Medical Association* 279(14): 1071–1075.

Oberklaid, F., C. Harris, and E. Keir. 1989. Auditory dysfunction in children with school problems. *Clinical Pediatrician* 28(9): 397–403.

Pangrazi, R. and V. Dauer. 1992. *Dynamic physical education for elementary school children.* 10 ed. New York: MacMillan.

Patton, H., J. Sundsten, W. Crill, and P. Swanson. 1976. *Introduction to basic neurology.* Philadelphia: W.B. Saunders.

Payne, V. and L. Isaacs. 1995. *Human motor development: A lifespan approach.* Mountain View, CA: Mayfield.

Radler, D. 1960. *Success through play: How to prepare your child for school achievement and enjoy it.* New York: Harper & Row.

Randolph, S. and M. Heiniger. 1994. *Kids learn from the inside out: How to enhance the human matrix.* Boise, ID: Legendary Publishing.

Riccio, C., M. Cohen, G. Hynd, and R. Keith. 1996. Validity of the auditory continuous performance test in differentiating central auditory processing disorders with and without ADHD. *Journal of Learning Disabilities* 29(5): 561–566.

Riccio, C., G. Hynd, M. Cohen, J. Hall, and L. Molt. 1994. Comorbidity of central auditory processing disorder and attention-deficit hyperactivity disorder. *Journal of the American Academy of Child Adolescent Psychiatry* 33(6): 849–857.

Riehle, A., S. Kornblum, and J. Requin. 1997. Neuronal correlates of sensorimotor association in stimulus-response compatibility. *Journal of Experimental Psychology Human Perceptual Performance* 23(6): 1708–1726.

*Roach, E. and N. Kephart. 1966. *Purdue perceptual motor survey.* Columbus, MO: Charles C. Merrill.

Rosenfield, M. 1994. Accommodation and myopia: Are they really related. *Journal of Behavior Optometry* 5: 3–11.

Sasse, M. 1979. *If only we'd known: Early childhood and its importance to academic learning.* New Victoria, Australia: Toddler Kindy Gymbaroo.

Schmidt, R. 1991. *Motor learning and performance: From principles to practice.* Champaign, IL: Human Kinetics.

Seaman, J. and K. DePauw. 1989. *The new adapted physical education.* Palo Alto, CA: Mayfield.

Sherrill, C. 1998. *Adapted physical activity, recreation and sport: Crossdisciplinary and lifespan.* Madison, WI: McGraw-Hill.

*Sherrington, C. 1906. *The integrative action of the nervous system.* New York: Scribner's Sons.

Sherrington, C. 1947. *The integrative action of the nervous system.* New Haven, CN: Yale University Press.

Sherwood, L. 1995. *Fundamentals of physiology.* New York: West Publishing.

Solan, H.A. 1994. Transient and sustained processing. *Journal of Behavioral Optometry* 5: 149–154.

*Vogel, G. 1995. Saccadic eye movements. *Journal of Behavioral Optometry* 6: 3–12.

*Wilbarger, P. and C.B. Royeen. 1987. *Tactile defensiveness: Theory, applications and treatment.* Annual Interdisciplinary Doctoral Conference, Sargent College, Boston University.

_____1997. "Mother's touch affects infant's brain." *USA Today,* Oct. 28, 4D.

Wilmore, J. and D. Costill. 1994. *Physiology of Sport and Exercise.* Champaign. IL: Human Kinetics.

*Young, J. 1978. *Programs of the brain.* London: Oxford University Press.

Index

About the Authors

Dr. Billye Ann Cheatum has spent 30 years devoting her life to the needs of children and adults with disabilities. She received her PhD in Physical and Special Education from Texas Woman's University in 1965 and has worked at Western Michigan University as an advisor of gerontology specialists, Coordinator of Special Physical Education, Special Physical Education instructor, and director of three disability laboratories.

Throughout her career, Cheatum received almost $2 million in federal grants. Part of the grant money was used to create SPELL (Special Physical Education Learning Laboratory). Located at WMU, this lab offers no-cost assessments of children and adults with special needs, individualized treatment programs, and follow-up. Federal funds also assist in providing laboratories for at-risk infants and toddlers and children exposed to drugs in utero. Cheatum has also published two books as well as a children's disabilities booklet with Dr. Hammond for the Michigan State Department. Now retired, she enjoys sailing, swimming, and snorkeling in her hometown of Kalamazoo, MI.

Allison A. Hammond is a sensory motor development specialist who provides sensory motor development programs to children through her private practice, The ResponsAble Child Clinic. She has received two master's degrees in adapted physical education as well as an EdD in Education Leadership with an emphasis in Special Physical Education. During Hammond's educational years as coordinator of the laboratories at Western Michigan University, she evaluated and planned special physical education programs for hundreds of children with a wide variety of disabilities including mental impairment, cerebral palsy, and learning disabilities.

Hammond has conducted numerous workshops and presentations concerning sensory motor development for parents. She has also trained teachers, occupational therapists, physical therapists, and administrators on the subject. Hammond currently lives with her husband Michael in Kalamazoo, MI.